ONLY HUMAN

ONLY HUMAN

Teenage Pregnancy and Parenthood

MARION HOWARD

A CONTINUUM BOOK
THE SEABURY PRESS • NEW YORK

Second Printing

The Seabury Press, Inc.
815 Second Avenue
New York, N.Y. 10017

Design by Nancy Dale Muldoon

Printed in the United States of America

Library of Congress Cataloging in Publication Data

Howard, Marion, 1936–
    Only human: teenage pregnancy and parenthood

    (A Continuum book)
    Includes index.
    1. Pregnant schoolgirls—United States—Case studies. 2. Teen-age marriage—United States— Case studies. 3. Parent and child—United States—Case Studies.
I. Title.
HQ799.2.M3H68   301.42'7   75-20460
ISBN 0-8164-9265-4

to an Unborn Child

NO BETTER THAN ME

I am only as human
   As Nature allows,
Governed by virtues
   And morals and vows,
Doomed to be judged
   By persons I see,
All in God's eyes
   No better than me.

Followed by snickers
   And comments and stares,
I try to pretend that
   I really don't care,
Carrying a child
   That's destined to be
Doomed in their eyes
   No better than me.

My mind has matured
   As my judgment has grown.
I know now I never
   Have *once* stood alone.
God has opened my eyes
   And now I can see
That those who will judge
   Are no better than me.

—*Tonia Wells*

CONTENTS

Introduction

At one time in our history, beginning family life at an early age was considered appropriate. Today it is frowned upon. As a consequence, young people find few institutions—family, schools, health organizations, social service agencies—prepared to help them if they become parents. Society is most often neglectful, and many times it is hostile or punitive.

Yet one out of every ten girls in the United States today gives birth to a baby before reaching the age of 18. Most are unprepared for the experience of being pregnant. Moreover, few teenagers have an adequate idea of what it means to be a parent.

There are a growing number of sex education and family planning books aimed at helping young people prevent pregnancy. To date, however, very little has been written for the teenager who becomes a mother or a father. *Only Human* is intended to fill that gap. It is a fictional account of three very different sets of young parents. The story follows them from discovery of pregnancy through the first year of their baby's life. The varied problems they encounter—telling their parents, obtaining health care, staying in school, making decisions about abortion, adoption, marriage, and finding solutions to financial, day care, and social needs—are typical of those faced by very young parents. Each of the couples, however, resolves their problems in a different way,

1

illustrating the range of experiences such parents may have.

Only Human is intended to reassure young parents that they are not alone in their feelings and experiences. Options and alternatives they may not have considered are pointed out. Ultimately I hope that this book will help young people make better choices about early childbearing and child rearing.

This book is also intended to help adults become more informed about the diverse needs of young-parent families. The purpose of the commentary which runs throughout the story is to clarify issues and add information of interest to teenagers, their parents, and those in the helping professions.

I wish to acknowledge my indebtedness to the young parents and concerned adults throughout the United States who, over the years, have taken time to talk with me about the problems of early pregnancy and young parenthood. I am particularly grateful to Dr. T. Berry Brazelton of Harvard University who first developed the format used in this book. Substantive comments made by Dr. Brazelton, Dr. Howard Jacobson of Rutgers University, and Dr. Luella Klein of Emory University were most helpful. I also appreciate the time that Connie Danielson, Elaine Epstein, Jane Hamilton-Merritt, Roger Ortmayer, Lucy Eddinger, and Dick Weber spent in reading drafts and offering suggestions. A special thank-you must go to my family for their patience and support.

Boston, Massachusetts
June, 1975

1. THE BEGINNINGS

Arlene hated her homelife. In fact, she tried to spend as much time away from home as possible. She had three brothers and two sisters. Her favorite sister, the only one she could really talk to and liked to be with, had become pregnant and had married and moved out the year before. Arlene felt that left her with no one despite the people around her.

Since her father's death, Arlene's mother always seemed to be tired and irritable. Arlene felt it wasn't just being a single parent that got to her mother. Her father had walked out on them six months before he was killed in a car crash. Arlene sensed that if her father hadn't done that, her mother might have felt differently about a lot of things, including his dying.

As it was, nothing seemed to go right at home any more. The family was alternately on and off welfare. When her mother had a job, she was forever yelling at Arlene about watching out for the younger kids while she was gone. When she was out of work, things weren't much better. She just found something else to nag Arlene about. None of the family liked being on welfare. But for Arlene, at least welfare meant her mother was home so she didn't have to run after the smaller kids.

Arlene had just turned thirteen. Often it seemed to her she was too big on the outside for the littleness she felt inside. At other times, she felt she was far more grown-up than anyone gave her credit for. Many times, for no apparent reason, she just felt sad.

Arlene spent hours studying herself in the mirror. Without her glasses, her hazy image seemed attractive enough. Once the glasses were firmly seated on her nose, however, she saw all the flaws—the receding chin that destroyed her profile, the too-broad nose that dominated her face in a front view.

There were a number of girls at school whose hair hung exactly as it should, whose makeup blended perfectly, whose clothes clung just right. As they walked, everything about them said "look at me." Whenever Arlene was near them, she felt awkward and uncomfortable. Sometimes she studied their appearances from a distance. When she tried to imitate them, however, whatever part she changed—a new style top, a hairdo—remained just a part. She never found the whole look.

Arlene had been missing school off and on since her father left them. When her mother worked, if one of her younger brothers or sisters was sick, Arlene had to stay home. Recently, she had begun taking off from school even when her mother was home.

At first she had nowhere to go, so she sat on the porches of people who worked all day. If they had a couch, she curled up on that. She liked to daydream. She made up romances based on things she'd seen at the movies or on television. Arlene was always the heroine.

Then Arlene discovered the Bot. The Bot, a small triangular park, and the run-down stores that faced it on two sides formed a gathering place for the freer teenagers. Most of those who came weren't from the neighborhood. For them, like Arlene, the take-out pizza, pool hall, drug and other stores offered some place to go. When time, money, or a store owner's patience ran out, there was always the Bot itself. One of the area's inhabitants had facetiously called the park, "the botanical gardens" because of its unsightly two bushes, one tree, scruffy grass, and decaying bench. The name stuck in the shortened form of the Bot.

Most of the group that came to the Bot were older than Arlene. Some had dropped out of school and were working full-time. They came only in the evening. Some were either between jobs or worked occasionally. Some didn't work at all. A few, like Arlene, were in school. All in all, during the day there might be only two or three people there. By late afternoon, however, more would have come. In the evening, there were always ten or twelve.

At first Arlene felt very shy and tried not to be noticed. In time, however, her regular presence (mostly after, but sometimes during, school hours) won her a certain acceptance. She was allowed to sit in the same booths, or stand around outside, with the others. Although she didn't say much, she loved hearing them talk. The frequent swearing and reference to various kinds of sex impressed her even if she didn't understand all that was meant. Once in a while she sneaked away from home and went to the Bot in the evening. It was one of those times that Arlene first saw Joel.

Joel had dropped out of school several years before. "I didn't flunk out or anything. I could have stayed," Joel frequently explained. "It was just that school and me—well, let's just say, we rubbed each other the wrong way."

Joel thought the teachers were fussy: "Even when I finally did one of their dumb assignments, if it had been accidentally scrunched in my books, or fingerprinted, they wouldn't take it." He hated the regimentation: "I had to raise my hand if I wanted to take a leak." And he disliked many of the other students: "If you want to see a real bunch of Smokey Bears, you oughta have seen those kids." But worst of all to

Joel, he felt picked on: "No matter what went wrong, the finger was pointed at me. So I decided to earn the blame I was gonna get anyway."

A number of months before he left school, Joel started doing little things to foul up the school system—like turning off every light switch he passed. But it was his biggest prank that parted school and Joel for good. One night he managed to steal all the lunchroom silverware and hide it in the boiler room. The next day the school cafeteria served spaghetti. Joel grinned wildly as kids tried to eat it with their fingers. Half the school population looked like they'd been attacked with orange spray paint.

The kids were furious but not as furious as the principal. "I never did find out why the principal blamed me," Joel noted whenever he told the story. "Maybe just a good guess." Because there was no proof, Joel couldn't be expelled. However, the principal did call him to his office and threaten him for over an hour with what he called "disciplinary action." "I decided then and there it was time to quit. I never even went back to seal shut the door of the teachers' john," Joel added.

Joel found a more appreciative audience in the Bot kids. He liked to perform for them. For example, when someone came along the street with a bag of groceries, he'd run after them with an overripe tomato in his hand. "I think you dropped this," he'd say. As they went to thank him, he'd either put it in their hand so hard it would squish all over them or else drop it politely into their bag of groceries where it would splatter over everything. He'd keep a straight face all the way back up the street. When he got to the Bot he'd let out a long yell of triumph and then collapse with laughter.

Joel had kept his latest job for a year, which meant he'd saved enough money to put a down payment on a new car. Before his father would sign for him, Joel had had to sit through four evenings of lectures about what had happened with the expensive record-a-month club he had joined. But, as he knew he would, Joel finally won out and his father signed.

The car was very important to Joel. Joel felt awkward with many of the kids his own age, maybe because he had dropped out of school. He knew he could impress the younger girls with the crazy things he did. With his green Mustang, he felt he could make an impression on the older kids too.

Joel had a set of false IDs. He felt it was ridiculous to wait three more years until he would be twenty-one to drink. After all he wasn't a school kid. He liked to go into the bar across from the Bot and then, with a drink in his hand, wander out to talk to the kids. Once in a while, when a number of other guys were there doing the same thing, they'd slip drinks to the younger kids in the Bot.

The one thing Joel didn't like getting involved in was the drug scene. Frankly, it scared him to see kids freak out. "I wouldn't even bother to buy pot," Joel confided to his best friend, "if giving it away didn't help my image."

When Arlene got to the Bot, hardly anyone was there. Occasionally that happened. It was one of those off-nights when everyone had something else to do. Only one other girl had come. They sat together in the pizza place. Jeanne was two years older than Arlene and much more sophisticated. Arlene found it difficult to talk to her. Jeanne evidently felt the same way for as soon as she finished her Coke, she got up to go. Almost as quickly, however, she sat back down. Joel had walked in.

"Where is everybody?" he asked.

Arlene waited for Jeanne to answer but she didn't. Finally Arlene mumbled, "I don't know." She knew he would be disappointed at not seeing other people.

"Jeanne and I were just about to leave," she added in a slightly louder voice. She hoped he'd think they had better things to do than stay at the deserted Bot.

Joel eased into a chair at the table and started to tease Jeanne about the red coloring she used on her hair. Arlene returned to her accustomed role as listener. She had seen Joel several times before but never up this close.

"He's so handsome," she thought. "If I bleached my hair, I wonder if he'd talk to me the way he does to Jeanne."

"C'mon," Joel finally said. "Let's get out of here."

Arlene sat as the other two got up. Joel turned to her.

"Well, c'mon," he said.

Arlene couldn't believe he meant for her to come. She got up so fast she bumped the table and barely managed to grab her glass before it fell.

Joel held the car door. "You first, little one," he said to her.

She climbed in the front seat followed by Jeanne. Joel slammed the door and headed around to the other side. Arlene's head whirled. Why had he asked her to sit next to him, not Jeanne? Perhaps because her legs were shorter and there was a bump in the car floor. Was that too simple an explanation? Maybe, but she didn't want to think further. She was lucky to be there at all.

They drove around aimlessly for a while. Finally Joel pulled up to a miniature golf course. Arlene had never seen one before. She hadn't the faintest idea of how to play. Joel put his arms around her and showed her how to putt with her club. Then he tried to do the same with Jeanne.

"Cut it, you clown," Jeanne said. "I know how to play *your* games."

Joel was his usual put-on self. One time he lay down with his mouth open next to the putting hole. "Ten extra points!" he called.

Arlene was having a wonderful time. Joel was the craziest

person she had ever met. While they were waiting for Jeanne
to putt on the last hole, Joel put his arm around her waist
and tipped her over against him. "You did all right," he said.
Her heart skipped.

"Hello!" Voices came from the outside. They were friends
of Jeanne's.

"Listen," Jeanne called back. "I just beat these two and
I'm ready to take on the whole pack of you."

Joel turned to Arlene. "I don't want to play again, do
you?"

Automatically Arlene said no.

"Then let's go," said Joel.

Arlene was a little startled and turned to look at Jeanne.
"We're going to go, Jeanne," she said, hoping Jeanne
wouldn't be too disappointed about having to leave.

"Okay," Jeanne answered. "You guys go on. I'm going to
stay and play."

Arlene didn't know whether to feel good or bad. She was
elated over being able to go with Joel but she wasn't sure
about leaving without Jeanne. However, Joel was already half
way to the car. She turned and followed him.

Once in the car, Joel drove to a dark spot around the other
side of the golf range. "Want one?" he said, offering her a
short squashed-looking cigarette.

"No, thank you."

She wished she could quickly think of something else to
say. She didn't want him to think she was straight. Even if
she had wanted it, however, she had tried smoking only once
or twice before. She had ended up in coughing fits each time;
she didn't want to do that tonight.

"Okay," Joel said easily. "No pot tonight." As he said it,
he put the cigarette away and moved closer to her. He began
to touch her gently. She didn't want to protest. If she acted
squeamish about that too, she would probably ruin any
chance of his ever again asking her to go for a ride. Then

before she knew what was happening, Joel was doing things she didn't like.

Joel had almost taken Arlene directly back to the Bot when they left the golf range. It had been a spur-of-the-moment decision to park the car. Joel knew Arlene was inexperienced. Even so, he was surprised she offered so little resistance to his feeling her. The more he did, the more he thought, "She'll stop me pretty soon." When he finally realized she wasn't going to, he momentarily thought of stopping himself. "Oh, what the hell," he thought. "I don't get it this easy every day." Even when she began to resist, he kept at her. At one point he thought, "Either she doesn't know how to struggle or I'm too ready."

Arlene finally realized that she had let Joel go too far and there was no turning him off. When they had intercourse, it hurt her and she thought it repulsive. It didn't feel like anything she had heard about and the sounds he made were disgusting.

After it was over and he had cooled down a little, Joel realized how shaken Arlene was by the experience. He began to worry.

"You're something else," he said, trying to be helpful as she put on her clothes. "I like a girl who knows how to turn a guy on."

Dimly Arlene heard the things he was saying. They went to a drive-in for a hamburger and fries. Arlene could barely eat.

On the way home, Joel put his arm around her. "You're prime time," he said, giving her an almost tender hug.

His gentleness and seeming sincerity made some of her bad feelings go away. Arlene began to think perhaps what she had done wasn't so awful after all. Here she was in Joel's car and he thought she was something special. Wouldn't it be great if he'd come to the Bot and ask for her? Everyone would turn around and look.

"C'mon," he'd say, putting his arm around her. "Car's outside. Let's go."

"Joel's girl"—that's what they'd call her. Maybe she and Joel would go dancing and to parties.

The next day Arlene skipped school. She spent all afternoon trying on her makeup and clothes—she had to look extra special that night. She was crushed when Joel didn't show up at the Bot.

In general, adolescence is a time for growth and change. The identity that the young person will carry throughout life begins to emerge during this period. As part of the process, young people begin to break away from their families. They critically examine their parents as well as society and its institutions. Adolescence is also a time of stress. In the search for a sense of self, for a belief in their own worth, adolescents often find themselves apparently in conflict with the world around them.

Adolescents also vary in maturity, ranging all along the developmental continuum from childhood to adulthood. Various measures of maturity, such as physical, social, and mental development, are not highly correlated during adolescence. Development in one area does not necessarily carry over into other areas.

Like other young people, both Joel and Arlene are struggling to mature. Both long for appreciation and acceptance from their peers. Each, however, for very personal reasons, is searching for friendship and understanding outside the normal peer network.

Joel's unequal development has left him isolated from his normal peers. He has not found the achievement either in school or the working world that can help him move forward. He needs someone to help him begin to channel his energy and creativity constructively while he catches up with himself.

The loss of her father and favorite sister have left Arlene feeling very alone. Most young people need to be able to retreat at times to the security of at least one meaningful person. It is important that someone—in Arlene's case, her mother, a relative, or even a teacher or counselor—sense the adolescent's need for sustained understanding and support at this time.

Parents who are faced with rebellious or moody young people, acting at times in hostile or destructive ways, may find it hard to remember that patience, consistency, and understanding may be needed more at this time of the young person's life than ever before.

CEIL AND RUSS

Ceil walked home from school slowly. She was trying to decide what to do about an article for the school newspaper. A voice from behind called her. She paused and Russell fell in step. She had known him for two years but they had been dating each other exclusively only about three months.

She smiled happily. "You got through basketball practice early."

"Yes," he answered. "You have time to stop somewhere on the way home?"

She hesitated. She really wanted to. "No, I guess not. I have a special choir rehearsal tonight and I've got to get my homework done before I go."

"What if I meet you after that?"

"Okay." She nodded.

He grabbed her hand, held it a minute, and then let go. "See you," he said and darted across the street.

Ceil's face, for a moment, reflected the indecision she felt. She'd had sex with Russ twice already. Both times she had not intended to—it just happened. After the last time, she decided definitely she would not do it anymore. Not only would her parents be mortified if they found out, but if word got around, their social reputations in the black community might be damaged. Besides, it really wasn't right. She had been brought up to believe that sex was something that should take place only in marriage. And marriage, well, that was so far away. Counting this year she had three more years of high school and then college. Her brother had just started college in the fall and his letters home made her all the more anxious to go herself.

Sex had complicated her life in a number of ways, she reflected. She hadn't told her girl friends. She didn't like keeping it from them but she wasn't sure how they'd feel about her if they knew. She wondered if Russ had told anyone. She didn't think so. She trusted him more than anyone she had ever met. He was very special. She liked to think she really loved him. At times she knew she did.

After they had had sex the first time, Ceil thought of trying to get some birth control device. However, she didn't know how to do it without risking disclosure. Certainly she couldn't go to her parents or the family doctor. Some of the girls in school probably were using birth control, but getting anything through them might mean being identified with them. She couldn't risk that either. They were not the kind of girls who were in her circle of friends. Perhaps most important, using birth control would be admitting she was going to behave in ways she knew her family, society, and even she felt she shouldn't.

No, tonight she would make sure things didn't go so far.

Russell walked home totaling up the things he had to do before he could meet Ceil as promised. He'd forgotten he had agreed to help his dad store away the screens and the lawn furniture. He also had to help his younger brother with his homework plus do his own. He quickened his pace.

This was Russ's last year of high school and almost everything was going great. He already had offers from several colleges. Russ was both a good athlete and a good scholar: colleges and universities were looking for promising blacks. Russ grinned. Moreover, he had gotten to know intelligent, funny, warm, sensitive Ceil. She was a no-contest first over most of the senior girls he knew. All in all, life was really good right now. He broke into a jog. To get everything done by 8:30 meant he would really have to push.

When Ceil got out from choir practice, Russ was there. She waved happily. Everyone's eyes were on her. She knew they envied her. A sophomore girl going with a senior basketball star. But then, she was the most talented and popular girl in her class, so why not?

Russ didn't have a car so they generally did things within walking distance unless they had time enough to take a bus downtown. Since it was a school night, it was too late to go downtown. The lateness of the hour also eliminated going to a nearby movie. Ceil's parents were fairly insistent on her being in at a reasonable time. The reasonableness varied with circumstances, but on a regular school night, ten o'clock was the limit.

"Want to get something to eat?" Russ asked.

Ceil knew eating meant they'd have a place to go. However, she was too stuffed from dinner to think of food so soon. "No," she said, "I overdid it on Mom's casserole tonight. Let's just walk for a while."

"I'm not hungry either," Russ said.

As they ambled along, Ceil tried not to think about the direction of their walk. When they reached the area where the new houses were being built, however, she knew what was coming. If they turned down that street, it meant they would come to sheltered spaces where there was no one around. "I should turn back," she thought.

But where else could they go? Although Ceil's parents always encouraged her to bring her friends home, there would be the usual round of "Hellos" and "Can I get you some Cokes or cookies?" That would take up precious time. Then, of course, there would be no real privacy. Even if her family cleared out of the family room, which they probably would do, she and Russ would have to remain a respectable distance apart and they would have to monitor their conversation just in case someone passing the door overheard them.

No, she had to have more freedom with Russ than that. "I'll be able to handle it when we get there," she thought.

Russ led her into the skeleton of a new house. In its shadows he took her in his arms and began to kiss her.

"If I act cold, maybe he'll get the message," she thought.

But her coolness did not deter him. He was gentle but persistent. She began to kiss him back and hold him tightly. Soon they both had too many feelings to want to stop.

Ceil had pictured intercourse as a melting together—a being so close that only thoughts and feelings of love were possible. But it didn't happen that way. Instead she experienced a confusing array of feelings: a wanting to and a not wanting to, a feeling guilty and a trying to feel free (but always alert in case someone came). As a result she never enjoyed it as much as she thought she should. And she also worried because she had not had an orgasm. But Russ had indicated that he found it all he wanted. That made up for some of her diminished pleasure. She did love him, she thought.

Russell heard something and got up from the ground hastily. He helped Ceil to her feet. They both stood silently—feeling vulnerable and guilty. He wished he had a car. Or better yet, that he knew a safe place where they could go and be alone.

Russ glanced down. Ceil looked scared. She was the nicest girl he had ever met. He had always thought that when he met someone he might marry, he would wait. Yet he couldn't wait with her. He felt confused. He didn't want her to be hurt by anything he did.

The noise was not repeated but the interruption had ruined the mood.

Each time, one of the nicest parts of their intimacy for Ceil had been being close and dreaming together afterwards. Now she felt cheated and unfulfilled. Neither, however, wanted to stay there.

They walked back to Ceil's house in silence. The farther they walked, the angrier Ceil became. Why had she been so weak?

Russ sensed something was wrong but he didn't know what it was. When they got to her house, Ceil coldly said good night and without even looking at him turned up the walk. Russ started to protest but stopped. After a minute, he turned on his heel and left without speaking.

Ceil walked into the house. She knew she had misbehaved toward Russ. Perhaps she should call him. However, she didn't know what to say. She was so angry. She just wanted to forget everything. She paused in the hallway and took a deep breath. Passing by the family room, she gave her parents a big "Hi" and motioned that she was off to study. Whenever she said she had homework to do, they left her alone. Also she felt she ought to wash up—she was conscious that she smelled different and wanted to get it taken care of before anyone came near her.

Ceil and Russ are, like many young people, ambivalent about the handling of sexuality in adolescence. Many times when there are strong group pressures, young people need to be told it is just as all right *not* to have sex as to have it. Ceil has no group pressure, but she needs reinforcement either for not having sexual relations or for facing up to the fact that she is having them and therefore needs to behave more responsibly. Russ also needs this kind of awareness.

Behaving responsibly involves a number of things. Russ already has some sense that it requires respect and concern for the other person's feelings and welfare. Ceil has some idea that protection against pregnancy is involved in sexual responsibility, but she probably sees this more as a concern for herself than for any child.

Since society does not encourage young people to have sexual relations (indeed it tries to prevent this through such worn-out methods as sexual ignorance, societal disapproval, limitations on freedom, moral exhortations, threat of punishment, and so forth), there is little help available for teenagers who need to think through decisions about sexual behavior.

Nor does society make contraceptive (birth control) information or services easily available to young people. Parental consent is most often required before prescription-method birth control can be given to those under the age of eighteen. Understandably, many young people are reluctant to disclose their activities to their parents.

However, public family-planning clinics, and private ones such as Planned Parenthood, often offer counseling and information services that may help the teenagers either tell their parents or else safely use non-prescription birth control methods. These agencies are listed in the yellow pages of the telephone directory under Clinics, Health Organizations, or Social Service Organizations, or in the white pages of the telephone book under specific names.

Until young people can secure counseling and medical services, the safest non-prescription pregnancy prevention method to use is a combination of a condom with a spermicidal foam, cream, or jelly. These are available without prescription at drug stores. The boy uses the condom; the girl uses the foam, cream, or jelly. If the girl is unsure whether the boy plans to use a condom, she should use the foam since it is more effective than cream or jelly when used alone. However, foam is not totally effective. Therefore, use of such contraceptives should be seen as a stop-gap measure only. As soon as possible, young people should seek contraceptive information and counseling and, hopefully, secure the birth control method that will best meet their needs if they plan to continue having sexual relations.

ERICA AND GARY

Erica lay flopped on her bed. As loud as the radio was, she barely heard it. She was trying to think of an excuse not to go to school the next day. Almost everything at school bored her. This was her last year and it seemed as if she had had everything before. Even the supposedly new things were just more of the same. She was tired of the regimentation: bells ringing; restrictions on lunch—when you had it, where you had it; having to sit in a study hall even when there was nothing to do.

Although it was only Monday, she was already dreaming of Friday. Friday evening she and Gary were going to another party. She had been steadily dating Gary for four years now. She couldn't wait to get married. Recently they had talked about it but he didn't seem to be in any hurry.

Gary had only been working a year. In that time he hadn't been able to save much money because he had bought a second-hand car and a new hi-fi. In June he was going to quit his job and go with his friend Chuck to California for the summer, something they had been planning since their graduation from high school a year ago. Erica guessed that the trip would take the rest of the money Gary would make between now and June. Although Erica knew Gary would be back, she was jealous. Why did he want to go off with another guy? Why not with her? What was she going to do all summer anyway? She knew she could be a waitress in the hill resorts again or maybe find some more permanent work at the plastics company. However, neither job appealed to her. She didn't know what she'd do in the fall.

"Yic." She turned over.

"Erica, turn that radio down!" her mother yelled from downstairs.

Erica pretended not to hear. Nevertheless, as she stretched, her hand felt for the dial and lowered the sound. Even though her mother said it was *their* home, at times she felt like a roomer with no rights. "Clean up your room." "Don't leave the towels spread around in the bathroom." "Put water in your glass before you set it in the kitchen sink." "Keep the front hall door closed." Oh, if only she could get out of here. She purposely let her feet hit the floor with a thud of resentment.

"Oh rats," she said. "Rats!"

Gary puttered with the carburetor in his car. His friend Chuck was underneath working on the muffler. Gary had paid, it turned out, far more than the car was worth. The motor was not nearly as good as he had been led to believe. But still, he wouldn't want any other car.

The first time he had seen the car was when a jobber had driven it into the parking lot at work. He went out to admire it on his lunch hour. He could hardly believe it when the same guy drove the car in six months later with a "for sale" sign in its window. It was a Mercury with black leather bucket seats and a vinyl sports roof. Even if there were some things wrong with the engine, Gary felt rich and important as he drove around. Chuck was putting some money into repairs now too. They wanted to get it in shape for the trip to California that summer.

"Remember, you said you'd call Erica and tell her what time we're going Friday night." Chuck's voice from under the car interrupted his thoughts. Gary hesitated. Erica would keep him on the phone for an hour if he called and he wanted to get the carburetor back together that night.

"Aw," he said, "I'll call her tomorrow night."

Even if she were angry, she would forgive him. They knew each other well. She was always getting mad about something. In fact, she seemed to look for things to get angry about. Sometimes he thought she did it just to keep him interested. Other times he thought it was to keep interesting things going for herself. Life was not terribly exciting in their town. And in a way her restless outbursts did keep things interesting. But at times he also got tired of them.

It would be nice just to get away for a couple of months and ramble around with Chuck. Of course, he would come back. But he would be changed when he did. He would take a firmer stand with Erica on some things.

Erica was miffed. Gary had not called her the night before

as he had promised. She wandered around the house aimlessly. Her parents were out for the evening and she had no one to talk to. She sighed. At school that day, she had found out that her best friend, Lizzie, had decided to go to junior college after all. Erica tried to feel happy for her but instead felt very let down. Because Gary had graduated, Erica was not regularly involved with the dating set at her school. However, her girl friends were all still in school. Over the years they had shared their successes, failures, love lives, and dreams. Now it seemed that she was going to be deserted by everyone. After graduation, one of her close friends was going to Chicago to get a job and live with an aunt. Another was getting married. Everyone had some kind of important plans. Now even Lizzie had plans. Erica didn't want to go to college but she didn't want to be left behind either.

When Gary did call, she yelled at him on the phone. "I want to talk to you," she said. "You get over here tonight or everything's off. Damn you and your car."

Gary was a little bewildered. He was used to Erica's ups and downs but she sounded particularly upset and he didn't know why. In the end, he said okay.

After she hung up the phone, Erica stormed upstairs to the bathroom. She talked angrily to herself in the mirror, turning away every once in a while so that when she turned back her arguments would have renewed impact.

Then suddenly she smiled. This was the time of the month she was most likely to become pregnant. She had thought of the idea before. She and Gary had been having sex for over a year now. They had always used something, usually a condom.

When Gary arrived he was surprised to find that Erica didn't seem angry at all. She was a changed person. She had hot coffee waiting for him and had fixed him a favorite snack. She was wearing a billowy see-through top and her best hip-hugger slacks. She leaned over and brushed against him as she poured his coffee.

"That's not fair," he said, reaching out to grab her.

She pulled back laughing. However, she continued to tease him while he ate. Finally he jumped up from the table and began to chase her. They ended up wrestling on the dining room floor. Erica wriggled away in delight. But Gary grabbed her again.

"Now you're going to get what you deserve."

Just before intercourse, Gary started to get out a condom.

"No," she said, pushing it back into his pocket. "I've been taking pills. It's okay."

Gary was surprised and started to ask her about it. She just giggled and pressed closer.

When Erica's parents came home an hour later, they found Erica already in bed and asleep.

At one point in our nation's history, adolescence was almost entirely skipped or at least shortened. Young people were expected to, and did, assume adult roles at earlier ages. However, for a variety of reasons, the adolescent period is now being prolonged. High school and college have replaced work institutions for young people in our society. As a result, the dependent state of youth has been lengthened.

For young people like Erica, who do not plan to go on to college, the last years of school may seem meaningless, particularly when confronted with a world which cannot absorb and generally does not reward youth with limited training and experience.

Erica has a further handicap in that she has not been brought up to think of herself as having a wide variety of options and choices about her future. Erica is one of the girls who, in a sense, seeks marriage and the family as a way out of her unchallenging personal situation. Her experiences are limited and so she doesn't see the alternatives that exist for young women today. She needs someone to take an interest in her, unlock her imagination and show her some of her potential.

In the future, one hopes that women will begin from early

childhood to prepare themselves for full- or part-time careers, meaningful avocations, and strong participation in community affairs as well as marriage, childbearing, and a share in child-rearing, if the latter are appropriate for them.

One also hopes that for young men like Gary, increasing technology will open up work opportunities of a more sophisticated and creative nature so that work will not be just a way to secure material things but also a meaningful experience in itself.

2. PREGNANCY:
The First Three Months

ARLENE AND JOEL

Arlene had just begun menstruating and her periods were quite irregular. Since she paid little attention to their timing, missing one or two had no meaning for her.

However, as time went on, Arlene's mother noticed she was acting out of the ordinary. Arlene seemed listless and was not as eager to get out of the house. On weekends, she took naps in the afternoon. Arlene also began to eat a great deal. She told her mother she had a queasy feeling inside and eating made her feel better. When her mother heard that she looked startled and asked Arlene if she had "done anything with anybody." Arlene denied it.

"You do and you'll get pregnant for sure," her mother warned her. "Just like Barbara did."

Getting pregnant had not occurred to Arlene at all. She only had a vague idea about how women got pregnant. She was pretty sure she wasn't. But Arlene wished her mother was easier to talk to about such things. Whenever anything to do with sex came up, her mother either pushed the question aside or else looked so embarrassed that Arlene herself changed the subject.

If only Barbara were still around. She could talk to her favorite sister about anything. Barbara had become pregnant her senior year of high school. Of course, Barbara and Jim had been going together a long time. Although Arlene remembered that Barbara said she hadn't planned to get pregnant, she didn't seem to be unhappy about it either. She moved out soon afterwards.

When Arlene's queasy stomach and tiredness continued, her mother's suspicions grew. She kept asking Arlene if her period had come. Arlene began to wonder more about pregnancy. She couldn't tell if anything different was happening to her. Pregnancy to her meant being very fat. When she stood on tiptoe to study herself in the bathroom mirror, she didn't look any fatter. She didn't feel a baby inside her either. She was sure she would know if one were there.

At about five weeks (three weeks after the first missed period) the baby is only about $\frac{1}{4}$-inch long. It has a heartbeat. The heartbeat, however, is too faint to be heard.

By the end of the eighth week, the baby has a head with the beginnings of facial features. Fingers, toes, eyes, and ears have begun to form. The baby is about $\frac{7}{8}$-inch long and weighs $\frac{1}{30}$-ounce.

By the end of the third month, the baby has grown to three inches or more in length and weighs two ounces or more. The baby squints, frowns, and opens its mouth. It practices breathing, eating, and movement. It can kick or pull up its legs, turn its feet, curl or spread its toes, bend its wrist, make a fist, curl or spread its fingers, turn its head. However, since the baby is still well down in the mother's pelvis, she cannot feel it yet. It is so small that its motions are not vigorous enough to be noticeable.

When Arlene's period did not come for an additional three weeks, Arlene's mother took her to the health clinic. Arlene did not want to go but her mother insisted. Arlene had seen a doctor only twice before—once when she had a very high temperature at age five and again at eight when she had broken her finger.

Her mother gave their names at the desk and indicated

what she thought the problem was. The receptionist looked unsympathetic and told them to be seated in the waiting room. Arlene felt very uncomfortable sitting in the yellow molded-plastic chairs. She felt everyone was staring at her.

"Mother, do I have to do this?" she asked.

Her mother nodded firmly.

Time dragged. Arlene fidgeted in her seat. Finally a nurse called her name.

"Go ahead," her mother said. "I'll be here."

Arlene got up reluctantly. She was frightened. She had no idea what to expect.

The nurse smiled at her—a weak smile but at least it was a smile. "Have you ever had a pelvic examination before?" she asked Arlene.

Arlene shook her head no.

"Well, before the doctor comes, I'll tell you about it so you'll know what's going to happen. First, however, I'm going to ask you to take off all your clothes. Here's a gown you can put on—put it on with the opening down the front. I'll be back in a minute."

Arlene took the gown, which looked like it was made from a starchy sheet, and put it on. It hung awkwardly. She could barely keep it up on her shoulders. She wrapped the two center folds across one another to keep them closed. She felt stupid holding it on.

The nurse was back quickly. "I'm going to ask you to lie down on this table. There," she said, "now bend your knees and put your feet in these metal holders called stirrups that are down here at the side of the table. That's it. Now move down toward them a little more."

The nurse covered her with a sheet and arranged it over her raised knees. "The doctor will be here in a minute. He will ask you some questions. When he examines you, he will insert two gloved fingers into your vagina. Then he will press on your abdomen with his other hand. That way he can feel if there are any changes in the uterus that are symptomatic of pregnancy. He will be done in a very short time. He will also want to examine your breasts for the same reason."

The doctor came in. He asked Arlene some questions about her periods, general health, and so forth. When he began the physical examination, Arlene clenched her fists, prepared for the worst. She was surprised when it didn't hurt. It was uncomfortable at times, but it didn't really hurt. While he was examining her, the doctor asked Arlene if she had had intercourse. She shook her head and stared at the formal medical certificates on the walls. Why didn't they have interesting pictures to help take her mind off the examination?

"Arlene," the doctor said gently. "A girl can't get pregnant unless she has intercourse—that's the only way. Did you have intercourse many times?" Arlene shook her head again.

The doctor was persistent. "When was the last time you had intercourse, Arlene?" He caught Arlene's eyes and held them. His look was serious. Arlene was scared.

"Just once in October," she blurted out.

"When in October?" he asked.

"Near the middle."

The doctor asked her a few more questions about her periods and how she had been feeling. "That will be all, Arlene. You can get dressed now," he finally said.

When Arlene was dressed, the nurse led her to a small office. Her mother was there waiting for her. The doctor came in soon after and sat down. He looked at both Arlene and her mother and then turned to Arlene.

"Arlene, I think you are about three months pregnant. We will give you a pregnancy test just to be sure but there is very little doubt."

Arlene didn't dare look at her mother; she just kept staring at the doctor.

"I'm going to give you a prescription now so you won't

have to make a special trip back next week. If you will call on Monday, we will have the results of the pregnancy test. If it is positive, as I am sure it will be, then just have the prescription filled. Also here is a card giving the hours of the maternity clinic. Your next visit should be one month from now. Do you have any questions?"

Arlene shook her head. Her mother got up and started walking out. The doctor handed Arlene another slip.

"Stop and ask the nurse where to go to get your blood test done and how to leave a urine sample," he said. "The nurse will also give you some information about diet and you can talk to a social worker about finances or other matters if you wish."

All the way home on the bus, Arlene's mother sat stonily. Only when they finally were in the house did she start to yell. Arlene was still so stunned at finding out she was pregnant she couldn't say anything. Although her mother yelled a number of different things, Arlene had trouble deciding what being pregnant really meant.

That night as she lay in bed, she began to dream about the future. She was going to have Joel's baby. They would get married just like Barbara and Jim. They too would get an apartment someplace. She wouldn't have to go to school anymore. She could stay home and cook special meals for Joel. Sometimes they would take the baby and go down to the Bot. Then even Jeanne would be jealous.

The next day Arlene's mother stayed home from work and refused to let Arlene go to school. Sometimes she was silent, at other times she scolded Arlene. Arlene thought it was really strange that her mother didn't ask whose baby it was. She acted as if Arlene had done it all by herself. Every time Arlene tried to say something her mother told her to shut up.

Arlene was miserable. She tried to ignore her mother. She dreamed about Joel, wondering when she could get out of the house to see him and tell him. She wasn't sure that he

would be at the Bot. Some kids had been picked up with
drugs a couple of weeks before. The police came regularly
now, checking out whoever was there. It had scared a lot of
the crowd off. But even if Joel wasn't there, there would
probably be someone there who could help her find him.

She wasn't quite sure what Joel's response would be. They
hadn't gone out. In fact, since the night they'd had sex, they
had only seen each other at the Bot. And she'd never really
talked to him alone. That made his reaction hard to judge.
Would he grab her and hug her? Would he want to go some
place together where they could talk about it in private?
Maybe he would just turn and yell to everyone else: "Hey,
Arlene's going to have my baby!" Every time she tried to
imagine what his reaction would be, she got very excited.

But Arlene had never seen her mother so angry. Finally
when her mother did ask who the father was, Arlene just
shrugged her shoulders. She was afraid of what her mother
might do to Joel, she seemed so upset. Her mother grabbed
Arlene by the arm and shook her.

"What does that mean?" her mother demanded to know,
imitating Arlene's shrug. Arlene burst into tears. Her mother
was making everything so mixed-up and awful.

Her mother finally softened. "Stop crying," she said,
patting Arlene. "I'm so upset because I love you. Your sister
got in trouble and ruined her life and now here you go and
do the same thing. You're so young too. My God, I don't
know what I'm going to do."

Arlene didn't reply. She wondered why her mother
thought Barbara had ruined her life. Barbara was very happy
with Jim. As far as what her mother had to do, Arlene didn't
know why her mother was worried. She was the pregnant one,
not her mother. It really didn't have that much to do with
her mother.

Arlene's mother made her stay home from school the next

day as well. Her mother missed work again. Arlene found out that her mother didn't care because it was her last day on the job. That also meant they would probably go back on welfare again. Her mother would be home all day and the way things were going, that meant Arlene wouldn't be able to get out of the house without permission.

On Saturday, however, she suddenly had a chance to sneak out for two hours.

Joel was anxious to get back to the pool game. Arlene had insisted that he come over to the end of the room to talk to her a minute. She was chattering on excitedly about babies. Only slowly did it dawn on him what she was trying to tell him. Arlene was pregnant and he was prime candidate number one for father. He was surprised. If some other chick had told him, he wouldn't have been so surprised. But Arlene? Why he'd only had her once. He mumbled something about being surprised. Then he patted her arm.

"Look," he said, "I've got this game to finish. We'll talk about it later."

Arlene was disappointed. He seemed so indifferent. Perhaps he didn't want the others to know right away. He would see her later. She stood at the end of the room waiting for him to finish. But when some other guys came in, Joel got into another game. Suddenly Arlene noticed the clock. She was late now. If she didn't get home, her mom would kill her. She was supposed to be looking after the younger kids. She had made them swear they wouldn't tell she had gone out. But she had to be back before her mother got home. Joel had gone to the john. She stood hesitantly. She couldn't wait. She'd have to catch him again.

But Joel wasn't around all during the week. Of course, she knew he didn't always come to the Bot. Plus her mother was making it so difficult for her to get away, she couldn't always come when she thought it would be the right time. At night she dreamed about Joel and what it would be like being married to him.

When Arlene finally did see Joel at the Bot, there was a big crowd of kids there. He was in the corner of the pizza place talking to one of his buddies. She walked over and touched his arm. He turned to her.

"Hi, Arlene, how you doing?" He gave her a big smile but immediately turned back to his friend.

"C'mon outside, I want you to meet somebody," Arlene heard Joel say to him.

Arlene started to speak. But Joel didn't hear her. He and his friend had already started toward the door. She followed the two of them outside, hoping to get Joel's attention again. Outside, in Joel's car, sat a girl Arlene had never seen. She was a pretty girl with long dark hair. She wore green eye shadow. Before Arlene could speak, she heard the girl say to Joel, "Is this the guy you've been wanting me to meet, Joel honey?"

Then Arlene heard Joel introduce this girl to his friend as "my girl." Arlene couldn't believe her ears. Tears came to her eyes and she rushed back inside. Jeanne came over.

"Arlene," she said, "what's the matter?"

Through her sobs Arlene poured out what she had seen.

"Oh, Arlene, wise up," Jeanne said. "Joel's had plenty of girls. This chick is just his latest—she'll be lucky if he doesn't get her pregnant."

Arlene burst out, "But don't you see? *I'm* the one who's pregnant!"

Jeanne stared and couldn't seem to say anything.

Arlene ran out the back door, down the alleyway behind the Bot stores. "Oh no, oh my God, no!" she kept crying. "This can't be happening to me. It can't be happening to me."

When she could run no more, she walked, tears streaming

down her face. At last she came to one of the neighborhood
porches where she used to curl up and dream before she
found the Bot. She threw herself down on the lounge and
cried uncontrollably. Finally she felt she had no more tears.
She tried to numb her mind so it wouldn't think and she
wouldn't have to feel.

When Arlene woke up, it was very dark. She must have
slept a long time. Her mother would be furious with her. She
didn't care. Nothing mattered. All her dreams were smashed.
She had nowhere to go, no one to turn to. She had never felt
so alone in all her life.

CEIL AND RUSS

As the time for her menstrual period approached, Ceil found
herself counting the days. If only it would come on time, she
would never do anything again. When her period did not
come, she felt a welling sense of panic.

"I can't possibly be pregnant," she thought. At the same
time, since she was very regular, she knew that for her, a late
period signalled something wrong. She wished she knew more
about pregnancy. Anyone she could trust to ask, however,
didn't know any more than she did and those who did know
more, she decided she probably couldn't trust.

Finally she chose the public library as the place to try to
find out if she could be pregnant. She looked up pregnancy
in the card catalogue. A number of books were listed. Most
were in the same number series. She tried to appear casual as
she walked along the shelves in the adult section. She didn't
dare take a book out of the library—someone might suspect.
She found one and took it off the shelf. A man turned down
the aisle. Ceil carried the book to one of the far tables at the
back of the library.

The book described the basic process of conceiving a child.
Ceil already knew that having intercourse was how women

became pregnant and that at certain times of the month women were more likely to get pregnant than at others, but she had only a vague idea of which time and what actually happened.

Despite adult misconceptions about the sexual sophistication of young people, few young people have accurate factual knowledge about sex. Ideas such as "you can't get pregnant if you do it standing up" and "you have to be older" are more prevalent than adults think. In one recent study, 98 percent of the teenage girls questioned said they knew what time of the month they were most likely to become pregnant. However, when asked what time of the month that was, half the girls gave an incorrect answer. Thus, giving accurate information about sex to teenagers is not just a matter of "filling empty bowls" as some adults like to think. Young people have acquired information already. Often, however, it may be erroneous enough to have negative consequences if they act upon it.

She struggled through the paragraphs of written explanation and drawings, trying to piece together what she needed to know. Some terms, such as "vagina," she knew; others, such as "cervix" and "fallopian tubes," made sense only when she looked at a diagram. She wished the books were written in street language rather than such fancy terms. However, she had to take what she could get. The book read:

> During intercourse, when a man's penis is in the woman's vagina, millions of sperm (the man's cells needed to begin life) are thrust out into the vagina.
>
> These sperm swim through an opening (the cervix) at the upper end of the vagina into the woman's uterus (womb). From there they swim through the uterus up into two tubes (fallopian tubes).
>
> Each tube leads to a part (ovary) of the woman's body that holds eggs (the woman's cells needed to begin life). If the sperm find an egg in the lower third of either tube, one

sperm enters (fertilizes) the egg and the process of developing a baby begins.

The fertilized egg in four or five days travels down to the uterus, implants itself in the uterine lining and begins to grow.

Nine months later a baby is ready to be born.

Ceil read the paragraphs several times in order to try to understand them. Even when she thought she did, though, this really didn't tell her what she needed to know. She turned the page. At last she stopped. She had found something reassuring. The book said that each month only one egg bursts out of one ovary at mid-cycle (that is, halfway between menstrual periods) and the egg could be fertilized for only about twelve to twenty-four hours. That made her chances of becoming pregnant seem much smaller. Surely she and Russ wouldn't have hit the exact twelve or twenty-four hours.

But when she began to read again, her panic returned. The book also said that once the sperm get to the uterus, they can live for four or five days. Therefore, there were five or six days each month in which intercourse could lead to pregnancy (four to five days before the egg bursts out and the half day after).

Ceil closed the book. She felt sick all over. Five or six days! She had been so sure she wouldn't get pregnant. It just couldn't happen to her. At the same time, it now seemed so easy to get pregnant. She wondered how people avoided it.

In particular, it should be stressed to young people that although women normally ovulate (release an egg) twelve to sixteen days before their menstrual period begins, a woman can become pregnant at any time during her cycle because she might ovulate early or late. Young women who are just beginning to menstruate often are more irregular than older women. Therefore they may be more susceptible to pregnancy during different times of their cycle.

As the days passed, every time Ceil went to the bathroom she hoped she would find that her period had come. Many times she went purposely just to look. Nothing happened. She grew more frantic. It was hard to study, hard to sit in school; she could only forget for a little while. She couldn't sleep at night. What if she really was pregnant? What would she do? Every day was more and more of a strain. She tried to keep her anxiety hidden from her parents. Finally she confided in one of her closest girl friends, Teri.

"I think I'm pregnant," she moaned, and for the first time began to cry.

"Oh, Ceil, how awful!" her friend responded. "What are you going to do?"

"I don't know. I'm terrified my parents will find out, and what if the school finds out? God, I'm so sorry. I wish I could take everything back."

"Well, are you really sure?" Teri asked. "Maybe you're just late or something. Sometimes my period is off."

"I've missed one period, Teri, and I'm due for a second one. If it doesn't come, I'll die."

When she was sure she had missed the next period too, Ceil told Russell. He looked as frightened as she did.

"I'll get the money for an abortion," he told her without hesitation.

Ceil nodded. Abortion would be a solution to the awfulness. "I don't know how to go about getting one, though," she confessed. "Plus I'm scared. I've heard stories."

"I mean a legal one," Russ said. "It'll be okay. Claire Scott had one."

Ceil looked surprised. Claire was treasurer of the senior class. "I didn't know that," she said.

"Most people don't," said Russ. "Look," he added, "we can't talk here. I'll meet you after school down by the new housing. Don't worry." He squeezed her hand briefly and looked into her eyes. "Don't worry," he repeated.

In many communities throughout the United States, abortion services are not readily available to young people. Even where they are, however, because of lack of knowledge about services, ignorance about pregnancy, fear of parental reaction, and so forth, young people often try problem-solving without adult help. The result can be getting to the services too late to be able to use them.

Young women who think they are pregnant and who think that abortion might be preferable to giving birth should immediately contact a counseling agency or an abortion center. Look in the yellow pages of the telephone directory under Social Service Organizations or Health Clinics. In the white pages look under Abortion or under the name of a specific organization. Most communities have counseling services. However, information operators in most major cities can give the telephone numbers of both abortion centers and counseling agencies in their areas.

The cost of abortions varies. Abortions done after three months of pregnancy can cost twice as much as those done in the first twelve weeks. In some states, welfare agencies will pay for abortions. Time payments can also be arranged.

Ceil waited nervously for Russ. What was taking him so long? Then in the distance she saw him coming. However, someone was with him. As he got closer, she saw it was Claire. Ceil was furious. She narrowed her eyes. She wanted to lash out at him and cry at the same time. How dare he tell someone else? She had trusted him. God, how could he do this to her? When he got up close she didn't even look at him. Her mouth was tightly drawn.

"Ceil, Claire can tell you all about it," he began.

Ceil didn't look at Russ. She tried to remain cool as she looked at the older girl instead.

Claire reached out and took her arm. "Gee, I'm sorry, Ceil. I know how you must be feeling."

"Sure, sure," thought Ceil, but at the same time she couldn't help but respond to the warmth in Claire's voice.

"In order to get an abortion," Claire went on, "you have to have a positive pregnancy test—that is, a test that says you are pregnant. You can get them several places. However," she went on, "if you go to the abortion center I went to, they do it for free. All you do is bring in a urine sample—one made the first thing in the morning before you have eaten anything. They'll let you know the next day. Then you can set up an appointment for the abortion."

Pregnancy testing is listed in the yellow pages of the telephone directory, often under a general heading such as Clinics. The cost is about eight dollars. One can call the health department and ask about where pregnancy tests are given or one can call a private obstetrician. Planned Parenthood can generally tell a caller where to get a pregnancy test and can also sometimes give information about available abortion services.

"Will my parents have to know?" Ceil asked.

"Yes," Claire nodded sympathetically. "If you're under eighteen years old, they won't do an abortion without your parents' consent."

Ceil's shoulders sagged. "I could never tell them," she said. "They'd die and so would I."

"I had to tell mine," Claire said. "Of course, they were upset. But it turned out my mom actually had one herself when she was young. Except she had to go to Chicago and some man did it in an abandoned building. He told her not to scream because someone might hear her but she did anyway. I guess it was a pretty awful experience.

"Mom said she was just glad abortion was legal and I wouldn't have to go through that. She even went with me and waited while I had it done. I wouldn't want to go through it again but it was okay."

"My parents aren't like that," Ceil said. "They don't approve of abortion, I'm sure. And I just can't have them finding out I've gotten pregnant."

"Well, there is one other way," Claire said hesitantly. "You can falsify your age."

"What do you mean?"

"Well, if you are under 18, they require a statement signed by your parents saying it is okay. That statement also has to be signed by a notary public, so you can't forge it. However, if you are 18 or over—nothing. So get some I.D. from someone who's 18. If you dress and act old enough, you might get by with it." Claire paused. "Listen, I know you've got a lot to decide but here's the number of the abortion clinic. They won't do an abortion if you are more than eleven weeks pregnant, so you have got to make your decision and really move if you've missed two periods."

Ceil was in agony all night. She was still angry with Russ for having broken her confidence. She didn't know how many people Claire would tell. Claire didn't seem like the type to spread gossip but Ceil had lost control of the situation. She felt embarrassed and hurt. The more she thought about everything the more frantic she became. Damn Russ, damn everything!

During the night Ceil had to urinate several times. In the morning she threw up. She came down to breakfast feeling giddy and depressed.

"What's the matter, Ceil?" her mother said. "You don't look well."

"Oh, I guess I'm just nervous," said Ceil. "We're having a history test today. I've gotten good grades so far, so if I can do well, I have a chance of getting straight A's this semester."

"Well," her mother touched her hair fondly. "I know grades count toward college. But remember they aren't important enough to make yourself sick over—there's a happy medium." She smiled.

Ceil tried to smile back but she found herself turning away instead.

"I've got to talk to you alone," Ceil whispered to Teri as they passed in the main hall that day.

"I'll meet you in the locker room before lunch," Teri offered.

"No, really alone."

"Come over to my house after school. It's my mother's bridge afternoon and she won't be back until 5:00."

Later when they met, Ceil poured out her problem. "So you see, I've got to get identification that says I'm 18. Can you get something of your sister's for me to use?"

Teri's sister was at college. Thanksgiving was only a week away and Ceil knew Marlene would be coming home just as her own brother was.

"I don't know," Teri said. "What if somebody thinks it's really her and it gets out. She'd . . ." Teri stopped talking as she saw the look on Ceil's face. "Sure," she finally said. "Sure, I'll get it for you."

Ceil waited. The week dragged. She continually had to urinate. She was also so tired that there were times she just wanted to slump down on the floor beside her desk and rest. As much as she needed to lie down, however, she was afraid to go to the school dispensary for fear the nurse might suspect something.

She began carrying crackers in her purse and nibbling them in class to help the nausea. Her English teacher caught her twice and gave her disapproving looks. Ceil immediately put them away. It was probably because she was a good student that the teacher didn't put her down in front of the whole class.

There are a number of bodily changes that can occur during early pregnancy: frequent urination, constipation, tiredness, nausea, swollen gums that bleed easily, breast enlargement, nervous upsets, and mood changes. Some, such as nausea, will disappear by the fourth month. Others, such as the need to urinate often, and tiredness, may disappear after the early months of pregnancy only to return in the last few months.

Women vary. Some experience few of these changes, others many. Most unfortunately, however, these early symptoms come at a time when a young person is likely to be trying to sort out feelings and make important decisions, often in an emotionally-charged situation. Certainly it is difficult enough to make sound decisions when a person is in peak physical and emotional health, let alone when she is feeling unwell and unsettled.

Finally Thanksgiving week came. Teri's sister had come home. Monday morning, before school, Ceil took the urine sample and her new identification to the abortion center. During the day she slipped the I.D. back to Teri. "I didn't need it," she said. "They just took my—I mean your sister's name."

The next day Ceil cut her study hall. It was strange being on the streets when no other students were. She kept looking around. She felt sure someone would see her and stop her. From a phone booth several blocks away she called the center.

"Yes, you're pregnant," the voice said.

Ceil gulped. She wanted to say, "Are you sure?" but she knew it was futile to ask. She just kept thinking, "I'm not pregnant and this is not me calling. This is something happening to someone else." At the same time, she heard her own voice say, "I'd like an appointment for an abortion."

"Can you come tomorrow?" the voice said.

Tomorrow! She was stunned. So soon. "Yes," she said.

"Then come at 7:30 in the morning. Now, I'll need some information. Your name is?" Ceil gave Marlene's name.

"Age?"

"Eighteen."

"Birthdate?"

Ceil hesitated. She didn't have the I.D. with her. She had

studied it before. Could she remember it? "March——." She said the date slowly. She hoped that was it. She was fairly sure but not absolutely. Her heart was in her mouth.

"Your address?"

Ceil gave Teri's address. All of a sudden she began to worry. What if the I.D. was traced to Teri's sister?

"Telephone?"

"Must you have that?" Ceil asked.

"Yes," the voice said. "But if you don't want us to telephone you, we will honor your privacy."

"No, don't call me," Ceil said and gave Teri's number.

"Bring $150 in the form of either a certified check or money order, another urine sample, identification, a sweater, and a sanitary pad. And don't be late," the voice said. "It will keep everyone else waiting."

Ceil hung up the phone. She felt weak in the knees. She didn't want to go back to school but she had to see Russ. She knew he had been trying to get the money ever since she told him she was pregnant. She hoped he had it.

Russ went with Ceil to the abortion center the next morning. Ceil still felt angry with him for having told Claire. At the same time, she needed someone desperately right now and he was being very involved and caring. Ceil was surprised to find so many of the other girls there had fellows with them too—only a few had either a parent or a girl friend. She studied the girls anxiously. Mostly college kids. She was afraid she looked young compared to them. Thank goodness Russ looked older.

One by one the girls were called to a reception desk. When Ceil was called, she gave the woman her money order, showed the identification she had gotten back from Teri, and answered several questions.

"Here is an information sheet describing what is going to occur today," the woman said, giving her a piece of paper. "We will also give one of the same sheets to the young man with you so he will know what's taking place while he is waiting."

Ceil took the paper and went upstairs to the clinic. She turned in her urine sample and was given blood tests and a preliminary physical exam to determine her stage of pregnancy. Other girls were being called in and out of the upstairs waiting room to do the same thing. Finally someone came up to Ceil and introduced herself as her counselor. The information sheet had said that the counselor would talk to her prior to the abortion, stay with her while it was done, and then see her afterwards.

The counselor and Ceil walked to a small, sunny interview room. All I have to do is get through this, Ceil thought, and I'm home free. But I've got to act 18.

"How do you feel about being here?" the counselor started off. Her face was pleasant and her voice was warm and encouraging.

Ceil fumbled a bit for an answer. She'd better not say she was scared, which was what she really felt. What would an 18-year-old say?

The more they talked the more Ceil relaxed and allowed her emotions to come closer to the surface. She was vaguely conscious of the counselor acting as if there were all the time in the world to talk. It was as if she were the only patient there, that no one else was waiting. As they talked, for the first time since she began to suspect she was pregnant, Ceil began to feel that someone really cared about the whole situation and about her special place in it.

Finally the counselor said, "I get the feeling you're not really happy about having an abortion."

Ceil hesitated and tried to think of the right answer. Instead she broke into tears.

"I don't know," she said. "I don't know. I don't want to have a baby, but I don't know whether or not I want to have an abortion either." She hesitated and then rushed on. "But

Russ is downstairs and he expects me to . . . and Teri
expects me to . . . and I can't not do it . . . I've got to."

"What about your parents?" the counselor asked. "Have
you told them? How do they feel?"

"Oh, I can't, I can't." Ceil told the counselor how she
thought finding out she was pregnant would affect her
parents. When the fact that she was not 18 slipped out, it
didn't seem to surprise the counselor. Ceil guessed she must
have known all along.

"Think about it for another week," the counselor finally
said. "You will still be eligible for an abortion here under the
twelve-week limit." Then she added, "You know I stand right
there with a woman when she has her abortion. Therefore I
have to believe what she is doing is right for her. If you
decide it is really right, then let's talk next week, but right
now I'm much happier that you are going home to think a
while."

Ceil smiled gratefully. She felt almost happy as she went
downstairs. All the problems were still facing her and they
were enormous. But one weight seemed to have been lifted
from her shoulders. She thought about the other girls she had
seen in the various waiting rooms. Like Claire, an abortion
was probably right for them. She was glad that they could
have it. But she also was glad that now she had more time to
think.

Up until the twelfth week of pregnancy, dilation (stretching
open) of the cervix followed by vacuum suction (a vacuuming
out of the uterus) and/or curettage (a scraping out of the
uterus) are the medical procedures used for most legal abortions. The process takes less than twenty minutes. Either local or
general anesthesia may be used. However, local anesthesia is
cheaper and safer, and the recovery time is shorter. Except for
some cramping the whole procedure is relatively painless.
Recuperation time is minimal, ranging from six hours to six
days.

After the twelfth week the most common legal abortion method is a saline injection (a salt solution is injected into the uterus). However, this means full labor for the woman, which is both painful and emotionally stress-laden. If pregnant adolescents choose to have an abortion, it is obviously important that they identify themselves before the twelfth week.

Russ was surprised when Ceil appeared so soon. None of the girls who had gone before her had come back to the waiting room yet.

"I decided not to have the abortion right now," Ceil told him.

Russ looked at her. The implication of her decision was enormous. He wanted to ask why. Looking around the waiting room, though, he decided he didn't want to talk about it where the others might hear. He stood up and helped Ceil on with her coat. "Let's just ride," he suggested.

They got on a bus that went way out to Parkside. For an hour and a half they sat and talked. There seemed to be very few answers, just lots of feelings.

"If you decide not to go back," Russ finally said, "I'll marry you. So don't worry. It's up to you."

During the next few weeks, Ceil's nausea increased—she threw up regularly. Because she was thin, as she approached the end of the third month she showed a little round bulge in her abdomen. She stopped wearing some of her clothes entirely and switched to the few full skirts she had. Ceil still had not told her parents. She worried constantly. She felt sure that she wasn't going to have an abortion but she kept putting off thinking about the alternatives. At times she imagined that she wasn't pregnant—perhaps it was all a mistake. Other times, she thought she might miscarry and her problems would be solved.

Ceil's face became pale. Her parents were worried about her and wanted her to see the doctor. She skillfully postponed making an appointment each time, but whenever her parents mentioned her health, Ceil grew more pressured and distressed.

Russ felt helpless. Ceil avoided him at times. At other times, when they met, she either angrily refused to talk about the pregnancy or else talked about it in circles. Russ sensed Ceil was in a real crisis and that he couldn't help her. Out of desperation, he finally called the abortion center and asked for the name of the counselor who had seen her—giving Teri's sister's name.

When Russ finally got the counselor on the telephone he asked her to see Ceil. The counselor noted that since Ceil was past her twelfth week of pregnancy, she couldn't have an abortion through the center. Russ said he knew that. "She needs someone," he pleaded, "and I can't help her. She won't face up to things and she's going to pieces."

The counselor finally told Russ that if Ceil would come in at the end of the day, she would stay late and see her.

Although a wide variety of counseling services—counselors in schools, mental health clinics, health agencies, hospitals, public and private social service organizations, YWCAs, special projects or programs—may be available in a community, self-referrals are unlikely unless a number of young people have had successful experiences with the particular service. Russ has put Ceil in touch with the only agency he knows to contact. Most often, it is when the plight of the young person comes to the attention of a professional—a teacher, a nurse, a minister, and so forth—that the young person is put in contact with an appropriate helping agency or service.

However it occurs, that first step is a most important one. Young people need to feel that the person they first turn to will respect them and keep their confidences until such time as they mutually agree others should be involved. If that basic trust can be established and carried out responsibly, it sets the tone for better following relationships.

Ceil was furious when she found out Russ had called the

center. Again he had intervened without her permission. In the end, however, she went with him because she felt too desperate to turn down any offer of help. When Ceil arrived at the abortion center, she found the counselor waiting for her in the reception area. Another woman was with her.

"Ceil, this is a friend of mine who works at the Family and Children's Service Agency. Would you mind if she sat in on our discussion? She's come by to give me a ride home but she also knows a lot about the problems of girls in situations like yours."

Ceil felt she could do little but say yes. Anyway, as long as she had come, it didn't matter that much whom she saw. Russ waited in the lounge while the three women went upstairs.

As Ceil and the counselors talked, it became clear that one of the major stumbling blocks to facing reality and to planning a course of action was the fact that Ceil was still unable to tell her parents. As they talked further, Ceil realized that although she was worried about her parents' reaction to the pregnancy, she also felt very ambivalent about marrying Russ and didn't want to face that. If she could just announce to everyone that she was getting married, it might help but—and here she hesitated—she felt so mixed-up. She loved Russ. But love as she knew it and suddenly being married with all that responsibility were two different things.

Ceil talked with the counselors for about forty-five minutes. At the end of that time, the social worker from the Family and Children's Service Agency told Ceil she would be glad to have her come and talk with someone in her agency, even herself, at any time. Furthermore she offered to go with Ceil to help tell her parents if Ceil wished. Ceil brightened at that offer but finally said no; she would do it alone. She agreed to report back to the Family and Children's Service counselor about what happened.

This kind of transfer of a person needing help from one agency to another is, of course, rare. Generally, formal referrals are made in which the person to be helped is responsible for calling the new agency, setting up the appointment, and introducing a new professional to the problem. Particularly for adolescents, who are naturally suspicious and somewhat distrustful of adults, such a process may be difficult. Moreover, being referred elsewhere for service may be viewed by the young person as a rejection.

Supplying the name of a specific individual whom the young person can see in the new agency, making a definite appointment time, or in some cases, even taking the adolescent to the agency and personally introducing him or her to the new service, may be necessary. Otherwise young people can easily get lost between the services.

Just as with other things, no one service is good for all people. Young people themselves should not be afraid to shop around for the kind of help *they* feel they need. Some cities have information centers or "hot lines" (listed under Social Service Organizations in the yellow pages, and often advertised on popular music radio programs) that can provide information about possible sources of help for young people.

Russ wanted to be with Ceil when she told her parents. He had already told his and to his surprise, although they were unhappy, they seemed to understand. They had urged him to marry Ceil if he loved her. He told them he did and that he had asked her.

The roughest part for Russ had been when his parents called a family conference to tell his younger brother and sister. Both looked up to him, he knew. Russ was worried about what effect knowing he had gotten a girl pregnant would have on them. He wanted to make sure they understood what a lousy situation it was to be in. At the same time, his respect and affection for Ceil made him feel disloyal when he talked negatively.

Ceil decided she wanted to tell her parents alone. She also

realized she had better do it before her older brother came home from college for Christmas vacation. He would be furious and she didn't want to face his anger at the same time she faced her parents. Ceil asked her parents to sit down. Perhaps it was because she felt so guilty that she approached the subject almost in an off-hand manner. Ceil's mother immediately put out her arms and rushed over to Ceil. Her father sat stonily. It was clear that he was very angry. When he began to speak he demanded to know who the boy was. Ceil hesitated and said that was not the most important thing.

"Who is he?" commanded her father.

When Ceil told him it was Russ, he demanded to know if he was going to marry her.

Ceil said that Russ had offered to.

Although it didn't reduce her father's anger, he did fall silent for a while. Ceil's mother asked how long she had known and said Ceil should have told them much sooner.

It was clear to Ceil that both her mother and father were worried about Ceil and her future plans. However, in the end their reaction was not nearly as bad as Ceil had anticipated. In fact their response made her feel even guiltier. She was terribly relieved she had told them. At the same time, deep inside she desperately wished they had punished her in some way. In a strange way she felt it would have made her feel less alone.

Ceil's mother called Russ's parents the next day and a meeting of both families was arranged for over the weekend. Ceil wished they wouldn't do that but her mother insisted it was a two-family affair.

Russ was as nervous as Ceil. They both felt embarrassed in front of the families. Russ spoke almost immediately. He said he was sorry that it had happened but that he was quite prepared to take on the responsibility. If he couldn't get a college scholarship large enough to support Ceil and the baby after they were married, he said, he would postpone going to college. Russ's family then said that they were prepared to help him go through college regardless.

As the discussion went on, Ceil began to feel more and more ignored. Ceil's going to college was not mentioned. She felt everything was being arranged for her, but without considering her. Finally Ceil blurted out: "I can't! . . . I can't marry you, Russ!" She turned to her parents. "I'm not ready. Don't make all these plans for me. I'm not ready to get married!"

Everyone sat uncomfortably.

"Well, that's your decision, dear," Russ's mother said at last. "But it is going to be our grandchild and we will love him and we think it is important that he has a father and his father's name."

Tears came to Ceil's eyes. She looked at Russ pleadingly.

At last Ceil's father said, "There are a lot of changes for Ceil to get used to all at once, as I'm sure there are for Russ. I think she'll see things differently once she's had a chance to think about them some more."

After Russ and his family had gone, Ceil burst into tears and ran upstairs. Her mother followed.

"Mom, I don't want to get married."

"I know, dear," her mother replied. "I guess neither your father nor I understood how strongly you felt about it. I know your father is thinking about the future of the baby as well as yours. We'll talk some more."

Later that evening when Ceil got up to go to the bathroom, she heard voices coming from her parents' bedroom. "But damn it," her father said. "She's so cocky. She doesn't act as if she feels guilty or sorry for what she's done."

Ceil's back stiffened. She wasn't going to go around in sackcloth and ashes, pleading forgiveness from everyone. She was pregnant. She hadn't intended to do it but it happened to lots of people. My God, you'd think having a baby was something that never happened. She went back to bed more determined than ever to show she could carry the pregnancy through on her own.

Several days later, Ceil learned that her mother had called Russ's parents and indicated that there would probably not be a marriage. Russ's parents said that they would contribute to the cost of Ceil's medical care. Ceil's mother had said they would not file a paternity suit. She said she trusted Russ and his family to contribute to the baby's later support as needed.

Ceil was furious again. She felt that whatever was worked out should be done between her and Russ—after all, it was their pregnancy. But she just turned her back and walked away. God, it was so complicated. All these people involved. It was her pregnancy but so many people were affected. And there was still the problem of school. Sooner or later her teachers would begin to suspect if they didn't already. Everything was so complicated. She went up to her room. She was tired and nauseous and fed up with the whole thing.

If a couple does not marry, a father can acknowledge his paternity voluntarily by signing legal papers stating that he is the father. In cases where the father is unwilling to acknowledge paternity, a court action can be brought by the mother to have the man legally declared the father of her child. By and large, paternity suits are brought as a protection for the mother and child. For example, the court can order the father to contribute financially to the child's support if he is unwilling to do so freely. However, there are other considerations in a paternity suit. If the mother later marries a man who wants to adopt the child, the legal father can withhold permission. Therefore, it is wise for both young people involved to have legal counsel.

In the case of Ceil, her parents do not want to file a paternity suit because they want to keep family relations smooth. Going through a court action, they feel, might damage these relations. And Russ has acknowledged his paternity, and his family has agreed to contribute to the child's support.

There is a statute of limitations, however, and paternity must be established within a set period of time. If a conflict arises after that period elapses, the young people will not be able to settle it in the courts.

Russ was angry and confused. He desperately wanted to do the right thing. By marrying Ceil he believed he would be taking responsibility for his actions. He felt hurt and rejected by her refusal to marry him. At times he felt she was denying him his right—that of being a husband and father. She was getting back at him in that way for his making her pregnant. At other times, when his guard was down, Russ realized that he too was somewhat ambivalent about marrying Ceil. He loved her, he knew. However, even though he had said he would put off going to college if necessary, he knew in his heart that he wanted desperately to go. He had counted on it, it was his future. If he went and took Ceil and the baby with him, it would change everything. He would make that adjustment if necessary. But still, deep in his heart there was that original dream—going to college just as he had planned and making a reputation for himself there. Damn, what a mess.

As the weeks went on, Russ became more and more confused. He felt guilty. Yet he didn't know what to do. He was often irritable and moody. At those times, his friends learned to leave him alone.

Although Russ has had several brushes with counseling through his contacts with the abortion center and the family agency workers, no one has actually offered to sit down and talk with him. Most community services are aimed at the pregnant woman and unfortunately see the young man involved as a secondary person. Russ needs to talk with someone just as much as Ceil. He, too, is a person with feelings, reactions, rights, and responsibilities.

The person Russ speaks with must consider the situation from Russ's point of view—see him as an individual with a full life

ahead and critical choices to be made. Ideally, the person who
counsels him should not be the same person who counsels Ceil,
although at some point joint counseling may become important.

ERICA AND GARY

Erica waited eagerly to see if her period would come. The
secret of what she might have done kept her on an edgy high.
When she did miss her period, she was ecstatic. She
immediately began to wonder how and when she would tell
everyone. Since she had already hinted to Lizzie that she
might be pregnant, she called her first.

"No, are you really? How do you feel? It's so beautiful!
What's going to happen to you at school? Have you told
Gary yet?" Lizzie asked all in the same breath.

Erica chatted on happily. "He's coming over tomorrow
night and I'll tell him then. I want to make it a really special
occasion."

When she told Gary, however, his reaction was not quite
as she anticipated.

"How'd it happen?" he asked. "We've been so careful."
He paused. "Jesus, that's really going to change things."

He stood up, put his hands in his pockets, and began to
pace. "It sure messes up everything. I suppose we should have
known something like this would happen sooner or later. It's
just that everything was going so well."

He looked over at Erica. There were tears in her eyes.
"Hey look," he said, "I love you. Don't worry. We'll work it
out. It's just that I thought we were so careful."

"Have you told your parents?" he asked later.

"No," Erica replied. That was the part she didn't exactly
relish. Now, based on Gary's reaction, she was really scared
about it.

"When do you want to tell them?" Gary asked.

"I don't know," she answered.

"Whenever you decide to do it," he said, "I'll come over. We've got to tell my parents too, you know."

Gary left early that evening. Erica realized, as she got ready for bed, that they hadn't even mentioned marriage. Not that she didn't know it was understood. But still, she missed having him ask her. But then, nothing was really going just as she had planned. All of a sudden, everything seemed so much more serious. She lay awake a long time. "I won't let anyone or anything ruin this. I'm going to have a baby and I'm going to enjoy every minute of it. This is my experience."

Gary drove back home slowly. He was still stunned by Erica's disclosure. His parents would give him hell for having made Erica pregnant before they got married. And Erica's parents? He really dreaded that. Erica's mother was just as temperamental as Erica—there was no telling what her reaction would be, but it wouldn't be good.

He kept wondering how they had slipped up. It must have been the pills Erica was taking. Perhaps she hadn't been taking them long enough or maybe she had missed a couple. One of the fellows at work had said that his wife did that. She started redecorating the living room and got so excited, she forgot her pills for four days. Later on, they had to cancel the order for the couch and the chairs—they couldn't afford to buy new furniture and have a baby too.

Gary began totaling up the money he had saved. It wasn't much but there were almost eight more months before the baby would be born. He didn't know how much it would cost to have a baby. His insurance at work wouldn't help—he had coverage only on himself. They would need a crib. Where would they live?

The more he thought about it, the more overwhelmed Gary felt by the problems to be solved. And then there was his California trip—his dream. It should seem small at a time like this, he realized. But it had been so real up until this evening, such a big thing. Now it was a big myth instead of a big reality.

"No way. No way," he said aloud without even realizing he had done so. He pulled into his drive. He mechanically shut off the motor and put his head down on the wheel. He was quiet for a long time. Finally his body shuddered and one sob escaped him. Then he straightened up, took the key out of the ignition, and went into the house to face his parents.

When Erica and Gary told her parents, a major scene developed. Erica's mother was furious and began to yell. Erica's father did not say much. He just sat.

The more Gary and Erica tried to reassure her parents, particularly her mother, the worse it got. The fact that they were going to get married did not seem to calm Erica's mother. She said they were too young to get married.

Then she ranted on about morals. Wringing her hands, she kept turning to Erica's father and saying "What did we do wrong?" Then she would turn back to Erica and repeat the same thing.

The more Erica's mother talked, the more worked up she became. She told Erica that she had not only ruined her own life, she had ruined theirs (meaning her parents') too. "What will your grandmother think?" "How can we face our friends ever again?" Finally she was at the point of shouting questions at Gary about his job and his ability to support a family.

Erica knew Gary was particularly sensitive about his job and money. She could tell the things her mother was saying were hurting. She began to yell back at her mother. Finally Erica's mother told Gary to get out of the house and never come back. Erica shouted that her mother couldn't do that and if Gary went, she'd go too. Then Erica ran out of the house with Gary following her.

They drove around for a while. Erica was shaken and

crying. Occasionally she burst out in a fit of anger. When she quieted down, the only place they could think of for her to go was Lizzie's. Gary drove her over there to spend the night.

Lizzie tried to comfort her but Erica thought Lizzie's ideas and comments were no help in the face of the awfulness of the situation. Finally Erica said she just didn't want to talk about it anymore.

In the morning, the phone rang. It was Erica's father.

"How does he know I'm here?" Erica asked.

"Oh, my parents insisted on calling yours last night," Lizzie said. "They said you couldn't stay unless your parents knew. I didn't tell you because I thought that was the last thing you needed to hear."

Erica hesitantly put the phone to her ear.

"Erica," her father said. "Your mother and I want you to come home."

"Oh, Dad," she sobbed and began repeating some of the things that had been said the night before.

"There, there," her father's voice soothed. "Your mother and I have been talking all night. It's going to take some more time for your mother to get used to things but I think we've got a lot worked out."

Erica was terribly grateful to her father. Normally he did not take such an active role in family affairs.

In the next few weeks, however, Erica found that her father's remark about her mother's needing time to adjust was something of an understatement. It was Erica's mother who had the pregnant mood shifts rather than Erica.

Erica had no nausea at all and was rarely tired. Nevertheless, there were times when her mother would make her stay in and rest when Erica would rather have been out doing things. At other times, her mother dragged her all over downtown looking at baby things and possible wedding gifts when Erica would have rather just relaxed and had some time to herself to think.

Indeed, at times the pregnancy seemed to have so changed things that Erica longed for a return to the old days when she felt isolated and somewhat alienated from her parents. But she knew now that nothing would ever be the same.

Erica's mother insisted Erica see a doctor right away. Their family doctor recommended an obstetrician of long-standing acquaintance.

Erica looked forward to her first medical visit as a chance to find answers to a lot of the things she was curious about. She also wanted very much to share her enthusiasm about being pregnant with someone not involved in her personal situation. Her happiness was dashed, however, by the cold, stern attitude of the doctor. He questioned her closely about when she was going to get married. It was evident that he didn't approve of teenage pregnancy in or out of marriage. Not until she was married, however, would she receive any tolerance at all. Erica wanted to ask many questions but it was clear that the doctor didn't care to spend much time with her.

Erica knew she needed medical care, but she left the doctor's office with a great deal of resentment. This is my baby, she thought. I'm not going to let any old moralistic physician make me feel bad and not enjoy it. I'm going to have a baby and nobody can take that away from me.

Unfortunately, not all physicians realize that pregnant adolescents may need special assistance. Young women often come to a doctor with inadequate knowledge about their bodies and themselves. They also do not have the peer resources of other, older pregnant women. Thus, ignorant on many matters and isolated from their peers, they need reassurance, an extra measure of understanding, and a wide variety of information about themselves, pregnancy, and childbirth. This information must be presented in ways that are appropriate to the age of the adolescent. Physicians who do not have the inclination or the time to provide this help should put their young patients in contact with community resources that can help. For example, hospitals or health agencies with teen clinics, or private organizations such as the Red Cross may offer health-centered group counseling for young people and/or preparation-for-parenthood courses.

Erica's parents both wanted Erica to finish school. Gary supported her parents' position, saying it was important to him as well to have her complete her education. Erica loved him all the more for thinking about her in that way when she knew he was under so much financial pressure. She did worry because going to school eliminated her being able to work before the baby was born. At the same time, she was glad to be able to do at least one thing that appeared to please her parents. Besides, she also felt her parents might not sign for her to get married if she quit school.

The wedding was quickly arranged. During the few weeks before the wedding, Erica's mother seemed to come to life. She loved planning the details. Even the embarrassment of having a daughter who "had to get married" seemed to get lost in the fact that her only daughter was to be a bride.

Erica thought the minister who married them was very nice except for one thing: several times he asked Gary and Erica separately, and then together, if they wouldn't like to attend counseling sessions prior to their marriage. Both Gary and Erica refused. Under the circumstances they both felt they weren't going to change their minds and Erica, in particular, resented his continued asking.

"Why does everyone want to see my pregnancy and our marriage as a problem? We are in love. We are going to get married. I am going to have a baby. Millions of people do that each year. Why pick on us?"

Gary sympathized with her attitude. He felt he had enough problems without talking to someone who might think up other ones.

Divorce rates for those who marry in their teens are
four times as high as those in any other age group. Indee
than one out of every two marriages among those of sch
ends in divorce within the first five years. Many of these early
marriages are the result of a pregnancy conceived before the
marriage. Marriage is seen as the only solution. Instead, several
years later, and often several children later, young women find
themselves faced with being the head of a household and often
the breadwinner too. With little education or training and no
work experience, they are generally ill-prepared for these
duties. Young men may find themselves with life-long commit-
ments which they will deeply resent.

Thus, marital and parental counseling—particularly discussion of the problems that are especially difficult or even unique
in young-parent families—is very important. Prevention of hasty
or ill-advised marriages among young people is one of society's
more important tasks and one that it has seriously neglected.

Everyone had reluctantly agreed that following their
marriage, Gary and Erica would have to live with Erica's
parents until such time as they could afford to move out.
Erica's mother put another single bed in Erica's room and
Erica shoved it together with hers. All the frills and girl stuff
now seemed out of place. She took many of the things down
but regardless of what she did, she couldn't make the room
look as it should. It looked plain junky, particularly after
Gary brought over his things.

There was so little storage space that they had to hang
many of his clothes on the backs of the doors. They bought a
cardboard chest to put some of his things in. However, it had
to be kept in the hall outside the bedroom door since there
was no room inside.

The guest room was temporarily converted into a nursery.
Erica's grandmother came to stay with them every summer
and had used it as her room. Because of that, the room
wasn't completely Erica's to redo. Moreover, if she and Gary

weren't able to move out by summer, Erica had no idea what they would do when her grandmother came. She longed for a place of her own. Rather than getting her out of the house as she thought it would, Erica reflected, her pregnancy and marriage seemed to be getting her ever more involved in her home and her family.

"Oh rats!" Erica said and sank back on her bed. Bang! Her head hit the sideboards between the two beds. She began to cry.

3. PREGNANCY:
The Middle Three Months

Arlene was very depressed. The days dragged for her and she dreaded each one more than the last. She hadn't gone back to the Bot. Jeanne had probably told everyone she was pregnant. How they must all be laughing.

In her mind, Arlene kept going over each time she had seen Joel since that night at the golf course. It had only been at the Bot. However, he had often called her over to join the group he was sitting with. And he had kidded around and given her playful hugs if she sat next to him. But then there were other times when he had appeared to ignore her too. Had it really been all in her mind? Every time she thought about it, she became more miserable.

"I hate him, I hate everything about him," she moaned over and over again.

If only things could be different. If only he would come to see her and say he cared about her. Then she wouldn't have to hate him and she could face people again. But even as she wished, she knew it wasn't going to happen.

Arlene was frightened about being pregnant. She had little idea of what to expect. More than anything, however, she knew she had this "thing" of Joel's inside her and she wished she didn't.

"Look," one of the older girls in her neighborhood finally said, "if you feel so bad, why don't you get rid of it?"

"How?" Arlene asked.

"Do something that over-strains you. Or drink something purging like mineral oil. That's what I've heard."

Arlene nodded soberly.

The girl lived in a five-floor walk-up apartment building. "Maybe run up and down the stairs in my place," she suggested.

"Why not?" Arlene answered. "It might work."

Arlene climbed up to the fifth floor as fast as she could. Then she ran down the stairs stomping on each step. She repeated the process two more times. Then she climbed back up slowly and sat down on the top step. She began to bump as hard as she could all the way down the stairs—counting the steps as she went. She had intended to do that again too, however she had hit her backbone several times on the way down and it hurt so much she couldn't bear to repeat it. She felt so stiff and bruised already; surely it must be enough. She waited expectantly for a couple of days. Putting clothes on her back was painful and every time she sat back against a chair, she winced. However, her period did not come.

Having her hopes raised and then dashed made Arlene more desperate. She bought two bottles of mineral oil. She drank them almost nonstop, gagging frequently. She threw up after the first bottle, and after the second retched over and over again. She coughed so hard she saw blackness and stars. She felt like she was going to die.

"Ohhh, ohhh," she murmured over and over again, dragging herself into bed. "Oh, I am so sick, so sick, so sick." She wished her mother were home to take care of her. However, she purposely had chosen a time when her mother would be out for the afternoon.

The next day she still felt very unsteady on her feet and

her head swam. "Whatever happens," she thought, "I can't go through that again."

She waited. By the following week, she gave up hoping.

Home remedy abortions almost never work. They can, however, be very dangerous. Illness requiring time in the hospital to recuperate is one possible result. Permanent disability can be another. Later on, for example, when the woman wants a baby, she may find she is unable to become pregnant or to carry the baby to full term. Some attempts at self-induced abortions can endanger not just the baby's life but also the mother's. Several thousand women still die each year from illegal abortions or attempts to abort themselves. With the expanding availability of legal abortion services, and a changing attitude on the part of welfare departments so that in many areas even the very poor can have abortions paid for, no young person should risk injury or death by attempting a self-induced abortion.

Arlene went to school to avoid being at home with her mother and her inevitable nagging. She was so upset by being pregnant, however, that she had difficulty even in the subjects that formerly had caused her no trouble.

Finally the gym teacher noticed Arlene was pregnant and sent her to the school nurse. The nurse, in turn, sent her to the principal. The principal called Arlene's mother. He said Arlene could not remain in school. His suggestion was that Arlene drop out this year and come back the next. However, since Arlene was under sixteen and therefore still subject to the compulsory school law, he added that she was eligible for home tutoring if a tutor were available. But when Arlene's mother told him she'd like Arlene to have a home tutor, the principal didn't seem too pleased. He said he would see what he could do.

Until fairly recently, compulsory education rules were almost always waived in the case of pregnant students. However, girls who are out of school a year because of pregnancy are much less likely to return to school and finish than are girls who remain in school during pregnancy. Recognition of the importance of education for all young women, and in particular, those who are about to take on the early responsibility of becoming a parent, has also helped to change this practice.

Arlene could tell that her mother was embarrassed about having been called by the school. Arlene wondered why. Surely her mother knew that sooner or later they would find out. Her mother also seemed embarrassed when the home tutor came. That seemed even stranger since her mother had asked for one.

Arlene didn't mind having a home tutor. However, staying at home made her feel very alone. Arlene didn't like school. But when she couldn't go, she discovered that it had a much more important place in her life than she had realized. The home tutor came two days a week for two hours each time. Between times, Arlene found she had trouble studying on her own. She felt bad about this because the home tutor was very nice. She told Arlene she had taught other pregnant girls and not to worry, everything would be all right. Arlene wanted to ask her more about the other girls. However, the tutor's time was short. As it was, they had trouble going over everything, particularly since many of the subjects seemed so much more difficult to Arlene.

Arlene spent much of her time at home daydreaming. If she were feeling really low, which was often, she tried to sleep so she could forget everything.

Being at home with little or nothing to do can add stress to the already trying situation of a pregnant schoolgirl. Nor is home tutoring the equivalent of education on a regular class basis. The situation is bound to have a negative effect on Arlene's already downward spiraling self-image.

Arlene's mother was always tense when the welfare worker

came. Today she seemed even more nervous than usual. She asked the worker if there would be money in their allotment for Arlene's pregnancy expenses. The worker did not seem surprised that Arlene was pregnant. He said, however, that until the baby was born, no extra money would be given.

States vary on this. In some states, the unborn child is declared to be a dependent, making the welfare mother eligible for Aid to Families with Dependent Children (AFDC). In the case of a young mother living at home whose family is already on welfare, the allotment will generally be given to the girl's mother rather than directly to the girl. In other states, such as Arlene's, the baby is not considered to be a dependent until it is born. This can create a genuine hardship, as expenses start well before the birth of the baby.

When Arlene's mother heard this, she grew very angry with the worker.

"Just how do you expect me to pay for her care? I've got all these kids. As it is, we are barely making it. When I can get work, I do. I don't want to be on your damn welfare but I'm stuck with it. Now just how do you expect me to pay for her care?"

The worker at last left. However, Arlene's mother did not stop talking. She ranted on to Arlene about how disgraceful it was that she wasn't covered. "What are we going to do?" she kept saying.

Arlene wished her mother wouldn't keep talking to her about it. She couldn't change the welfare rules. Furthermore, she didn't have the slightest idea of what to do. Everything was such a mess. Now she was the cause of the family's problems. As much as she hated what her mother was saying, she knew some of it was true. How *were* they going to manage? She wished she could rip her insides out, curl up and die, do anything. Instead she sat at the kitchen table feeling miserable and listening to her mother talk on and on about the dumb welfare people.

Arlene lay awake late into the night. She cried for a while but it didn't do any good. In the morning, everything would still be the same. Finally she got up and dressed. She took a paper bag from behind the refrigerator and put a few of her clothes in it. She thought of leaving her mother a note. If she turned on the lamp to find a pencil and paper, however, she might wake someone so she just left.

The pavements outside were wet with rain. Arlene stopped under a street light and in the cold mist counted out how much money she had. It wasn't much. She didn't know how expensive the train fare would be. She decided that rather than take a bus to the train station, she had better walk.

It took her an hour. She was frightened being alone on the dark streets. At the same time, she drew back into the buildings, and one time went around the block, to avoid people she saw coming. Her heart was beating wildly.

At last she got downtown. There was a doorman by a hotel. She asked him where the train station was. He looked at her suspiciously but pointed it out. Arlene found out that the train she wanted did not leave for an hour.

"And it's the last one goes there this evening," the man told her when she bought her ticket.

Arlene sat down on a hard wooden bench in the nearly deserted station to wait. She looked around. There were no other women there. Just a soldier, a college student, and some men who looked like they were there just to sleep. Arlene studied the gum wrappers on the floor and the dirty half-open ashtrays. She was very cold. Her shoes were wet and the station was damp and drafty. She couldn't wait to get on the train if only to get a little bit warmer.

Arlene was afraid she'd miss the train so she got up periodically and walked to the gate where the train would leave. But there was no place to sit there so she had to walk back across the station to her seat each time. Finally the train was called. A few more people had arrived at the station.

Arlene followed them down to the dim train platform and then on to the lighted train.

The train was not much warmer than the station. After what seemed to be a long time, it started. A little heat came on. Arlene slumped down in her seat. Her mouth was turned down; her eyes stared vacantly. What would she do if Barbara didn't want her either?

When she got off the train, Arlene went into the small station house to ask how to get to her sister's apartment. However, there was no one inside. One other man had gotten off at the stop. By the time Arlene got back outside, he had already gone. The streets leading away from the station were empty and dark. Arlene stood for a while not knowing what to do. Finally she went back into the unheated station and curled up on a bench. She took some of the clothes out of her paper bag and put them over herself as best she could to try to keep warm. She did not sleep, but at times her mind drifted off so that she wasn't completely aware of where she was. She had no idea how much time she had spent in the darkened station. Finally she heard a car door slam. She sat up, grabbing her falling clothes. She was still stuffing them into the paper bag when a man came in. He didn't notice Arlene. However, when she rolled the top of the bag closed, he turned, startled.

"Well, I'm usually the first one here," he said. "You are an early bird."

"Can you tell me," Arlene began and pulled the slip of paper with her sister's address out of her pocket, "how to get to this address?"

"You mean, you're not waiting for a train?" he asked.

Arlene shook her head no.

"Have you been here all night?" he asked.

"Only since the last train," Arlene answered. She didn't want to get involved with anyone. "Can you tell me how to get there?" she asked again.

"Let me see," he answered. "That's between . . . Yes," he said. "There's a bus pulls in here that goes back out that way, I'm sure. You can ask the bus driver but I think that it will take you where you want to go. It's a Number 5 bus."

"When will it come?" Arlene asked impatiently.

"About half an hour," he said. "It gets here about five minutes before the first train leaves."

"Where will it come in? I mean, where do I get it?"

"Out there," the man pointed. "See that oval sign—that's where the bus stops."

Arlene went over to the door and looked. She didn't have a watch and didn't want to miss the bus. She straightened her shoulders and went outside to stand in the cold morning wind.

An hour later, Arlene sat in Barbara's bath tub trying to get the deep numbing chill out of her bones. A cup of tea was on the toilet seat next to her and she occasionally reached over and took a sip. Her eyes closed ever so slightly. She felt very tired. Through the closed door she could hear Barbara talking to Jim.

"She's pregnant."

"Well, what's she doing here?"

"Look, I haven't got the full story. The minute I opened the door, she began crying so hard, I couldn't understand half of what she said."

"Well, she can't stay here."

"Look, let me find out what's going on, huh?"

"Well, I've got enough—what with the baby up half the night and the television upstairs. . . . I don't need a . . ."

"Jim," Barbara said firmly. "Look, just go to work and let me find out what's going on. There's no point in getting worked up over something you know nothing about."

"If those people upstairs watch television till one o'clock again, I'm going to go up there and . . ."

"Jim, honey, let me talk to them today. I'll see if maybe they can't put their TV on a different wall or something."

Arlene thought Barbara's voice was soothing. She heard Jim's tone soften and then some quiet laughter. Finally the front door closed. Barbara knocked and came into the bathroom. Arlene expected her to start asking questions. Instead Barbara took a big warm bathrobe off the back of the door.

"C'mon," she said. "Dry quickly and jump into this. You can crawl into our bed. I'll bring you a hot water bottle for your feet."

"Barbara . . ." Arlene started to say.

"Shhh . . ." Barbara said. "We'll talk later. The baby's still sleeping so be quiet when you go into the bedroom."

Arlene crawled into bed. Barbara took hold of her hand for a minute and then kissed her on the forehead.

Arlene was surprised. Barbara had never kissed her before. It reminded Arlene of what her mother used to do when she was a very little girl. Then the warmth of the covers and her own sleepiness took over and she drifted off to sleep.

Arlene was awakened by her sister's footsteps. She turned around in bed quickly. She had forgotten where she was. Her eyes met her sister's. Barbara's look said firmly, "Be still and be quiet." It was then that Arlene noticed her sister was carrying Jimmy. The little boy let out a small cry of protest as he was put down in the crib. But before Barbara had unfolded the blanket to put over him, he was asleep.

Arlene quietly slipped out of bed. She had slept through the baby's getting up, playing, and two of his feedings. This was his afternoon nap.

Over the lunch Barbara fixed for her, Arlene poured out her story: how she hated living at home, how she hated Joel and what he had done, how she was not doing well in school even with the home tutor.

"Please let me stay here. Please don't make me go back,"

she begged. "I'll be very good. I'd help you with little Jimmy and maybe I could get a job or something."

Barbara listened sympathetically. Finally she said sadly, "I'd let you stay but I don't know about Jim. He's carrying two jobs now and he's so tired. Then there's that television . . ." She rolled her eyes to the ceiling. "That reminds me, I've got to go up and talk to them."

Arlene slumped down in her chair. If Barbara said no, where else could she go? There was nowhere.

Barbara looked over at her. "But I'll ask him if you can't stay at least for a while . . . till something can be worked out. Don't worry," she said. "I'll ask."

For the first time in weeks, Arlene smiled. "Oh thank you, thank you." She wished she could think of some way to better say what she meant.

"Don't thank me yet, because I . . ." Barbara started to say but the cries of little Jimmy interrupted her. "That was a short nap," she said. "There are days when he does this to me." She left to get the baby. Arlene sighed.

The rest of the afternoon was spent helping her sister, talking, and playing with the baby. Arlene hadn't felt so happy in a long time.

That night Arlene slept on the living room couch. She could hear the voices of Barbara and Jim from the bedroom long after they had gone to bed. In the morning Barbara told Arlene Jim had agreed to let her stay while she was pregnant. After the baby was born, however, she would have to leave. Their apartment was just too small for another baby, particularly a newborn one likely to cry around the clock.

It was more than Arlene had hoped for. She didn't even mind when Barbara insisted they immediately go down to the corner phone booth to call her mother or that she go home and pick up more clothes right after.

While Arlene gathered up most of her wearable clothes, her mother stood in the bedroom doorway not speaking.

Then at the last minute, just when Arlene was about to go out the front door, her mother thrust five dollars into her hand. "You take care, you hear," she said.

To Arlene's surprise, the following Monday morning Barbara made her get dressed and go down to the local school. "I heard something about their having classes for pregnant girls," she said.

Arlene hated the thought of more school. Particularly a strange school where she knew no one. More important, she enjoyed being with her sister.

The local school sent Arlene to the administration building. After enrollment, she was sent to the location of a special school for pregnant girls. Barbara went with Arlene to the special school. She told Arlene once more how to get back to the apartment and then left. Arlene hesitated at the door. She wanted to turn and run. However, she knew she couldn't stay with Barbara unless she went in. To her surprise, she found the building full of girls, most of whom looked even more pregnant than she did.

As the morning wore on, Arlene was introduced by the school's administrator to the three teachers, a number of the girls, a cook, and a custodian. Arlene couldn't believe how friendly everyone was and how immediately she was accepted. Some of the girls showed her things they had been making for their babies in sewing class. At lunch she sat with both girls and teachers. There was a lot of laughter. It seemed strange to Arlene to find so many girls who were pregnant and able to smile and laugh. She wondered if any of them had had as bad an experience with their boyfriends as she'd had with Joel.

The formal classes were over at one o'clock. However, school was not over then. Arlene was told, "There's group counseling on Monday afternoon; Tuesday, a health person comes—a nutritionist, nurse, family planner, someone like that. On Wednesday, there are clinic visits for the girls who are not seeing private doctors."

Arlene said she didn't have a doctor yet.

"Being at the clinic with other kids your age is great," a girl responded. "You don't have older ladies looking at you like you should drop outta sight or something. They also have group discussions. They take lots of time to explain things. One of the girls found out she was Rh negative and they told her all about it—us too."

Tests can determine if a woman has Rh negative blood type. If she has, there is further concern only if the father has Rh positive blood. Without special attention the baby can experience severe jaundice and anemia at birth or soon after if the mother is Rh negative and the father Rh positive. The physician, however, can take precautions during pregnancy and following to assure a healthy outcome if this fact is known to him.

"What goes on on Thursdays?" Arlene asked.

"Thursdays is private counseling or handicrafts such as instruction in knitting. Fridays there is a special session of some kind."

"Last week someone from an adoption agency came and talked to us," another of the girls said. "This week I think it's going to be a lawyer."

Arlene went home to Barbara's feeling a little bit like Alice in Wonderland. She had never seen so many pregnant girls. And although most of them were older, there was one she was sure was younger than she was.

"I'm not the only one," she kept saying to Barbara. "I didn't know so many other girls had this happen to them, too."

In the United States today, one out of every ten girls will give birth to a baby before reaching the age of eighteen. The school system in Barbara's community has cooperated in the establishment of a comprehensive service program for school-age pregnant girls. There are over 400 such programs in the United States at this time. The general goal of such programs is to see that pregnant school-age girls are provided or have access to:

——early and consistent prenatal and postpartum care, including family planning and pediatric health services, to improve the health of mothers and infants;

——continuing education on a classroom basis during pregnancy and following the birth of the baby to assure that the young mother stays in the educational mainstream;

——counseling on a group and/or individual basis to help young parents solve problems that either may have led to or may have been caused by the pregnancy.

There are many different organizational models for such programs. Most often the school system provides the teachers and educational equipment and services. The school system often provides housing also. The local health department may participate by providing the services of a nurse and lectures by the medical staff. It may also offer a teen clinic where girls can be grouped for prenatal care. Local public and private social service organizations may contribute the services of social workers. Other community agencies and organizations can participate by offering additional services, such as day care, vocational counseling, and job training and placement.

In the following weeks, Arlene found herself less reluctant to go to school. Arlene especially liked to talk with the other girls. She felt closer to some than others, but there was an unspoken understanding among all of them. Most of the time the girls talked about things all girls talk about. When they talked about babies, however, Arlene was generally silent. She was just beginning to feel her stomach push out. The baby still seemed so unreal to her. It was even hard for her to connect Barbara's little Jimmy with having a baby.

"Maybe it's because of Joel," she thought. "I just don't want to think about it at all."

Arlene tried to help Barbara as much as she could. She

walked around the grocery store amusing Jimmy while Barbara did the shopping. She couldn't help but notice, however, how carefully Barbara counted up everything in the shopping cart before she took it to the checkout counter. Sometimes she took things out of the basket and put them back.

"Having a baby is very expensive," Barbara said. "You just don't know. Even a healthy baby needs all kinds of medicines—daily vitamins and lots of immunization shots from a doctor. A baby grows so fast, he never even begins to wear out his clothes, and the strained food is so expensive."

"But you're happy, aren't you?" Arlene asked.

"Oh yes, I'm happy," Barbara said, and then hesitated. "It's just that there are so many problems."

"Mom thinks you really messed up," Arlene hurried on. "But I think everything is great."

"Well," Barbara hesitated. Then she looked directly at Arlene. "You know, Jim had to drop out of school so we could get married. People hold it against him that he doesn't have a high school diploma. He'd like to go to night school to finish even now. But he earns so little on his regular job, we can't make it unless he works part-time in the evening too.

"I'd like to help out," she went on, "however, it would cost me more to get someone to care for Jimmy than I could make. People would hold it against me too because I don't have a high school diploma. That's why I think it's so important that you go to school. I don't want you to end up like me."

Arlene paused and wondered. She felt she would give anything to be like Barbara, married to someone like Jim with her own apartment and her own things. And there was Barbara saying she should be something else. She didn't know what to think.

With an unprecedented 75 percent of all youth graduating from high school and a high proportion of those going on for additional education or training, it is becoming not just a luxury but a necessity that every young person finish high school. Education for the young pregnant girl involves not only improving her competency as a mother—from being able to read and understand the label on a medicine bottle to being the teacher of her child—but preparing her for other life responsibilities including the ability to grow and mature with her husband, contribute to family support as needed or desired, and perform citizenship functions.

CEIL AND RUSS

Ceil continued to hide her pregnancy from school personnel and her classmates. Once her nausea went away, it was easier to act normally. However, her blouses as well as her skirts were getting tighter. She could wear only two of her dresses. Unless she left her slacks unzipped, she couldn't wear them at all. Sometimes she wore slacks with a long sweater but she was always afraid the sweater might ride up.

Ceil's mother, on the other hand, was most concerned because Ceil had not had any medical care during her first three months of pregnancy. She insisted Ceil see an obstetrician right away. The doctor, an efficient but friendly woman, also expressed concern.

"Ceil," she said, "I can understand your not wanting to involve other people at the beginning, but you must begin to think of the baby, not just yourself.

"It takes more than nine months to have a healthy baby—a woman who is healthy *before* she becomes pregnant has the best possible chance of having a healthy baby. Once any woman becomes pregnant, however, she should see a doctor and dentist immediately, particularly if the woman is as young as you are. You need to stay healthy to give your baby a good start in life."

Doctors are concerned because the younger the mother is, the greater is the possibility that she may experience complica-

either the pregnancy or the delivery. Younger women
more likely to give birth to low-birth-weight babies—a
on associated with various kinds of handicapping conditions, including learning disability and mental retardation.
Therefore, it is essential that the school-age mother seek out
quality prenatal care as early as possible and continue going for
care throughout pregnancy.

The doctor went on. "Most of the young girls I see are not
at all prepared for being pregnant. My first job is to oversee
your health, but I also want to help make this as positive a
time in your life as possible. So don't hesitate to ask me any
questions at any time. Knowing answers will help you go
through the pregnancy and childbirth experience with dig-
nity."

After Ceil had been examined, she dressed and joined the
doctor and her mother in another room.

"The baby seems to be coming along fine," the doctor
said. She then wrote out two prescriptions. "These are for
pills containing calcium and iron. Most pregnant women
need them. Let me caution you, however. Take no other
medicine, not even aspirin or laxatives, unless I say you can.
Drugs can harm your baby.

"Now, before you go, there's one other very important
area to talk about," the doctor added. "And that has to do
with the right nutritional diet."

Ceil liked the doctor very much. But the minute she heard
the word nutrition, she thought, Oh no, here goes. She had
had nutrition in the ninth grade and it was one of the most
boring subjects she had ever had. And very little at school
bored Ceil. The last thing I need, she thought, is a lecture on
the green leafies.

"Imagine your baby were here right now," the doctor said.
"What would you be feeding it?"

"Milk?" Ceil said.

"And when it got a little older and could have some solid food, what would you be feeding it?"

Ceil didn't like playing games. She wished the doctor would get to the point. "Well . . ." Ceil hesitated. She really didn't know much about what babies ate. However, she did know it had to be soft, squishy stuff. "I suppose applesauce, strained carrots . . ." Her voice faded away.

The doctor said, "All right. Now the important thing to remember is that you are feeding your baby right now. Just as you didn't mention you'd be popping greasy french fries or chocolates into the mouth of your baby after it's born, so you should begin to think about what value they have for your baby now." The image of feeding a baby french fries or chocolates stuck in Ceil's mind.

The doctor went on, "You need calories but you want to avoid calories that don't have nutrients in them. 'Empty calories' is the popular way to say it. In other words, cut out things like candies, Cokes, cookies, and starchy foods like french fried potatoes.

Standard diets given to pregnant women are generally not adequate to meet the needs of pregnant teenagers. Because their own bodies have not completed growth and development, they have additional needs. Since caloric restriction may be poorly tolerated, higher levels for weight gain during pregnancy may be necessary. Moreover, diets especially rich in protein, calcium, and other essential nutrients are required.

"I know it's hard for teenagers to think about drinking lots of milk, eating vegetables, fruits, lean meats, fish, or chicken —at least in the quantities we're talking about," the doctor added. "However, it's not just you that's eating. You have to remember that. You're already a mother with a baby to feed."

Mother. The doctor had called her a *mother.* It gave Ceil such a strange feeling. "Mother" meant her own mother or the mother of one of her friends. She had no association with herself and "mother." Somehow even though she had thought of having the baby, she hadn't thought of herself as a mother.

For the first time it seemed real to her that there was a person inside her—not some vague thing that came with a condition called pregnancy. She thought back and realized how careless she had been about eating. She had been so upset about being pregnant, it seemed she'd either skipped whole meals or just shoved in whatever food was available at the moment.

The doctor was right. She *had* thought only of herself. Even now, however, it was hard to forget all her own feelings and think about someone else's welfare—some tiny unknown being. Nevertheless . . . "Green leafies here I come," she mumbled to herself.

The doctor looked at her. "Do you have any questions?"

Ceil shook her head no and then said quickly, "Oh yes, when will my baby be born?"

"Well," the doctor sighed. "If I knew, it would make my job a lot easier. The length of a normal pregnancy can vary anywhere from 240 to 300 days, but about 280 is a good estimate. To figure it out, take the first day of your last menstrual period and add seven days, then subtract three months. That will at least tell you roughly when you can expect to deliver."

Ceil's mother asked how soon Ceil's condition would become too noticeable to hide. "She hasn't yet told her school," her mother said, "and wants to wait till as late as possible. Also what do you think about her climbing all those stairs? And what if she got bumped in the halls? I'm just not sure she should be there much longer."

"Well," the doctor said. "Let's face it. No one tells a housewife she's too delicate to do housework or care for other children or shop at the grocery store or go to the movies because she might get bumped. Ceil can certainly go to school right up until the time of delivery if she wants."

She went on. "Ceil should be able to keep up almost any activity she's been involved in. Her desire to do some things may change, particularly in the last months of pregnancy, and of course, if she gets tired she should rest. Particularly in the last months, she should not overdo it. But basically she can do almost everything she is doing now. Certainly keeping up with her normal routine is going to help her mental state. I favor minimal disruption to a woman's life. After all, pregnancy is not an illness.

"As for other people knowing she is pregnant . . ." The doctor paused. "Ceil's thin and therefore she's going to show a lot sooner than the girl with extra fat, who can look like she's just putting on some more weight. She'll have to be in maternity clothes no later than the beginning of the fifth month or at least be wearing clothes of a looser style. Whatever she does, she should not wear tight clothes—tight bras, tight girdles, tight panty hose or slacks. In other words, what she wears should not interfere with her blood circulation. Clothes should hang from her shoulders, not her waist or legs."

Weight gain during the middle three months of pregnancy may average from ½- to ¾-pound each week. The baby grows from six inches (fourth month) to twelve inches in length (sixth month). The baby's weight goes from about ¼-pound to 1½ pounds during the same period.

However, in addition to the baby's growth, the woman's body is growing too. Her breasts are becoming larger, the uterus that holds the baby is expanding, the placenta (the tissue that filters nourishment to the baby via the umbilical cord and then carries away the waste products) is developing. There is an increase in the amniotic fluid, the watery substance the baby swims in until it is ready to be born. As a result, the mother does not merely thicken in her abdomen; she gets larger throughout much of her torso.

---

ct that her body shape was going to be noticeably
made it impossible for Ceil to put off telling the
much longer. She determined to get it over with by
doing it the following Monday. Ceil's mother wanted to go
with her but Ceil insisted she would be embarrassed by her
mother's being there. As she waited outside the counselor's
office, however, she wished she hadn't been so insistent.

The counselor suggested they go immediately to talk to
the principal.

"I am really surprised," the principal told her.

Ceil knew what he was thinking. She was considered an
unusually good student and one of the "nice girls."

"A couple of years ago, we would have just asked you to
leave." The principal got up. "However, the school board
passed a resolution based on something that came out from
the U.S. Office of Education. I think I have a copy of that
somewhere." He began searching through some notebooks
he kept on the bookshelf behind him. "Ah, here it is." He sat
down and passed the open notebook to Ceil. Ceil glanced
down at the open page but the principal was already talking
again.

The paper the principal has shown Ceil contains a statement
made by the Commissioner of the United States Office of
Education in 1972. It reads in part:

*Every girl in the United States has a right to and a need for the
education that will help her prepare herself for a career, for
family life, and for citizenship. To be married or pregnant is not
sufficient cause to deprive her of an education and the
opportunity to become a contributing member of society.*

*The U.S. Office of Education strongly urges school systems to
provide a continuing education for girls who become pregnant.
Most pregnant girls are physically able to remain in their regular
classes during most of their pregnancy. Any decision to modify
a pregnant girl's school program should be made only after
consulting with the girl, her parents, or her husband if she is
married, and the appropriate educational, medical, and social*

service authorities. Further, local school systems have an obliga-
tion to cooperate with such other state, county, and city
agencies as health and welfare departments and with private
agencies and physicians to assure that pregnant girls receive
proper medical, psychological and social services during preg-
nancy and for as long as needed thereafter. . . ."

"Anyway as I was saying, it used to be we would have had
to ask you to leave. However, the new board ruling is that
you should be able to stay if you want. We had one girl who
became—had a circumstance like yours last year. She chose
not to stay.

"If you want to remain, I will try to see that the situation
here is as helpful to you as possible. I want to warn you
though: not everyone is going to accept your being in school.
Some students may not and certainly some teachers will not.
However, I will be available if any real trouble comes up.
The rest will be up to you. If you conduct yourself as I know
you are capable of doing, there should be little problem."

"I want to go to school," Ceil said. "So I want to stay."

"All right." They talked for a few minutes more.

As Ceil got up to leave, the principal looked directly at
her. "Ceil," he said, "I'm sorry."

Ceil didn't know how to respond. She had been all right
until he said that. She just nodded and walked out the door.
She felt bad. She wasn't sure why. Then she realized. She was
ashamed. She tried to reason with herself. After all, she was
no different a person today than she had been the day
before. The only difference was that today the principal
knew she was pregnant. But there was that heavy feeling of
having done something very wrong, the same feeling she had
had after she told her parents. Maybe it would have been
better if the principal had punished her in some way. And
that new policy—or whatever it was. Now she had to prove
to everyone that it was right—that a girl could go through
school pregnant without being a disruption. All the responsibility was back on her.

Within a short time word got around school that Ceil was pregnant and Russ was the father. She had known it would. Most of the kids accepted her pregnancy. Some weren't as anxious to be with her, but that was the only difference. But if there was any malicious talk or gossip, she didn't know about it.

"If I weren't so well liked, it might be more of a problem," she thought.

Ceil stopped seeing some of her girl friends. She also dropped out of a number of school activities. She wasn't forced to do either; she chose to. Even though physically she felt much more like herself, she didn't feel very energetic. The emotional upheaval—what to do about the baby, how to relate to Russ—left her feeling drained much of the time.

To compensate, Ceil withdrew into herself more. She concentrated on studying.

There is a trend throughout the United States for more and more school systems to allow pregnant girls to remain in regular school. One major fear—that more girls might become pregnant—has been fairly well dispelled. Past policies of removing pregnant girls from their regular classes are not known to have reduced the number of pregnancies. Moreover, the results of a three-year pilot program in which girls remained in regular school classes showed that fewer other girls in the school became pregnant than previously. As one obstetrician involved in that pilot study likes to point out, "I never heard of a case where one girl made another girl pregnant anyway."

Restrictions against participation in extracurricular activities are also being removed. Once applied to both young parents, this unfair practice was often particularly hard on young men since excellence in athletics can result in college scholarships.

As she promised, Ceil called the social worker at the Family and Children's Service Agency after she told her parents about the pregnancy. She also went to see her. The counselor helped her begin to think about the many problems that had to be solved. Did she want to keep the baby? What were the problems likely to occur in her own family if she kept the baby? Who would care for the baby if she went on in school? What plans did she have for long-term financial support of the baby? What did she want to do about her relationship with Russ?

It was painful for Ceil, thinking about these things. She didn't know what to do about so many of them. Particularly in relation to Russ, her feelings often seemed to change from day to day. The last time she had seen him, he had talked about marriage.

"Maybe," he had said, "after I am through college we can get married."

"Well," she said angrily, "you mean after the baby's all grown and you can just sit back and take credit for what a fine child you've got."

As soon as she said it, she wondered why. She was the one who was refusing to marry Russ right now. Yet she was attacking him as if he were neglecting her.

"Look," he replied. "As I've said, all I want to do is what's right by you."

"That's what I mean," Ceil responded, tears coming to her eyes.

"Ah the hell with it," Russ said, getting up. He left her sitting by herself at the lunch table.

Russ was confused. Ceil's moodiness drove him wild. Their relationship was on one day and off the next. The week before, Ceil had told him not to come to see her. Then Sunday she called him and angrily asked him why he hadn't come by to find out how she was.

Russ had been working with a counselor at an inner-city youth center. Russ refereed and coached sports for young kids who had been in trouble. It required swallowing his pride, but Russ finally asked the counselor if he could talk to him. At the end of several conversations, Russ felt differently about a number of things. First of all, he was surer that the decision not to marry, although primarily Ceil's, was in his best interest too. If he started off a marriage resenting so much, it would be much harder for them to make a go of it. And what would he have to offer her if he quit school?

Once he stopped feeling guilty about not marrying Ceil, a great weight was lifted from his shoulders. However, he also had to stop feeling guilty about his parents' having to foot the bill for her. They had told him any money he earned he should continue to save for college. He wanted his money to go for Ceil's bills, and their money to be used for college. After a while, he realized it was just a numbers game he was playing. His ego and self-respect had gotten all mixed up in short-term, rather than long-term, thinking. If he really cared about helping Ceil financially, he had better get his education so that he could take on that responsibility. What he could contribute now was so little compared to the total cost of her support.

Finally, because he had offered to marry Ceil and his family was paying for most of the medical care, Russ had believed the rest was her problem. The counselor helped him see that he was so wound up in his own feelings that he really hadn't been thinking about what Ceil must be feeling. Russ began to understand, for example, how grand and proper he had been with his regular inquiries as to how she felt. Mouthings about her health, he finally realized, were superficial in contrast to what was really going on in her life.

"I do care about her and what's happening," he told the counselor. "I wish I could live her life for her right now or at least take on some of the painful things she's going through."

"But you know you can't do that," the counselor said.

"I know, but I can be there to listen and care when she needs me." Russ very much wanted Ceil to know that.

He called her and asked to see her. She said she was busy.

He asked if she would listen on the phone for a while then. He had planned to say things differently. However, he told her the way it was: that he had been to see a counselor several times and that he thought he had his head on a little straighter.

"Rather than trying to do what's right—whatever that is—I just want to be as honest as I can," he said. "I know you've got so much to work out. I haven't got everything all figured out either. But I care about you enough to want to keep trying to figure things out. And I want to keep sharing them with you when I do."

In the end he heard her sobbing. His heart sank. "Oh Ceil," he moaned. "That's the last thing I wanted to do—make you cry. Can't I do anything right?"

"No, no," Ceil was saying. "What you said was fine. I just feel so . . . relieved. I've been so alone. Don't you see, when you said something about wanting to do what was right by me," she took a deep breath, "it meant I couldn't trust anything you did to be because you really cared. It made even the nice things you did seem cold and ugly." She began to sob again. "I think I better hang up now," she finally managed to say. "Thank you for calling."

Russ hung onto the phone long after he heard the receiver click. He felt so full. Then he sat down and wrote Ceil a long letter in which he repeated the things he had told her on the phone. When he finished, he didn't know whether or not to mail it. But he decided writing, even awkwardly, would at least show her the telephone call was only the beginning.

Russ read the letter twice more slowly. Then he put it in the mail box.

Russ has long needed to talk to someone outside his own situation. He has found that his friends are not objective enough, and his family is already settled in their attitudes. The function of the counselor has not been to tell Russ what to do.

Instead the counselor has tried to help Russ examine his options. He has also tried to show Russ how to look at some of these options a little differently.

Moreover, what both Russ and Ceil are learning is that once decisions are made, they are not necessarily irrevocable. Many times throughout the pregnancy and following, previously-made decisions will be called into question and reexamined from different perspectives. Some decisions will remain the same. Others will be changed—not because they were necessarily bad decisions but because the situation and the people involved have been changing.

ERICA AND GARY

Erica and Gary were married on a Saturday. The following Monday, the principal called Erica into his office. She thought it was probably about being married. She hadn't kept it a secret at school. Moreover, the formal wedding notice had been in the Sunday paper.

"Sit down." The principal motioned to the chair in front of his desk. "I understand you are married."

"Yes," Erica answered, wondering why he didn't sit down too.

"Are you pregnant?"

Erica reddened. The first reply that came to her mind was, "It's none of your business." However she couldn't think of a nice way to say that. Until she knew what was going on, she thought she had better be polite. After some hesitation, Erica just said yes.

The principal didn't look surprised. It was almost as if he expected and wanted a yes answer.

"Well, I'm sorry. You can't stay. We don't allow pregnant girls in school."

"But, I'm married," Erica protested. Erica had not expected a questioning about her pregnancy and she felt somewhat bewildered.

"That doesn't matter," the principal said. "We can't have you corrupting the morals of the other students."

"Corrupting morals?" Erica questioned him without thinking. "What do you mean?"

"You know perfectly well what I mean," he replied.

"But I've only got five months to go to graduation." Erica was pleading now. "My parents want me to go to school. Please, I have to stay."

"See here, I can't spend all day talking to you about this," he said coldly. "You can go across town to adult night school if you want and finish there. If you want to do that, the clerk in the office will make arrangements for you. Regardless, she'll show you how to withdraw from here completely. That's all."

Erica started to say something, but the principal repeated, "That's all" and motioned her out the door.

Erica stood outside the principal's office trying to take in what had happened. The bell rang. She'd be late for English class. Then what he had said dawned on her. She wasn't to go to English class. She wasn't to go anywhere in the school. For a moment, she didn't know what to do. Finally she walked out the front door without saying anything to anyone. The walk home was one of the saddest ones she ever remembered.

As Erica expected, her mother flew into a rage when she heard what had happened. "As soon as your father gets home tonight, I'm going to call his lawyer friend. The principal can't do that. You're married!"

When her father heard the story, however, he urged Erica's mother to calm down. There was an hour or so of discussion. Then Erica's mother called the lawyer anyway. The lawyer didn't seem too pleased about having been called at home. But he said he would look into it. Toward the end of the week, Erica and her parents met with the lawyer in his office.

"This is the situation," he began. "There have been some

court cases on this matter. Most recently two significant court decisions have supported the right of pregnant girls to stay in school and young mothers to return to school following the birth of their babies."

The court cases the lawyer is referring to are: *Perry v. Granada Municipal Separate School District* (300 F. Supp. 748, Miss. 1969), in which the court upheld the right of young mothers who were not married to return to their school following the birth of their baby, and *Ordway v. Hargraves* (323 F. Supp. 1155, Mass. 1971) in which the court upheld the right of an unmarried girl to remain in her regular school classes during pregnancy.

The lawyer continued, "You could take the school department to court and you might well win because there is some precedent. The advantage would be that it might make it easier for the next girl who becomes pregnant, although that is not necessarily so, since court cases are not self-implementing."

"What does that mean?" Erica's mother asked.

"It means we might win the case for Erica," the lawyer explained, "but it would not necessarily apply to another girl. Another family might also have to sue. On the other hand, if the school system loses once, they probably won't fight a second time."

He paused, then went on, "Now the disadvantage is that court cases take time. Because of the circumstances, we might get a fairly early hearing. Even then, however, Erica would be out of school for some time unless I could get a restraining order."

Erica sank back in her chair. She wished her mother would ask what a restraining order was. She wasn't sure whether that meant she would be restrained or the school would be restrained or the principal would be restrained or what.

"And let's face it," the lawyer summed up. "Erica won't be going back to school after the birth of the baby because she's a senior so—for a couple of months in regular school, you'll be exposing both yourselves and Erica to a lot of publicity and comment, not to say some expense."

Erica finally could not contain herself. "But it's not fair," she said. "I've been pregnant for three months already and haven't corrupted anyone's morals in school. Besides I know for a fact that one boy in my class got some girl pregnant last year. They never kicked him out. He never had to go to night school. He's going to graduate with my class in June." The adult sense of justice always unhinged Erica.

"Well," the lawyer said, "the one thing you must remember is that the local school system is given broad powers by the state education agency. From what I can tell from my research there is no state law on this subject. What happens is up to the local school board. And apparently our school board doesn't have any policy. So what it comes down to is just the practice in each individual school."

Erica's mother interrupted. "And that means the principal can keep or push out pregnant students as he chooses."

"Unless someone challenges him either by going to the school board and getting them to establish a positive policy, or by bringing a lawsuit that makes him comply with a favorable court ruling," the lawyer finished.

The situation in Erica's state is not unlike that in many others. Very few states have laws (or educational bylaws, which have the effect of laws) that stipulate what happens if a student becomes pregnant. Local school systems, therefore, make their own decisions regarding this matter. Sometimes the local school board sets up a policy; sometimes it is left to school administrators to decide what to do. The result is that pregnant students in the same state, the same community, and even in the same school may be treated differently.

In a number of communities where school systems have treated pregnant girls punitively, professionals—such as those connected with health or social service agencies—as well as parents and other laypeople have put pressure on local school boards to establish policies permitting and encouraging the education of pregnant school-age girls and young parents. In some of these communities, court cases have been brought to force school systems to permit expectant students to remain in school. Sometimes just the threat of a court case has been enough to bring about change. Legal aid groups have been helpful in this area. In other states, laws have been passed to liberalize policies uniformly with respect to pregnant girls. Those concerned with women's rights have also been active in this area, continually pointing out the injustice of forcing pregnant girls to leave school while allowing fathers-to-be to remain in class.

Erica's parents debated the subject all evening. Erica's mother was for going ahead with the lawsuit. Erica's father was for letting it drop as long as Erica could go to night school. Gary was neutral. Erica herself supported first one argument, then the other. She was, by now, enjoying the uproar and particularly the thought that she might get back at her school principal. However, as the debate wore on and other considerations were raised, retaliation toward the principal seemed less and less important.

Finally Erica said, "I'd really rather stay in regular school. But if I go to night school I might be able to get some kind of a job for a couple of months. As long as I can graduate at the same time anyway, I guess it's more important to try to earn money. So," she sighed, "let's not sue the school system or anything like that. Let's just drop the whole thing."

Erica's mother objected for a while. But eventually she quit talking, much to everyone's relief.

Erica's case points up the fact that pregnant girls and young mothers need educational options. Certainly adult school, day or night, is no substitute for continuation of education in regular school. And it is certainly inappropriate for many young adolescents to be mixed in with adults, or to be out late at night and traveling longer distances to attend school. Nor are other forms of alternative education any more acceptable. If, however, a young mother is truly incapacitated by pregnancy, home tutoring is a valid option. Adult day or night school may be the best solution for a few girls.

The choice of whether to remain in regular school, attend adult school, enroll in special classes for young mothers, or receive home tutoring should be the student's. It should be based on a genuine assessment of each individual's situation, not some arbitrary classification of where or how pregnant girls or young parents should be educated.

Erica started night school the next week. Classes were held in an old school building. Erica felt uncomfortable since most of the people there were so much older than she was, or else were what she called the real "problem" kids. She missed seeing and being with her friends. Also the subjects were taught differently and seemed less interesting than in regular school.

"Now I know what a plant feels like when you pull it up by its roots and plunk it down in some hole," she told Gary. "Even if it's better earth and you give it a lot of water, the poor things droops over and kinda shrivels for a while. And believe me," she finished dramatically, "night school is not better earth and I have yet to feel the water."

Erica also hated the fact that going to night school cut down on the time she had with Gary. He was gone during the day when she was home and she had to rush to school soon after dinner, leaving him for most of the evening. It made her feel less married than she thought she should feel.

Erica has a number of major changes to adjust to—being married, being pregnant, and working out new relationships with parents and peers. At this particular time, young women often look to school—the one meaningful institution in the lives of young people—for stability. It is one thing they can cling to that isn't changing. Erica does not have that resource. Instead she has the added burden of adjusting to a new school routine.

After Erica began night school, Gary felt awkward about being alone with her parents each evening. He tried spending some evenings with his parents. At first he also looked up his buddies. Chuck was as friendly as ever. However, since the California trip was off, they had less to talk about. More important, because Gary had to be so careful with money, when Chuck and the others went for a beer or to the movies, Gary had to make excuses not to go. That embarrassed him. So, most often, he parked outside Erica's night school. He listened to the car radio or sat back and daydreamed.

Some nights he was so glad to see Erica come out of the school door that he galloped halfway across the school grounds to meet her. At other times, he sat in the car and barely looked at her when she got in.

Once in a while Gary picked fights with Erica just as she used to do with him. He felt bad even as he did it. He knew life was no picnic for her either. It's this no man's land I'm in, he thought. He understood that it was natural that Erica was involved with the development of the baby and her own feelings. But it was also her home they were living in, and her parents they were living with. Erica was still busy with school, too. The things Gary liked and had been planning for all seemed to have been taken away from him. And he felt nothing yet had been given as a replacement. "I was just at a point of feeling like I was on my own and taking care of myself when—oh hell, it doesn't matter now," he muttered to himself.

Early marriage thrusts many young fathers back into a dependency state at the same time that it adds much responsibility. For those who have not yet achieved independence or a feeling of competence in managing their own lives, it can create particular problems. The process of growing up combined with additional burdens may be especially taxing to a young person with limited inner resources.

Finances were something Gary and Erica worried about constantly. They both wanted to get out of living with her parents. Yet they had no idea when that would be. Although Erica's parents were contributing to their support by providing them with housing and meals, Erica and Gary were expected to manage the rest. Clothes, insurance, car expenses, costs related to the pregnancy and birth of the baby, and so forth were left up to them. Every time Gary and Erica sat down and tried to line up their income with the expenses they already had and the ones they expected to have, they became depressed. There was so much to pay for.

Erica finally found a part-time job in a cleaning store. No one wanted to hire her full-time because she was only going to work until the baby was born. Her job was to open up the store at seven in the morning, and take in the clothes to be cleaned and give out the ones that were ready to be picked up. At noon someone else came in and took over until closing time. The job paid less money than Erica had hoped to make. But any amount will help, she told herself. Having to be at work so early meant Erica now got up before Gary. She woke him when she left for work. She got home about twelve-thirty, had a quick lunch, did laundry or other housework, and completed her homework. Gary got up soon after Erica left. He arrived home from work just in time for dinner. They saw each other briefly after dinner, then Erica left for night school. Their lives seemed more messed up than ever. "It's just for a short while," they told each other.

At first Erica tried to stretch their time together by sitting up with Gary at night to watch TV. But she found herself falling asleep on the couch next to him at an earlier and earlier hour. Finally, she gave up and went directly to bed almost as soon as she got home from night school.

Erica stopped seeing a private doctor and went to a public health maternity clinic to help with expenses. It meant a savings of about $400 in total costs, including delivery.

"The doctor my mother took me to rubbed me the wrong way, anyway," she told Gary.

"What about this place though?" he asked.

"Well, I do feel sorta like a computer punch card at the clinic, the way they treat me. I see a different doctor every time, so I don't know anyone. But," she added, "at least I'm treated like everyone else."

Erica knew she was defensive about her pregnancy and marriage. She wanted everything to be as normal as possible, even though she also realized a number of circumstances made the situation abnormal. She liked the anonymity of the clinic because she thought it helped with the appearance of normalcy.

What she didn't like was the fact that there was no one at the clinic she felt she could talk to about many of the questions she had. For example, she wondered how long she could continue to have intercourse without hurting the baby, but she was too embarrassed to ask anyone. She also worried about other things, such as whether her stomach would get so big that she wouldn't be able to fit in the desks at night school. Although the clinic gave her pamphlets and she was told various things at various times, it was hard to absorb it all and so much seemed cold and medical, not relevant or personal.

Young people may be too shy or embarrassed to ask questions that are bothering them. Moreover, they often have needs and concerns that are not the same as those of older pregnant women. Being young, dependent, unwed or newly wed, unfamiliar with adult treatment creates a difference. Having a body that has yet to complete its own growth and development at the same time that it nurtures a baby further makes standard clinic care inappropriate for pregnant young women. In general, the younger the girl, the more likely she is to need and benefit from a setting or approach geared to her level of maturity and understanding.

Erica resents being made to feel that hers is a "problem pregnancy." However, she needs to understand that women with normal pregnancy situations may have problems too. In particular Erica needs someone willing and able to relate to the situation and needs of a young person.

The person Erica turned to for help was Lizzie. Erica's mother felt Erica should still be seeing the private doctor. She used any questions from Erica about pregnancy as an opportunity to point that out. So Erica stopped asking her anything. Lizzie's lack of knowledge was made up for by her enthusiasm about the pregnancy. From the very beginning she had been the only one besides Erica to be happy and excited. Even though they no longer saw each other in classes, Lizzie called Erica almost every afternoon after she got home from school to find out how things were going.

"Tell me how you are feeling," Lizzie would say.

Erica then responded with thoughts about her physical, emotional, or mental state, whatever struck her fancy. It was so nice to have Lizzie to talk to.

"If I saw more of Gary," Erica thought, "I might be telling him all the things I tell Lizzie." However, Erica realized Lizzie was a ready-made eager audience available at the same times Erica was. Gary was not. Furthermore, Gary often seemed tired or not genuinely interested in every new tidbit Erica had to tell about pregnancy. With Lizzie, Erica could chatter on for half an hour about the minutest thing. Lizzie never seemed to tire of listening. There were times Erica suspected Lizzie was being a special friend—no one could be all that interested. But then Erica was so interested in all that was happening to her, she felt that she couldn't be boring Lizzie.

Erica shared all her clinic pamphlets on pregnancy with Lizzie and together they talked about them and tried to piece together the needed information. It was Lizzie who finally discovered the pamphlet which said that Erica could continue to have intercourse up until the last few weeks of pregnancy. "It says at that time there is danger of breaking open the sac surrounding the baby and causing a premature birth if you have intercourse. Also you want to avoid any possibility of bacterial infection," Lizzie noted. "And about stretch marks, you can't do anything about them, so relax," she added.

Lots of times, however, what they were curious about wasn't in the books and they laughed about things they imagined. For example, Erica said, "Can a woman get pregnant during her pregnancy? If so, could she just go on having a child every couple of months or so?"

"Like a baby factory," Lizzie said gaily. "Kachoom, kachoom," and she imitated a stamping machine stamping out babies.

During the middle three months of her pregnancy, Erica thought she felt physically the best she ever had in her life. She had bursts of energy that she didn't know what to do with. At times, she just had to dance, she had so much vitality. When someone told her that the baby could feel the movement of her body, she liked dancing even more. She turned on the radio at home and danced while she dusted. She turned on the radio at work, and danced between waiting on customers. She was delighted with the thought that she was communicating with the little person inside her. The first time she felt the baby's movement, almost like a flutter inside her, she burst out laughing. The baby was communicating back—perhaps dancing too!

"I've never ever been happier in my whole life," Erica thought.

Before a baby is born it can hear—hear its mother's heartbeat, its mother's voice, loud music, and so forth. The baby can also feel the rhythm of the mother's movements. The baby can see light—for example, if the mother stands in bright sunshine. Thus the baby is aware of its mother and her environment long before it is born.

The mother will become more aware of the baby about the middle of her pregnancy. At first she will feel a very faint movement. It may not occur again for days. Then the movement will gradually become more noticeable. It will grow stronger and more active each day until the mother can look down at her abdomen or watch it in a mirror and see her baby's movements.

4. PREGNANCY:
The Last Three Months

ARLENE AND JOEL

Arlene now looked forward to going to school. She even hated to see the school day end. Since the pregnant girls came from many different schools where they had been studying in different books at different levels, class sizes were kept small. Also the teachers spent time with the girls individually.

Arlene couldn't get over the relaxed attitude of the teachers. Girls were constantly transferring in and out, absent for illness, out two weeks for childbirth, yet the teachers didn't seem one bit flustered. She also marvelled at how they were able to make school subjects seem so much more interesting. The English teacher let the girls read Dr. Spock's book on baby care in class. In gym, the girls did prenatal exercises. In math class, they took a trip to the grocery store. There they learned about unit pricing and how to figure out which things were the best buys. The girls even studied nutrition by helping plan the menus for the hot lunch they were served each day at the school.

"School here sure is different," Arlene told another girl. "I really feel like I'm learning things."

"So am I." The girl sighed. "But with no boys or nothing,

what else is there to do but study?" She winked at Arlene as she said it. However, Arlene took it seriously.

Studies of pregnant girls show that their grades often improve in special educational programs such as the one Arlene is in. For the first time, many gain a sense of pride and achievement in school work. Some who never thought of going on for higher education are motivated to do so.

Arlene also felt she was learning because the teachers seemed so interested in her. They noticed everything. When she tried extra hard, even if she didn't succeed, they complimented her on trying. If she did something well, she was praised.

"I wish my baby would never be born," Arlene thought. "I'd like to stay in this school forever." However, Arlene knew that normally the girls came back to the special school two or three weeks after the baby was born. Then after their sixth week medical check-up, the girls went back to regular school. No one stayed beyond that unless it was close to the end of a grading period.

Arlene looked forward to the afternoon program. She particularly liked the group counseling sessions. The bolder girls asked questions she also wanted answers to. Many admitted things she, as yet, couldn't admit. Some girls planned to get married, many did not. Arlene found that almost all of the girls thought they were in love at least at the time they became pregnant, although the reality of pregnancy was making many of them reexamine their feelings and the relationship with the boy.

Sometimes the sessions became heated.

"Why does everyone think that if a girl becomes pregnant, she's the kind that sleeps with every boy she meets?" one girl asked the counselor angrily. "That's just not true. Most of us have known the fathers of our babies a long time—at least two years. And if you are only fifteen, that's a long time in your life. Furthermore, most of us haven't had intercourse that much!"

Research evidence supports the girl's statement. Most school-age pregnant girls have just begun to have intercourse. They are not promiscuous. Particularly if they are in senior high school, their pregnancy is likely to have been the result of a continuing relationship with one boy.

In the group counseling sessions, Arlene learned to begin to respect her own feelings more. "It's really all right to feel bad about some things," she decided. "A lot of other girls do too." Most importantly, she found she wasn't the only one who had problems. It meant something to her to know that.

Arlene had an individual counselor she was less enthusiastic about. She knew the woman was trying to be helpful. But I can't answer her questions, Arlene thought. I don't know what I am going to do when the baby comes. I can't face going back home, yet Barbara won't let me stay. I want to stay in the special school forever, but I know I can't.

She was glad each time the appointment was over. "She's a very nice person. It's just that counselors can't really do anything to help you. They can't change Joel. They can't change my sister."

Arlene later acknowledged, however, that the counselor did do some good things even if they weren't the things Arlene most cared about. For example, Arlene had no one to pay for her medical care. "Barbara and Jim certainly can't afford it," she had told the counselor. "And my mom was told I wasn't covered by welfare."

The counselor insisted Joel be found. "If he fails to assume financial responsibility voluntarily, a paternity suit should be brought to force him to do so," she stated. This turned out to be complicated because Arlene's mother had to be involved and Joel had to be located. That meant two trips back home.

After the counselor and Arlene had visited the Bot, Joel got word to Arlene through her younger sister. "You bring that suit and I'll have three other guys in court to swear they all had intercourse with you too," was his message. It unsettled Arlene so much that she broke down crying in the counselor's office.

"Don't worry, Arlene," the counselor soothed. "I think once he's had time to think about it and understands a little better, he may reconsider trying such a stunt."

Joel couldn't believe his ears. The kids at the Bot told him Arlene had come by with a woman asking what his full name was and where he lived.

"You guys didn't rat, did you?"

"No," they all said. "But they've got you for sure. The guy at the drugstore gave out your last name. Arlene remembers the letters on your car license plates too."

"Look, I can get other guys to swear they had her too," Joel said immediately. "They'll never prove I knocked her up." He hung around the Bot that evening until a couple of the older fellows came. He cornered them and immediately explained his problem.

"You guys go to court for me?" he said.

"Sure, sure," they answered, patting him on the back. "We'll bail you out. Let's get a drink now—that's what we came for." But Joel was still worried. He had forgotten all about Arlene. She'd disappeared from the Bot. He presumed she was off some place. Who'd ever think she'd come back trying to pin something on him?

He still had an uneasy feeling when the phone rang in his home later in the week. His dad answered it. "It's for you," he said. "Some woman."

Joel went to the phone hesitantly. "Yah?" he said softly,

turning his back to the living room. After listening a while, he said, "I don't know what you're talking about," and hung up.

"Who was that?" his father said.

"Oh, I don't know," Joel said. "Some crazy woman. She must have had the wrong person."

He went to his bedroom. They *had* traced him. The woman had wanted him to come in and talk to her. "I'm not about to go and talk to anyone," he said to himself. "I want no further part in this whole mess." His palms were sweaty. He hoped to God she wouldn't call again.

She didn't, but several days later when Joel got home, a letter was waiting.

"You got this," Joel's father said.

He could tell his father was curious. Joel didn't think anything of it. Then he saw that the return address was some official-looking agency. Right away he knew what it must be about.

"Well, aren't you going to open it?" his father asked.

"No, I'm sure it's not important. Maybe just advertising or something," Joel said. The minute he said it, however, he wished he hadn't. It sounded like a phony answer, even to him. He swallowed and said, "Oh well," as casually as he could and opened the envelope. He was more aware of his father's eyes on him than he was of the paper he was supposed to be reading.

"Oh, it's nothing," he said, putting the letter back in the envelope.

"Nothing," his father said. "What is it?"

"Look," Joel said, trying to shove it into his pocket. "I gotta get cleaned up. Sharon's coming by to watch the basketball game on TV."

"Let me see that," his father said and grabbed it out of his hand.

"Dad, give it back," Joel pleaded, but his father had already begun to read it.

"Joel, this says paternity! What the hell have you gotten yourself into now? Did you do this?"

"Look Dad, it's okay. I can get a couple guys to go into court with me and say they all had her. I can handle it. It'll be okay."

"*Okay?* First of all, you did do it, didn't you?"

Joel was silent.

"Yes, if you say you'll get others, of course you did. You're not denying it. You're *handling* it."

Suddenly his father raised his voice. "How old is this girl?"

"About thirteen or fourteen, I don't know."

"Thirteen or fourteen! Did you ever hear of a thing called statutory rape? A girl that young—you can go to prison! And you want other boys to lie for you? Did you ever hear of perjury? Do you know what they'd get if they lied in court? Oh sure, you're going to handle it. Handle it, my foot!"

Joel stood in amazement. His father was angry, furious. But more important, his father was telling him he was in trouble. And the way his father said trouble, he meant real trouble. It had never occurred to Joel that he could go to prison. And if anything went wrong and those other fellows also got in trouble. . . . Well, he'd rather be in prison than out where they could get him.

When Sharon rang the bell half an hour later, Joel's father was still raving and Joel was still standing in the same spot. Joel turned and buzzed her up to the apartment. When he went to let her in, his father came to the door behind him.

"Sharon, I'm sorry," his father said. "But you better go on home. Joel can't see you tonight."

Sharon looked at Joel perplexedly. Joel looked back at her.

"I'm sorry, Sharon," his father said and shut the door in her face.

"Dad, why'd you have to go and do that?" Joel said.

"Why? *Why?* I'll tell you why. You and I are going to have

a very, very long talk. And I'll be surprised if you ever go out with any girl again after that."

Joel was scared enough. He didn't say any more. He just went into the living room with his father for what he knew was going to be a long lecture.

By the end of the evening, his father had covered every subject from A to Z and back to A again. He had also wound down a little. Enough, anyway, that Joel could explain what had taken place with Arlene. At the end Joel thought he better mention Sharon. He knew his Dad liked her: Sharon had a way with his father. Joel reasoned that if his father thought he was serious about Sharon, it might help. He was going to need every bit of his father's help that he could get.

However, his father exploded again. "Are you doing anything with Sharon?"

Joel hadn't expected that response. "You dummy, you left yourself open for that one," he thought.

"No Dad, Sharon's a nice girl," Joel replied. Actually he and Sharon had had sex a couple of times. That was one of the reasons he liked her. But he told himself this was no time to be honest.

His father simmered down again. Finally it was agreed that they would meet with the woman who wrote the letter, as she requested.

"To keep it out of court," his father added. "We'll probably have to give them everything they want. And if I know anything, that means money. And you, my boy," he emphasized, "are going to be the one who pays. I'm not picking this up for you. You get free room and board here. I don't care if it means you don't have any money to go anywhere for the next ten years, you are going to pay for this one. I bailed you out of the record club, I cosigned for that gas-eater of yours, but this one is all yours. No sirreee, not a cent from me for this. This one is all yours."

Joel went to bed somewhat in a state of shock. However,

he knew he was over one big hurdle. When his father cooled down further, things even might be worked out a little better. If the money was needed all at once, for example, he could borrow it from his father and then stretch it out in small payments over a long time. That way he could still have money to run the car and go places with Sharon. He went over various plans several times and then finally fell asleep.

Toward morning, he dreamed he was in a jail. The jailor kept coming with a key to unlock the door. It turned out the jailor was Arlene and she was very pregnant. She would open the door to his cell and say, "Go on out, you're free." When he looked behind him through the jail window, however, he could see his father and the guys who had agreed to swear in court for him. They were angry and had clubs and chains in their hands.

"I don't want to go out. I don't want to go out," Joel would cry and then Arlene would smile sweetly and say, "Okay, it's up to you." She'd lock the door again. As she walked back up the aisle, a thin hand would reach out from the end cell, begging to be let out. Arlene would ignore it. Then the whole thing would start all over again. Arlene would come toward him and unlock his cell. He kept trying to see into the end cell to see who the person was whose hand kept begging to be let out, but he couldn't see. Finally, for some reason, he could see into that last cell. Joel woke up in a cold sweat and sat bolt upright in bed. It was Sharon and she too was pregnant! He desperately wished morning would come when he knew everything would look different.

Arlene had missed the special session conducted by the adoption agency. Because of her circumstances, the counselor suggested she go to the agency and talk with someone there. Arlene hated leaving the school and going out in public, even for an afternoon. Now that she was showing quite a bit, people gave her looks or made remarks. One stranger on the bus had exclaimed, "Why you're too young to be pregnant."

A pregnant girl with Arlene said, "That's funny, 'cause she is."

However, Arlene felt embarrassed. Not until the school arranged transportation to take her to the agency, did Arlene agree to go.

Arlene already had ambivalent feelings about keeping the baby. Barbara had said that she couldn't stay following the birth of the baby. Arlene understood. Even now being there was sometimes awkward. Arlene slept on the couch. She couldn't go to bed until Barbara and Jim did. So she sat up with them watching TV. Sometimes if she were sleepy, she drank Cokes and ate potato chips to help keep awake. She knew the people at the clinic said she shouldn't eat such stuff. However, Barbara said she'd had Coke and potato chips during her pregnancy and her baby was fine. Besides it was hard not to eat when Barbara and Jim were eating.

Although Barbara has had a baby of her own, she received no special help during her pregnancy with questions regarding childbearing and childrearing. As a result, she passes on to Arlene a mixture of personal experience and hearsay information. The point, of course, is not that Coke and potato chips will harm a baby, but that they do not provide sound nutrients for the mother. Furthermore, if a girl tends toward being heavy, as Arlene does, such eating habits can lead to excessive weight gain and potential problems in pregnancy and childbirth.

Barbara has also told Arlene a number of old wives' tales, such as not to eat strawberries or your baby will end up with a red mark on its face. Doctors and nurses often say wistfully that they get only an hour or two a week to try to take out of the heads of pregnant school-age girls all the misinformation everyone has put in during the rest of the week.

Arlene also knew Barbara and Jim often went to bed before they wanted to because she was there.

"If I can't stay with Barbara after the birth of the baby, the only alternative is to go back home," she told the adoption worker. "Baby or no baby, I don't want to do that. But if I do have to go home, maybe not having the baby would be good. But I'd be an awful person if I didn't love my baby, wouldn't I?" she continued.

"And do you think if you gave him up, it would mean you didn't love him?" said the worker.

"Yes," Arlene said.

"Did it ever occur to you it might mean you loved him more?"

"What do you mean?" Arlene said.

"I mean that for a mother to give up her baby does take a lot of love generally. It means that she loves it so much she is able to think beyond herself—think really of what is best for the baby."

"I never thought of it that way," Arlene said. "A lot of the girls at school think it's awful to give up your own flesh and blood. Almost all of them are keeping their babies."

"Each person is an individual with individual circumstances, Arlene, remember that. What is good for someone else may not be good for you and the other way around. Those girls won't be around living your life for you or living your baby's life for it. Therefore don't make your decisions on what other people say. Make your decisions on what is right for you and right for your baby."

After Arlene left the adoption agency, she thought about what the worker had said. The more she thought about it, the more she thought maybe adoption would be the right thing for her to do. The worker had assured her that there were many very nice people who wanted a baby and couldn't have one. They would love the baby very much. And because they might never have had a child otherwise, they would feel very special about the baby.

The worker had said she should take her time to think

about it. But the more Arlene thought, the more she was
convinced that was probably what she would do. Not just
because she loved the baby so much either, but because she
hated Joel so much.

Arlene's dinner didn't fill her up that evening. Later on she
split a homemade pizza with Jim. The next morning at the
breakfast table she told Barbara, "I shouldn't have had that
pizza last night. It's left me feeling very funny."

"Is it like the heartburn you've been having? Maybe you
should take milk of magnesia or something."

"No, it's something else."

"Well, maybe you shouldn't go to school then," Barbara
suggested.

"No, I'm . . . I'm okay to go," Arlene said. "Besides this
afternoon there's a tour of the labor and delivery rooms at
the hospital so I especially want to go today."

However, about eleven o'clock Arlene went to the school
nurse. "I ate a pizza last night," she said, "and I've got
stomach cramps. Can you give me something for them or let
me lie down for a while?"

The nurse had Arlene stretch out on a cot. "What kind of
stomach cramps do you have?" she asked.

When Arlene described what she felt, a concerned look
passed over the nurse's face. "I think we better get you to a
hospital," she said.

"Why?" Arlene said.

"You may be having your baby."

"No," Arlene said. "My baby's not due for a month and a
half yet."

"I think we better get you to a hospital anyway," the nurse
said. "Your baby may not know what month this is."

From there on everything was a blur to Arlene. When she
finally realized she was in labor, she became very frightened.
She felt unprepared. As much as she had been told things at
school and at the clinic, it had all seemed somewhat of a

dream. She had a month and a half to go. She hadn't started thinking seriously about having the baby. "I haven't even had my tour of the labor and delivery rooms," she thought foggily.

She remembered the school nurse saying once, "At the hospital they tell us they know the girls from the program just by the way they behave." Arlene felt she wasn't behaving well but then everything was so unexpected.

Premature labors are often lengthy and Arlene was in labor a long time. She was heavily sedated toward the end and remembered little or nothing about giving birth. The baby was placed in an incubator immediately and rushed to an intensive care section.

In the seventh month, the baby weighs almost three pounds and is about fifteen inches long. Its development is almost complete. Its eyelids are opening and it is able to turn its eyes in all directions. The baby may suck its thumb continually.

In the eighth month, the baby gains almost 1½ pounds and its length increases to about 16½ inches.

During the ninth month, the baby gains several more pounds and probably weighs at least six or seven pounds. It is about twenty inches in length. The baby's skin is smoother and less pink. It has developed an insulating layer of fat which serves as a source of food and a protective coat after birth. The baby has paper-thin fingernails, which have grown out over the ends of its fingertips. In nine months, one cell has multiplied to two billion. The baby weighs six billion times its original cell weight.

A baby born prematurely during the seventh or eighth month has a 50 to 90 percent chance of survival. The longer the baby is carried, the better are its chances of survival.

Arlene was not allowed any visitors since she had been through a difficult labor. She felt dopey and exhausted. She remembered thinking just before she dozed off: "This is all my fault. I've done everything wrong. Now the baby is fighting for its life and it's all my fault. I'll make it up to the baby."

It wasn't until the next morning that she realized she didn't know whether her baby was a boy or a girl. Either no one had told her or she didn't remember what they had said.

CEIL AND RUSS

Ceil decided to try to avoid maternity clothes. To her they seemed inappropriate. "The maternity clothes I've seen all look like they were made for some cutesy lady in the suburbs," she told her mother. "And considering I won't ever wear them again, they cost too much. I'm a schoolgirl who happens to be pregnant, and that's what I want to look like," she finished.

Ceil still had to buy some clothes, however. She bought a maternity skirt and a pair of maternity slacks because nothing else would cover her growing stomach. The other clothes she bought were nonmaternity things in sizes larger than she usually wore. She hoped she could take them in to wear afterward. One outfit that worked well was a red and white striped jacket in a large size. Underneath it she wore a semi-fitted red dress. Toward the end of her pregnancy, she was still wearing the outfit. She didn't dare take off the jacket, however: she couldn't zip the dress. With her maternity skirt and slacks she wore loose-fitting sweaters and tops and, occasionally, her father's shirts.

At school Ceil now sat sideways at her desks. Although she could fit frontwards, it wasn't comfortable. Whenever she arched her back to help with the backstrain, she bumped her stomach.

To Ceil's embarrassment, her baby was much more active. At times when Ceil was sitting in class, her sweater twitched on her stomach. Although the other students didn't notice, Ceil always blushed.

Often Ceil had a burning sensation in her stomach that

came all the way up to her throat. The doctor had told her to take some cream or a tablespoon of milk of magnesia before eating to help prevent it. But that didn't always work. Once in a while she even belched after lunch. Whenever no one laughed, Ceil was grateful.

"I can't believe all the things going on with me physically," she confided to Russ. "I know I'm not sick, so they're not scary. But I feel so different. I'm aware of myself all the time."

As her pregnancy progressed, and Ceil showed more, the other students began to treat her differently. When the bell rang and she got out of her seat, they waited until she was erect and steady before following her out the door. Her friends helped by standing in line for her lunch.

So when one of Ceil's girl friends said, "I'm getting a ride home today. Can we take you too?" Ceil assumed it was more of the "handle with care" treatment she'd been getting.

"Sure," she answered. Actually she was glad to get home as soon as she could these days. It felt good to plop down with her feet up before dinner. If she could, she liked to get her homework done then too. She found herself wanting to go to sleep earlier and earlier.

When Ceil got out of the car, her friend said, "Wait a minute, Ceil." The girl took a heavy white box from the trunk of the car and carried it up to the house. She set it down on the porch.

"We talked it all over and . . . well, anyway, we didn't know whether or not you'd want a formal baby shower," she said. "And to be honest, when one of the moms heard about it, she sorta squelched it. So a number of the girls went together on the box—it's sort of a non-shower shower. I hope you like them."

Ceil was so surprised she didn't know what to say.

"Anyway," the girl continued, "my brother just drove so I

could get the box to you. I didn't know how else to do it. He's waiting so I've got to go. See you Monday, and . . ." she hesitated, "Happy Baby!"

"Thank you," Ceil managed to call as her friend ran down the walk. She opened the door and went inside with her books. Then she came back out and picked up the box. Ceil knew she should be excited or happy. But those weren't her feelings. "It's just like them to do something like this," she murmured almost angrily. She carried the box inside and up to her room. Then she came back downstairs, poured herself a lemonade, and turned on the television.

Her mother noticed the package later. "What's that big box on your bed?" she asked.

"Some of the girls gave it to me," Ceil said.

"Well, what is it?"

"I haven't opened it," Ceil said.

"When are you going to open it?" her mother asked, puzzled.

"Oh, sometime later, I suppose."

"What if one of them calls you. It wouldn't be polite not to have opened it."

Ceil hadn't thought of that. However, she sat in her chair.

"Why not do it right now?" her mother suggested.

Ceil got up reluctantly. She couldn't think of any excuse other than that she just didn't want to open the box. And that didn't make sense even to her.

Ceil put the box in the middle of the living room floor. She took off the lid and parted the tissue paper. Inside were over a dozen items for the baby—a clown rattle; a music box; a comb and brush set; a receiving blanket; a kimono, cap and booties set; baby powder. Her mother watched with pleasure while she finished taking out all the gifts. It was just as if she were having a baby shower. Ceil felt all the girls were sitting around her smiling. Suddenly Ceil grabbed at the baby things and began to shove them back into the box. Later on she would like them, not now. Not so soon. She wasn't ready yet. She wasn't ready to have the baby yet. She had to go through midterm examinations next week, and . . .

She rubbed the pink satin covering on the little music box. She had gotten it wet. However, as she rubbed, another tear fell.

"Ohhh," she whispered to herself. "Ohhh." Ceil stumbled to her feet and ran upstairs leaving the presents scattered on the floor.

Her mother looked after her. "Oh Ceil," she said softly. Tears came to her eyes.

The eighth month was difficult for Ceil. She was very big now and her ankles were swelling. She would have liked to have dropped out of school. However, she had only one month to go until the end of the school year. "If I can just stick it out, if I can just hold on," she said.

The baby generally will weigh six or seven pounds by the time it is born. However, the total weight gain of the mother may be twenty-four or more pounds. The weight comes from the increase in the size and weight of the placenta, uterus and breasts, along with an increase in the amount of amniotic fluid, interstitial fluid, and material blood. Storage of nutrients, mostly fat, may account for some of the additional weight as well.

"It's not just a matter of your holding on," the doctor reminded her. "The baby's due date is only a week after school ends and, as I have told you, you have to be prepared to have your baby a number of weeks either side of that date."

As her size increased, Ceil noticed that some of the teachers looked at her disapprovingly when she came into class. She tried to ignore their glances. In the hallway, she overheard one of the teachers say to another as she passed,

"Just look at her. The brazen hussy! I don't know what the principal's doing allowing that girl to be in school. If I had my say, she'd be in the alley where she belongs."

Ceil cringed. Earlier in her pregnancy she would have turned and said something. Now she felt unprotected and insecure. Rather than anger, she felt hurt. She saw Russ starting down the stairs at the end of the hall. She quickened her pace. "I've got to catch him," she thought. "I've got to say something to him."

"Russ," she called as she got to the top of the landing. Several students turned around and looked up but he didn't hear her. "Russ," she called again, a little more desperately. The boy going down the stairs behind Russ looked up, saw her, and poked Russ.

"Hi," Russ called. "I'm late for baseball practice. I'll see you after school." He turned and went on down the stairs, waving his hand as he left.

Ceil stood at the top of the stairs for a moment. Then for the first time since she had become pregnant, she went to the school nurse. "I don't feel well," she said. "I'd like to go home."

Russ was surprised when Ceil wasn't waiting outside the gym door. After practice she usually met him and he walked her home. Since their telephone conversation a month ago, things had been going well. Of course, there were ups and downs. But at least it was clear that he wanted to continue to work at the relationship. He tried hard to see things from Ceil's point of view. At the same time, he attempted to keep his own feelings straight. Russ debated about going back into school to try to reach Ceil on the telephone. Maybe she had the baby early. A worried look came to his face. He decided to go directly to Ceil's house and find out.

Russ was surprised when Ceil herself answered the door. After what he had imagined, he expected to get no answer.

"Ceil, you're home," he said. "How come you didn't meet me after school?"

"I left early," she replied. "C'mon in."

Russ could tell Ceil was feeling down. When he tried to find out why, however, she pushed his questions aside. He decided to stop asking.

They talked on about nothing in particular. "I hear the place they have for the senior prom is the best ever," he finally said.

"Oh," said Ceil. "I wanted to talk to you about that. I want you to go."

"I didn't mention it for that," Russ replied. "I don't want to go. If you can't go, it doesn't mean anything to me."

Ceil secretly bristled a little. Absurd as it was, she would have liked him to ask her. She pressed him harder than she meant to. "No," she said. "I want you to go. I would feel so awful if you didn't get to go to your own senior prom just because of me. You'll make me miserable if you don't go."

Russ objected. "I really don't want to go."

"Russ," she said, her voice rising. "I said you should go."

Russ could tell Ceil was becoming very emotional but he didn't understand why. "I'll think about it," he said.

"Don't think about it," she said desperately. "Go! If you don't, it will mean you really don't care about my feelings."

Russ looked at her in wonderment. All he could finally think to do was nod. He made an excuse about leaving soon after. He could tell Ceil was getting agitated. He thought the best thing to do was go home.

After he left, Ceil sat despondently. She had wanted to go to the senior prom with Russ almost more than she had ever wanted to do anything. And she really didn't want Russ to go with anyone else. What was she trying to do? Was she trying to force him to ask her to the prom? Did she need that kind of public declaration of his support? Or did she, she thought, want to punish herself in some weird way by having him go without her? "Ohhh," she leaned her head back against the chair and shook it slowly from side to side. "I don't know. I don't know. I don't know."

On the way home, Russ accidentally ran into Claire Scott. They talked casually for a while. Claire asked him how Ceil was doing. Then suddenly, almost from out of the blue, Russ found himself asking Claire if she would like to go to the prom with him. She accepted. Afterwards he wondered why he had done it. He had meant what he said to Ceil: he really didn't want to go to the prom without her. Now here he was taking Claire. Not that there was anything wrong with Claire. He just felt that he shouldn't and didn't want to be dating at this point. "Why, *why* did I do that?" he mumbled. "I've got to get out of it." But he didn't see how he could right now, just after he'd asked her. Maybe later he could think of something.

Until her ninth month, Ceil mostly had been reading books about pregnancy—the stages of pregnancy, what to expect at each point, the development of the fetus, and so forth. Now she had two interests—what would happen to her in getting the baby born, and what she would have to know right after in order to care for the baby. "It's funny," she thought, "I had no interest in baby care until now. Nature must help a pregnant woman's interest to shift."

Ceil had seen her doctor regularly—once a month until the eighth month, every other week during the eighth month. In the ninth month, she was to go every week. The doctor took her blood pressure, weighed her, analyzed the urine sample she brought, checked the position of the fetus and listened to its heartbeat. Then she asked Ceil if she had any questions.

Ceil confessed to her doctor that she was concerned about labor. "I'm afraid I won't know when I'm having labor pains. How can I tell?"

"Well," the doctor said, "I can never be sure what it is going to feel like to a patient. Everyone is different. However, it may feel like big cramps. Or it may feel like a crescendo pain that travels from the back forward to the abdomen. If you have such pains and they increase in force, regularity, or length of time, you are probably in labor.

"However," the doctor continued, "there are other signs that you may be starting labor. If they occur, I want you to tell me about them. A mucus-like discharge tinged with blood may appear. This substance has acted as a plug in the opening to the uterus. It means that the uterus is now ready for labor. It can happen, incidentally, before or after labor begins so don't rely on it entirely.

"Another thing to watch for is a gush of watery liquid. This is the amniotic fluid the baby has been floating in. It also means the uterus is ready for the birth process. Most often this does not occur until toward the end of labor. But it can occur one or two days before. If it does, I want you to call me. The baby will then be unprotected and it's important that you call me so we can prevent infection.

"And, of course, as you have mentioned, there are actual labor pains. The contractions may come ten to thirty minutes apart and last ten to forty seconds. When they are about eight to ten minutes apart, I'll want to know and I'll probably tell you to come to the hospital. But you may call me if you have questions or are concerned."

Ceil nodded. But there was a frown on her face. "Something's bothering you," the doctor said. "You have some concerns."

"I'm still wondering if I'll know."

"You'll know," the doctor reassured her. "However, some women have occasional cramping toward the end of pregnancy—pains which are not regular. Sometimes they think they are in labor when they are not. It is nothing to be

embarrassed about. Call me. We'll discuss what's going on
and whether I should see you. Anything else?"

"What if the watery fluid breaks while I am in school?"

"Well, it could happen. I don't think it will. But it's not as
if you'll have a pailful of water, anyway. Sometimes there is
just slow leakage. If you are concerned, you can wear a
sanitary pad the last week or so. That would absorb most of
the moisture. Your clothes would take up some of the rest so
you won't be standing in a puddle."

"What if labor starts in school?"

"Even if it does, you aren't going to deliver there. The
reason you hear about people delivering in taxicabs is
because it's so unusual—that is, it makes news. People don't
give birth in grocery stores or any of the other places
pregnant women go—banks, movies, health clinics. So there's
no reason why you should do so in school.

"Don't worry, Ceil," she said. "First labors tend to be
longer than subsequent ones, anyway. So I am quite sure
we're going to be seeing each other in the hospital for a good
while before the baby comes."

Ceil smiled. She hesitated, then asked, "What about—
what if the baby won't come out?"

The doctor sensed that Ceil felt a little reluctant about
asking her such questions. "Don't feel bad about asking me
these things," she said. "Every pregnant woman wants to
know them. Now, as to your question, I like to reassure all
my patients that 90 percent of the childbirths in this country
are normal. That is, the baby's head comes out first and no
instruments are necessary. So you see, it's only a small
percentage of babies that have trouble coming out. Even
then, however, we have ways of successfully helping the baby
into the world.

"If a baby is turned around inside your uterus so that it
might emerge feet first, or with its face not in the direction it
normally is, we may try to rotate the baby to the correct

position before birth. Or we may use other skills or tools to see that it is safely born. Forceps, a curved, tong-like instrument which is shaped to fit the baby's head on either side, may be used to help the baby through the birth passage. If necessary, we can make an incision in the abdominal wall and in the uterus and lift the baby out. This, which is called a caesarean birth, happens rarely. It's major surgery so recuperation takes longer, but it's a safe procedure. However," she finished, "I don't think you need to worry about that or for that matter any of the other special techniques. Remember 90 percent of women have their baby normally. I don't think you'll be any different. Anything else?"

"Well," Ceil said. "I wonder . . ." Finally she blurted out what worried her most. "How much . . . how much will it hurt?"

The doctor smiled. "I like to be philosophical about this. You've been pregnant for nine months. The little person coming into the world will probably be around for sixty or seventy years. The short spot of time when both of you are going to experience discomfort is not significant in contrast to all that. However," she went on, "that really doesn't answer your question, does it?

"Some women mind labor more than others. With the use of anesthesia, childbirth can be made much more comfortable than it used to be. I don't use complete anesthesia because of its effect on the mother and the child and because it can impede labor. We will use injections of fluid into the spinal area toward the end of your labor and from that point on, although you will be awake and aware, you won't feel pain at all.

"Prior to that time, if you need a painkiller, we can give you something else. The idea is not to slow down your labor but to let it proceed at its natural pace and help you as much as possible in the process."

Ceil nodded. She dreaded the thought of labor. She

thought about it quite a bit and it worried her. She knew that the contractions were necessary to open up the neck of the uterus—the cervix—to let the baby out. She also had read that the average first labor was something like fourteen hours. Once the neck of the uterus opened up, the baby would be born in about an hour. After the baby was born, usually in only a few minutes, the placenta would be expelled since the mother and baby no longer needed it. She didn't mind the thought of having the baby or having the placenta come out. It was all those contractions to open up the cervix that she was worried about. "I wonder if I'll be able to stand it," she thought.

When the ninth month came, Ceil felt very tired. The pains in her lower back were replaced by leg pains and cramps. However, her spirits were greatly improved. "Mother, look at this," she said, standing in front of the mirror and lifting up her maternity top. Her belly looked enormous. It was firm and hard. Ceil looked closer. "How can I stretch so much? I must be carrying a giant!"

"Well, you're the one who picked Russ," said her mother. They both laughed. As a basketball star, Russ was one of the tallest boys in school.

Ceil looked at her mother adoringly. "You've been great, Mom," she said.

"Why, thank you," her mother said, blushing. "I think you've been doing pretty well yourself."

Ceil meant what she said. It seemed in the last couple of months that she and her mother had grown very close. In some ways, even though she was about to become a mother herself, she had felt more childlike these last months. She liked being at home with her parents; she enjoyed the warmth and security of their house. She liked being cared for by her mother, much as her mother had done when Ceil was smaller. Her mother made her special things to eat, helped her fix her hair, and came to say goodnight after she was in bed. Often her mother sat on the edge of the bed and talked with her about Russ, or the baby, or her future.

"Do you think I'll make it through the end of the school year?" Ceil asked, turning back to her image in the mirror.

"That is something I can't answer," her mother replied.

"I hope I do," Ceil said. "I've been so tired that I haven't been able to do anything it seems, except go to school and sleep. I'd like to have a little time just to shop and buy one or two things for the baby myself. Not that I don't appreciate Dad's having gotten the crib and buggy for me. But it's just that I'd like to pick out something myself. Part of the fun of having a baby must be planning for it. I mean looking at things in baby departments, making things, and stuff like that. I've been so busy I haven't had time to do any of it."

"I know, dear," her mother said. "I hope you do have time." Then she added, "You know, I would have gone with you any Saturday."

"I know, Mom," Ceil said thoughtfully. "But for a long time, I couldn't even think about the baby. It was all I could do just to think about me. Now I feel more ready. But I've been so tired and with exams coming up, I better not go right now."

"I understand," her mother said. She walked over and gave Ceil a hug from the side. "We'll have some time."

Three weeks later, with an enormous sigh of relief, Ceil cleaned out her school locker. She had made it—she didn't know how. But she'd gotten through the whole school year and she had a week and a half to go before the baby was due. Russ took the things that needed to be carried home and helped her down the stairs. Despite how big she was, he felt she was very fragile. Ceil was chattering on happily. However, there was a frown on Russ's face. The senior prom was only a week away. His parents had shaken their heads in wonderment when they heard he was taking Claire. Even though he felt awkward about going himself, he had defended his behavior to them.

"Parents are funny like that," he said to Ceil. "As often as not they force you to talk or act in ways you really don't intend." Russ had told Ceil a number of weeks before that he'd asked Claire and was very sorry he had.

"Look, I told you to," Ceil said once more. "And honestly I don't feel any resentment toward you 'cause you're going. You can tell me about it. If you don't go, how will I ever know how it was?" And Ceil was telling him the truth. At this point, she really didn't care. She was just waiting. It was almost as if life had stopped. Nothing could go on again until the baby came. She certainly didn't like to be far from home. She slept a lot during the day. Other than wanting some time to shop, she felt she was in limbo.

Ceil made her way out of the school door into the bright sunshine. When school was out each year she had a free feeling. Today, however, she had the gayest, freest feeling she had ever had at school's end. "I can't believe I've made it," she said over and over again.

"You'll probably look back at this next year," Russ said, "and wonder how you ever did it."

Next year. The thought struck Ceil. Next year. It was hard to imagine what next year would be like: when she wouldn't be pregnant, when she would have a baby, when Russ wouldn't be in school but away at college.

Ceil started to say, "Nothing will ever be the same though." But she thought better of it. Russ had enough without her starting up now. Instead she said, "If we walk slowly, I'd like to walk home. It would be such a great thing to do on this absolutely glorious day."

"Sure," Russ said. "If you think it's okay."

"The doctor said walking is a terrific exercise for pregnant women," she replied.

They walked along without saying much, enjoying the

warm June afternoon. Suddenly Ceil stopped. "What's the matter?" said Russ.

"I don't know," Ceil said. "I just felt something unusual."

"You okay?" Russ asked anxiously. "Hey, let's take a bus, or I could call a cab."

"Oh no," Ceil said. "I'm just fine. It was just a funny feeling for a minute." They turned to cross the street. A car passed in front of them.

"There goes the school's morals squad," Ceil said, motioning to the two teachers driving past.

"What do you mean?" Russ asked.

"Oh," Ceil answered. "They used to make nasty remarks when I passed in the hall."

"You never told me that."

"Well, I was going to and then I thought, It's my problem, not his."

"Anything that's a problem for you . . . ," Russ stopped. "Ceil, are you okay?" he said. "You look a little funny."

"I'm fine," Ceil said. They crossed the street and continued on. Shortly before they got to her house, Ceil stopped again. "That was the third time," she said.

"Third time what?" Russ asked.

"Third time I've had a pain. I'm pretty sure now."

"Do you think you're going to have the baby?"

"I think so," Ceil said.

Russ stepped in front of her. "Now you just stand here. I'll run down to your house and get your parents to come with the car."

"Don't be silly," Ceil said.

"But you shouldn't walk any more."

"Look, it's only a block. I can walk that. I'm okay."

As Russ went to take her arm, Ceil could tell that he was shaking a little.

It's so funny, she thought. When I thought of going into labor, I thought I'd be hysterical. And here I am calm as anything, even feeling good about it, and there is Russ, all upset. There must be something about being a mother that prepares you more than the father.

When Ceil got home, her mother called her father at work. "He was just about to leave the office anyway," she reported. "He's coming right home."

"Don't you think we ought to get her to the hospital?" Russ said.

"I don't think so. Not just yet," her mother said. "We'll start timing the contractions, but from what Ceil says, they must be about twenty minutes apart. We may have a long wait until they get closer together."

"Would you like something to eat?" Russ said to Ceil hopefully and then looked at her mother. It was clear that he thought someone ought to be doing something.

"No," Ceil said. "The doctor told me not to eat anything after labor starts."

Ceil sat down in a living room chair with her feet propped up. Russ popped up and down off the couch. He walked over to the window and looked out. When he looked back at Ceil, he had a panicky look on his face.

Ceil looked at her mother appealingly.

"Russ." Ceil's mother went over to him. "I know it's going to be a wait. Why don't you go on home. Tell your parents because I'm sure they'll want to know. When the time comes to take Ceil to the hospital, we'll call you. You can come to the hospital then if you want. Right now there's nothing you can do and Ceil will probably want to go upstairs and get some things ready."

Russ nodded. "Okay," he said. "But you will call me, won't you?" He hesitated. "Do you think I'll have time to get home first?"

"I'm sure you will. And don't worry, we'll call you."

Russ went over to Ceil. He knelt down by her chair. "I love you," he said. "Don't worry, everything is going to be fine."

He kissed her on the forehead. It was the first time he had ever kissed Ceil in front of either of her parents. He was conscious of Ceil's mother when he did it. "She won't mind," he thought foggily. "It's my baby."

Ceil looked back at him tenderly. "Sure," she said. "I'll see you after it's all over."

After he had gone, Ceil said to her mother, "Thank you. I couldn't think of what to tell him. I had no idea he'd be so upset."

One of the problems of single parenthood in particular is that doctors are unlikely to involve the male partner, even when he is willing. Ceil has had a warm, understanding doctor who has taken the time to allay her fears and answer her questions. However, never once has the doctor asked Ceil to bring Russ in with her, nor has she offered to communicate with him in other ways. Thus, although Ceil has been thoroughly told about pregnancy, labor, and delivery, Russ has little idea of what to expect. At one special school program for pregnant girls, a fourteen-year-old father walked his pregnant girlfriend back and forth to school each day. When she had the baby, however, he ran away from home for two weeks. No one had sought to involve him or help him with whatever problems he had.

At this particular moment, Russ feels very responsible for what is going on. Yet he has only piecemeal information and his own imagination to either help or hinder his ability to cope.

Ceil's mother answered. "I am sure he will be all right. But sitting here waiting was only going to aggravate him. Besides, I'm sure you would like to change and put on something else before you go to the hospital."

It was, as her mother had suggested to Russ, a good number of hours before Ceil's contractions got close enough to call the doctor. Even after she was settled in the hospital, her labor went slowly. Ceil was given a number of drugs during labor. She had a caudal anesthesia administered close to the time of delivery. After that, she thought her labor had stopped because she felt nothing. However, it had not and she was awake throughout the birth process. In the delivery room, someone raised her head so she could see the baby's head and shoulders emerge.

During the first stage of labor (the opening up of the neck of the uterus), most women are given sedatives or narcotics. A stronger anesthetic may be given when the baby starts to pass through the birth canal. The tendency today is not to use total anesthesia, which puts the woman to sleep, but a regional anesthesia, which frees the woman from pain but leaves her awake. There are numerous kinds of regional anesthetics. In spinal anesthesia (saddle block), the drug is injected into the spinal canal. In caudal anesthesia, the drug is injected into the lower end of the vertebral column. Epidural anesthesia, a particularly reliable and safe form of caudal anesthesia, is given through a catheter placed outside the spinal column. Regional anesthetics, however, may not be available in every hospital. Specially trained doctors are needed to administer regional anesthesia. Regional anesthesia is also expensive, so cost is another factor limiting its use. In place of regional anesthesia a strong, localized anesthetic affecting much of the birth canal and surrounding area may be used.

"Is it a boy or a girl?" Ceil asked.

"It's just a baby so far," the doctor said. Then the rest of the baby came out. "It's a boy," she told Ceil.

Ceil put her head back down. "A boy," she thought with a smile. She remembered all the times when she had hated Russ during her pregnancy. How, at times, she had wished she were having any baby but his. At those times, she thought, "What will I do if it's a boy and it looks like him? I couldn't stand it." Now, however, she thought: "A boy. That's just fine. It really isn't so much Russ or me, it's a whole separate person. And it's a boy. Maybe it will be a little like Russ. That will be fine too."

ERICA AND GARY

During the last three months of Erica's pregnancy, a calmness settled over her immediate household. Tempers, even that of Erica's mother, seemed to die down. Erica and Gary began shopping on Saturdays. Since they had so little money, they looked for used rather than new baby furniture. The only piece of baby furniture they had was an old highchair given them by Gary's aunt. With a little looking they located a playpen at a garage sale and then a used crib in a secondhand furniture store.

Erica had read that a baby spends about half its time in bed. A firm, flat mattress is very important, the book had said. Therefore, they thought they better buy that new. They also bought a new, small dresser in an unfinished-furniture store. On the top of the dresser they fastened a thick, plastic-covered foam-filled pad. That saved on both space and money since Erica would be able to use the dresser top as a changing table.

Furniture and equipment needed for a baby is generally that which helps in managing the baby's basic functions: sleeping, eating, eliminating wastes, and exercise.

Sleeping:
   A crib is the most important piece of furniture for a baby. Baskets, bassinettes, cradles, and even smaller-size cribs are soon outgrown. The best investment is the large-size crib. A firm mattress for good support is essential.
   An infant seat—a molded plastic shell with a mattress pad—is useful but not necessary. In it the baby can half-sit, look around, be fed its first solid food, and go to sleep. The baby can be carefully carried in it as well. These seats are outgrown within six months, however.

Eating:
   A highchair or feeding table is helpful as the baby grows.

Highchairs are easier for the parent to feed the baby in. If they have a removable tray, they can later be used to bring the child to a proper height for sitting at a regular table. Babies must be closely watched so they don't fall out of a highchair, however. Feeding tables, on the other hand, are often promoted as usable for eating, playing, and exercise. A separate eating place can help the baby understand what is expected at mealtimes.

Elimination of Wastes (Cleanliness):
   The baby can be changed in any safe place that it will not roll off. Changing the baby's diaper while it is lying down is a constant activity throughout the first year and even much of the second. Thus it is helpful to have one place to change the baby that is waterproof and within reach of changing supplies (diapers, cotton, powders and ointments, diaper pail, etc.). There are changing tables sold in stores, or one can be made, as Erica and Gary have done, from another piece of furniture such as a dresser.
   The baby can be bathed in any small basin until it can be safely supported in the bathtub.

Exercise:
   A playpen can be helpful to the parents in providing a safe place for baby's exercise and play. The advantage of the playpen is that it is portable and can be moved from room to room and even outdoors. A child-proofed room, i.e., one that has been arranged so that the baby cannot tip over objects, poke into electrical outlets, and so forth, or a child-proofed house can allow the child greater freedom and can stimulate the baby's exploration and curiosity.
   Swings, walkers, and bouncers are not necessary.

Mobility:
   The other major kind of furniture used by a baby has to do with mobility for the baby and the baby's parents. When the baby is very small, a body sling can be used to carry the baby. A backpack can be used within a relatively short time, too.
   A baby carriage—one in which the baby can lie flat and sleep—and, later on, a stroller are important to the mobility of both child and parent.

A car seat or car bed is necessary for automobile travel. Check carefully in a consumer's guide to see that the seat has an approved rating. Only a few kinds will actually protect a child against injury in an accident.

Gary spent evenings in the basement, removing paint from the used furniture. After this was done, he intended to paint everything a matching color. When he told a sales clerk at the paint store that he needed yellow paint for baby furniture, he was advised to get paint without lead in it. "Nontoxic paint is what they call it," the clerk explained as he showed Gary the paint can label.

The possibility of lead poisoning is one problem young parents should be aware of. Paint on furniture, on window sills, and peeling off walls, particularly in older buildings, may contain lead. Since babies chew on everything and pick up and put things in their mouths indiscriminately, it is important to see that the surfaces they come in contact with are lead-free. Lead can also come from other sources, such as excessive use of canned products. Many health departments offer free tests for lead poisoning (a blood sample is all that is needed). Lead poisoning is curable but must be detected as soon as possible to prevent harmful effects such as brain damage.

Erica bought some teddy bear decals for the front of the dresser and the end of the crib. "These will make them look like a matched set," she told Gary proudly. "Plus it will make the crib look newer."

Gary was pleased and grateful to have something to do. At last he was participating and contributing. Moreover, Erica's father often came down to the basement to sit on the bottom steps and talk to Gary as he worked. Erica's father was a quiet man and conversation with him was usually difficult. However, when Gary was working on the furniture, talking seemed easier. Even the long pauses were acceptable. Gary began to feel more at home. At times, he even thought of himself as one of the two men of the family.

Toward the end of the seventh month, Erica, for the first time, began to feel some discomforting effects of being pregnant. For example, she was often short of breath. Also, as time went on, she began to have to urinate frequently.

Anywhere from several weeks to a few days before labor begins, the baby's position shifts forward and lower down into the pelvis. Its head moves down into the birth canal (nearly all babies are born head first). When this occurs, there is less pressure in the abdomen. The pregnant woman can breathe better. However, increased pressure on the lower organs makes her urinate more often.

Erica also noticed a discoloration in her ankles and asked the doctor about it.

"Well," he said, "the human animal walks upright. Other animals walk on all fours and the baby is carried freely between their legs. However, in the human female, the baby is carried over two legs. The result is a strain on the pelvis, rectum, and legs. That's why you have backaches. That's also why the thin-walled veins in the legs, which have extra blood to carry and pressure from above, sometimes break. You have what is called varicose veins. Heredity has something to do with it. It's likely your mother was troubled by them too."

"Will that purple look go away?" Erica asked, studying her ankles.

"Yours don't look that serious to me. I suspect they will become largely unnoticeable after you have had your baby," the doctor said reassuringly. "However, to help with both the swelling of the ankles and the varicose veins, keep off your feet as much as you can. And prop your feet up on something whenever you can." The doctor paused, then went on. "The swelling you have had in your ankles is fairly normal. However, if your hands or face swells, I want you to let me know immediately. That can be serious. One way to judge is by your wedding ring. If it gets so tight that you can't get it off, call the clinic right away."

One of the symptoms of toxemia in pregnancy, a serious illness which can threaten the life of both mother and baby, is swelling of the face or fingers. Toxemia is preventable by constant prenatal care, good diet, and alertness to symptoms that may indicate a problem, such as continuous headaches, blurred vision, sudden weight gain, a decrease in the amount of urine, or as has been mentioned, swelling of the face and hands.

"Make sure you get eight or ten hours sleep a night during this last three months especially," he added.

"You don't have to worry about that," Erica sighed. "I couldn't stay up past ten o'clock if I wanted to."

Even though she was experiencing some of the discomforts of the later stages of pregnancy, Erica continued to work at her job in the dry cleaning store. She sat on a stool behind the counter and put her feet on an upside-down wastepaper basket as often as she could. Since the job had become routine and she knew the management and what to expect, she also brought school books and did her homework between customers.

Night school was going well enough, she acknowledged. "But I still resent the fact that I couldn't go to day school even if I wanted," she told Lizzie. "It bugs me even more when you tell me about the plans for your graduation. I earned the right to be there. All night school has is an informal thing. You go and pick up your diploma and stand around with coffee and cookies."

"Maybe you could graduate with us anyway," Lizzie suggested. "You'll have all the same credits."

"The head of the night school already asked the principal for me. He said no," Erica answered. "The night school man was very sympathetic though," she continued. "Maybe because he has all different kinds of people in his school, he can tolerate a wider range of circumstances. I just don't know. Yuk."

The more Erica thought about graduation, the angrier she got. It wasn't just for herself that she wanted to go, she decided. It was because all her friends were graduating too. It was a moment they had all worked for and had expected to share together. Finally, she told Gary, "Even if I can't go up on the stage, I can be there to see Lizzie do it. After all, he can't stop me from going to graduation and being in the audience. Everyone's relatives and friends are invited. And I'm as much or more a friend of the kids in my class than anyone is."

Gary thought going to see Lizzie graduate was a fine idea. Erica's mother and dad weren't so sure. However, Erica was determined to do it anyway. Her mother's eyebrows raised a little further when she saw what Erica put on to wear the evening of the class graduation. It was the outfit Erica looked the most pregnant in. And, at the end of her eighth month, Erica looked very pregnant indeed.

Erica and Gary purposely left for the school auditorium early. Erica chose seats in the first row, directly in front of where the principal would stand to make his remarks and then give out the diplomas. She chatted happily with Gary, delighted at finally being able to do something to get back at the principal.

Finally, the processional music began. Everyone's head turned. Down aisles on either side, Erica's class began filing into the auditorium. The boys wore black gowns and caps. The girls wore white gowns and caps and each carried several long-stemmed red roses tied with red ribbon. The girls looked so beautiful and grown-up that Erica caught her breath. Deep inside she felt a pang of loneliness and jealousy. She caught Gary's hand and held it. Her life was so changed. If she hadn't gotten pregnant, she could have worn a cap and gown and graduated with the others. Her parents would have been here. They would have been so proud. Her mother would have been dressed to the teeth. Her father would have been one of the fathers standing up to take flash pictures as she came down the aisle. For a moment she desperately wished she hadn't come. However, she soon caught sight of Lizzie moving down the aisle. She relaxed. She wouldn't have missed Lizzie's graduation for the world.

The class filed onto the stage and remained standing. The audience got up for the invocation. Then everyone sat down.

The principal stepped forward to introduce the graduation speaker. Erica watched him carefully as he peered out into the audience. Finally, his glance fell on her. It was more than she could have hoped for. Surprise, dismay, shock, anger—it was hard to describe. But to Erica it was perfect. She sat up a little straighter and smiled pleasantly. The principal was for a moment transfixed. Then he reddened. Several people in the front row looked at her. They could tell something was going on. The principal quickly looked away and began to intro- duce the speaker. She liked to think that when he mispro- nounced the speaker's name and had to say it twice more to get it right, it was because he had seen her sitting in the front row.

After the speaker and the address by the class valedicto- rian, the principal returned to hand out the diplomas. He once again stood in front of her. Erica was aware that he was very careful not to look in her direction—so careful that she knew he must be terribly aware of her presence. She shifted in her seat with delight.

He began to call out the names.

Erica beamed when Lizzie or any of her other close friends walked across the stage to receive their diplomas. After all the diplomas had been given out and the last student had returned to stand at his seat, the audience began to applaud. Erica again got that choked-up feeling. She had struggled through twelve grades to be able to be up there too. It just didn't seem fair. She really was terribly sorry she had come. It would have been so much better not to have known what it would have been like. She looked down at her hands to avoid letting her facial expression show.

The recessional started. The class moved slowly off the stage at both sides clutching their diplomas and smiling broadly. Suddenly, Erica became aware that the processional had been halted on one side and there was some confusion. She looked up to see Lizzie making her way down the row toward her. Before Erica could figure out what was happening, Lizzie thrust her bouquet of roses into Erica's arms. Then Lizzie looked up at the principal and gave him a defiant stare that said, "So what can you do to me now? I've graduated." Then she returned to the recessional parade. The students began filing out again, while people in the audience craned their necks to see what had happened.

Erica clutched the roses against her bulging form. Wonderful, crazy Lizzie. Only she would have thought to do that. Suddenly Erica felt very grown-up. Both she and Lizzie were out of school now. They had graduated. They were entering the real world at last.

Even though she no longer had night school, Erica kept herself very busy after graduation. Faithfully, every afternoon, she did exercises given in the prepared-childbirth classes she had begun attending. She knew the exercises wouldn't guarantee a painless childbirth. However, she had been told they could help ease the labor and delivery. She especially practiced the breathing exercises.

Natural childbirth, or as it is now beginning to be known, prepared childbirth, is of interest to many pregnant women. It involves exercises (physical preparation) and elimination of mental anxiety and fear about childbirth (psychological preparation) in an attempt to eliminate undue pain. Pain-reducing drugs and instruments may or may not be used during delivery, depending upon the progress and condition of both mother and baby. The intention is not to do away with modern medical skills, but to take fuller advantage of the natural processes of childbirth by preparing the mother for the experience. Erica has started such classes late. Beginning about two months before childbirth is much more usual.

Erica liked to sew. Since she had almost a month to go before giving birth, she decided to make a layette herself, or as much of it as she could. Although a layette was supposed to consist of clothes and other articles every baby needs, Erica found each book she read listed different items. Even when they listed the same items, the quantity specified was different. By putting all the lists together on a scratch sheet, Erica was able to come up with the kinds of things she would probably need:

For the baby's clothing:
Nightgowns (sleepers, kimonos)—Very young babies sleep and are awake in the same kind of clothes. Later on, stretch suits are very good for both sleeping and waking times.
Undershirts—Depending upon the climate these may not be needed. Some mothers put them under other clothes for added warmth. Others use just a shirt and diaper in warm weather. They come in different sleeve lengths.
Sweater, cap, booties, and bunting or coat—Depending upon the time of year and the climate, the baby may need just one or all of these things. Baby blankets are used to provide added warmth as needed. Baby shoes are not needed until such time as protective foot covering is necessary for outdoor walking. A baby's feet are strengthened if he or she is allowed to go barefoot even after beginning to walk. All the baby's clothing should be easy to put on and launder, and should be made of soft material.
For the baby's diaper needs:
Diapers (cloth);

Diapers (disposable kind for traveling or emergencies);
Plastic pants (the kind that permit air to circulate);
Diaper pail;
Cotton balls, washcloth, tissues, or other cleansing materials;
Vaseline and/or ointments and powders for control of diaper
    rash;
Diaper pins.
For the baby's bed:
Waterproof sheeting (a washable covering to protect the
    mattress);
Absorbent mattress pads;
Crib sheets (preferably fitted);
Blanket (Depending on climate and time of year, both a
    lightweight one and a heavier one may be needed. Crib
    blankets may also double as blankets for a buggy, depend-
    ing on size.);
No pillow.
For the baby's bath:
Soft towels and washcloths;
Baby soap;
Baby shampoo.
For the baby's feedings:
Bib;
Bottles (four- and eight-ounce sizes). Even if breastfeeding,
    bottles are necessary for water and juice;
Nipples;
Tongs.
For the baby's general care:
Receiving blankets;
Thermometer;
Baby laundry soap;
Nail scissors (baby scissors come with a blunted end).

   The numbers of things needed varied so much on the
different lists that Erica was confused. Finally a neighbor

told Erica: "Look, it depends on how often you do a wash as much as anything. If you wash every day or every other day, it's one thing. Twice a week or once a week and you're going to need a lot more things. Babies grow so fast, buy the least amount you think you need. If you find you really need more, buy more. I guarantee that by the time you find out you could use more, the baby will be in a different size and maybe in different type clothes."

Doing small amounts of final shopping and finishing up things for the layette filled much of Erica's time in the last month. Now that she and Gary had more time together, the planning for the baby had truly become a joint effort. At night they endlessly discussed boys' and girls' names. Sometimes they giggled so hard at some of the concoctions they made up that only the coughing from the other end of the hallway reminded them they were not alone and were making too much noise.

Erica and Gary liked best those times when her parents were away for the evening and they had the house to themselves. Then they did what they called "playing house." Erica cooked special dinners and they wandered all over the house together. They laughed, giggled, and even lightly wrestled sometimes, mindful of the big stomach between them.

In June Erica had packed her bag of things to take to the hospital, since the doctors at the clinic had warned her to be prepared weeks in advance. However, July came, and then Erica's due date came and went, and still nothing happened. Lizzie still called daily and Erica was beginning to feel embarrassed. When at last she felt her first labor pain, it wasn't a surprise, it was a relief. She woke up Gary. Later she supposed she should have said something sensational. Instead she just said, "Finally."

Their getting dressed woke up Erica's parents. Her mother wandered into the room sleepily. "We won't go to the hospital with you, dear," she said. "They won't allow us in the labor room and I don't think there's much point in sitting around the waiting room. Gary, you call us the minute you hear. We'll come and see you as soon as we can. I know everything is going to go just fine," she said, giving Erica a hug.

Before they had gotten out the door, Erica's mother had woken up a little more. "You got your bag?" she said. "You have any papers you need? Did you leave your ring at home, watch at home . . ."

Erica was glad her mother had been so sleepy to begin with. It was just as well for Gary that her mother wouldn't be at the hospital. It would have driven him wild.

They stopped at the admitting office in the hospital. Erica was supposed to be preregistered; however, the clerk couldn't seem to find her records. So they had to give the information all over again: name, address, phone number, Gary's occupation, and so forth.

Prior to going to the hospital, it is extremely helpful to find out what the exact charges of the hospital will be, and what their policies are (husbands or boyfriends allowed in the labor room and/or delivery room, visiting hours, number of visitors, and so forth). It is wise to fill out pre-registration admission forms in advance. The doctor can tell patients where to get the forms or can obtain them for patients. These may be mailed in. It is especially important to fill them out if the patient does not have insurance.

Erica's contractions were getting closer together. "I can't believe this," she kept saying to herself. "I'm going to have a baby and here they are wanting to know how old I am."

Although it seemed like hours, filling out the forms actually took only a few minutes. Just as they finished, someone came up to the admitting clerk and said, "Here it is. It was just misfiled. We had it under 'G' for Gary instead of under their last name."

Erica groaned. "I hope they do better with the babies," she said to Gary. Gary looked too nervous to appreciate her humor.

She joked on anyway. "Oh here he is, we just misfiled your son. We have him under 'T' for tonsilitis rather than under 'N' for nursery."

A nurse with a wheelchair arrived. Erica sat down, feeling very important. She was wheeled to the elevator to go upstairs with Gary tagging along behind. The nurse directed Gary to a waiting room. Then she turned to Erica. "If you have any valuables—money or otherwise, we'll put them in the hospital safe." Erica shook her head. She had already been told to leave her valuables at home and she had done so. The other possessions she had were labeled along with her clothes and put somewhere. Erica didn't know where, but later on they showed up in her room.

Since new mothers generally are in the hospital for at least three and often five days, a number of personal items must be brought for their stay: toothbrush, toothpaste, hair brush, cosmetics, deodorant, nightgown, robe, slippers, sanitary belt, and support bras or nursing bras. In addition, writing materials, magazines, books, and a portable radio may be desirable. Items for the baby's trip home—diapers and pins, plastic pants, nightgown, receiving blanket and sweater or heavy blanket if needed—can either be brought with the mother's things or by the person coming to take the mother and baby home.

Erica put on a hospital gown. A nurse shaved the hair around her vagina and washed the area with a warm sterile solution. Erica was also given an enema. Erica asked a lot of questions. She had waited so long. She was so happy at last to be having her baby that she didn't want to miss anything. Someone took her blood pressure. She thought it must be an intern since he didn't look quite old enough to be anyone else. He asked her questions about her contractions—both the frequency and severity. He listened to the baby's heartbeat by placing a stethoscope on Erica's abdomen. He also checked to see how far the cervix was dilated. Then Erica was shown to a small hospital room. "Is this a labor room?" she asked.

"Yes," the nurse replied.

Erica looked disappointed. It didn't look different from any other room. It had a bed, a chair, a sink, and a clock. No pictures were on the walls. And it was painted that awful institutional green. "I thought labor rooms were, well . . ."

"What did you think they were?" the nurse asked.

"Well, I thought they'd be fancy and have lots of equipment and maybe lots of people."

"There will be enough people coming in and out of here," the nurse said. "Don't worry. As far as fancy goes—well, we'll save that for the delivery room."

"Oh," said Erica, not knowing whether the nurse was kidding her or not.

Erica lay down on the bed. The nurse stayed with her for a few minutes and then went out the door. Erica was alone. A contraction came. She practiced the breathing she had been taught in the education-for-childbirth classes. In through the nose, and then slowly let the air out through the mouth. She hoped she was doing it right. Suddenly there was a familiar "Hi!" It was Gary.

"Hi!" she said. She was delighted.

"They said I could come in for a while. Can I do anything for you? How's it going?"

"It's all so interesting," Erica said.

Gary laughed and Erica laughed with him.

"No, I mean it. Isn't this a silly room? Look, no pictures."

They talked on for a while. Another contraction came. Erica tried breathing again as instructed.

"Let's talk about names," she said. "You talk."

Erica was surprised how fast the time went. Finally

someone came in and told Gary he'd have to go back to the waiting room. "See you, hon," he said.

A doctor came in and examined Erica to determine how much the neck of the uterus had dilated. Over the next hour or so, this was repeated along with other kinds of checks such as a check of Erica's pulse rate. She was given some pills for pain. Erica was beginning to feel terribly poked and examined. It was as if she were on display and everyone that came by dropped in to see what was going on.

The nurse chided Erica when Erica asked if she could charge admission. "Just be glad so many people are concerned about you and your baby. What if no one came?"

Erica thought the nurse might be just putting her on again. However, there was some merit in what she said. Finally Erica was given a pain-killing injection as her contractions came closer together. "We're going to take you to the delivery room now," the nurse said.

One of the first things Erica noticed were the bright lights in the delivery room. And it was, as the nurse had promised, fancy. That is, fancy in terms of the kinds of gadgets and machines standing around. It looked to Erica like an operating room.

Erica was transferred to the delivery table. Her legs were covered with cotton leggings for warmth and sterility and were lifted onto holders. She was covered with sheets until only her face, hands, and vaginal area were exposed. There were people at her head and people at her feet, and it seemed that there were even some people at the side. This is so interesting, she thought to herself.

Just as she was beginning to figure out what everything must be and who must be who, she heard a cry. She couldn't believe it had happened so fast.

A nurse's voice said, "You have a girl."

A girl, she thought. Gary's voice saying "Roxanne Lynn" flashed through her mind. Yes, the baby was only out one minute and it had a name. A new person and a new name.

The baby was held upside down and mucus and blood were sucked from its nose and mouth. The umbilical cord was cut and a clamp put on it.

"It doesn't hurt the baby," the nurse said to Erica.

Then the baby was wrapped in a blanket and laid in a small crib at the side of the delivery table. Drops were put in its eyes to prevent infection. Erica could see the tiny reddened person kicking and could hear her crying. She wanted to go over and pick her infant up but she knew it wasn't possible. People were still clustered around her.

"Okay," the nurse said. "The afterbirth—your placenta—has just come out. Now the doctor is putting in the stitches where he made a small incision—an episiotomy—in the vaginal wall to let the baby come through more easily."

Erica could not feel anything. She just kept looking to the side at her baby. Her baby. Her heart leapt with joy. She looked around the delivery room. Everyone was smiling at her. Within a short time, she was ready to be moved from the delivery room. On her wrist was a pink plastic bracelet with writing on it. It matched the smaller one that had been put on her daughter's wrist.

"That way we can't mix up mothers and babies," someone said.

Erica called over the nurse who had been so nice to her throughout delivery. "Do you think you could get me the small print purse I took with me to the labor room?" she said. The nurse looked at her questioningly. "It's got my makeup in it," she said.

"Sure," the nurse said, suddenly smiling. She was back in a minute.

Erica quickly powdered her nose and put on some lipstick. She brushed back her hair. In her small hand mirror she studied her face. She looked pretty good, she thought, for just having had a baby. She was transferred to a cart and wheeled out of the room and down the hall. Someone brought the baby to her and laid it against her breast. She sighed in happiness and looked at the tiny creature. Suddenly Gary was there beside her.

"She's beautiful, and you're beautiful," he said.

Then the baby was whisked away through one door, and Erica was whisked away through another. After she had been settled in bed for a while, Gary was allowed to see Erica again. He was so excited. "I've been down to the nursery to see our baby," he said.

Erica was almost jealous. "Tell me," she said.

"She's beautiful!" he exclaimed. They were so excited talking about the baby that it seemed unfair when a nurse told Gary he'd have to leave. "See you tomorrow," he said. "And thank you, thank you for my beautiful daughter." He kissed her.

Erica was so elated that she thought she would never get to sleep. She had a small radio and listened to it long after she assumed she should have fallen asleep. They were reporting news about oil prices and small wars and stocks. It was hard for her to believe that there was any world beyond the small area of her room and the nearby nursery where her precious daughter slept.

5. PARENTHOOD:
The Early Months (0-3 months)

ARLENE AND JOEL

Arlene was in a large maternity ward of the hospital. Not many beds were occupied. That added to the strangeness Arlene felt. Several beds down was an older woman. A younger woman, probably in her twenties, was across from Arlene. The only woman even likely to be in her teens was in the bed farthest from Arlene. The first morning Arlene watched as the other women were brought their babies.

"Your baby will have to stay in the incubator," the nurse told Arlene. "When you feel like it, you can go to see him." Arlene felt too tired and lonely to go. Joel was responsible for all this. She felt as though it was his baby, not hers.

Barbara came to see Arlene in the afternoon. "I got someone to look after Jimmy this time," she said. "But I probably won't be able to come again. Anyway as long as you're okay, that's the important thing. The nurse told me your baby would have to be in the hospital a couple more weeks so you can come home with us as soon as you get out."

Arlene brightened. At least there was one good thing about the early birth.

"I'll keep calling the hospital to see when you're getting out and I'll come get you when you do," Barbara added.

Arlene nodded. "I hope it's soon."

Visiting time from then on was a lonely time for Arlene. Everyone else had visitors. The husbands came with flowers or other presents. They sat and talked eagerly with the new mothers. Arlene watched them enviously. It was painfully obvious she wasn't married—no one was coming to see her. Sometimes she chose visiting time to go to the bathroom, where she lingered as long as she could. Other times she stayed in bed and pretended to be asleep. The only bright spot was when the head teacher at the special school unexpectedly came with a stuffed toy for the baby. Arlene thought it was the nicest thing anyone had ever done.

Arlene finally went to see her baby. Looking through the glass into the tiny incubator was like looking at a creature in a jar. The baby didn't look like the sort of baby Arlene had imagined. He was scrawny. His head seemed much too big for his body. His eyes seemed too large for his head. The yellow tinge to his skin made him appear sickly. Arlene felt so removed from the baby that she only went to see him once more while she was in the hospital.

Arlene was allowed to go home after the third day. Before she left, the hospital pediatrician talked with her. "The baby is doing well for his weight and early birth. The care he needs does mean he will be kept in the hospital for several weeks. Do you want him circumcised?"

Arlene looked blank.

"That's a cutting off of a small part of the skin that normally covers the head of the penis. It's a method of making cleanliness in that area easier and preventing infection. It heals in a few days."

Arlene didn't know what to say.

"Most parents do have it done," the doctor told her.

"Okay," Arlene said.

"Also," the doctor continued, "one of his feet is turned in an awkward position. A cast will have to be put on that foot before he leaves the hospital."

Arlene was stunned. She hadn't known there was something wrong with her baby.

"You'll have to take him to an orthopedic doctor at least once a month for several months after that. With the foot correction, I am sure the baby will be able to walk normally."

Arlene had a rush of guilt. She remembered bumping down the stairs, taking the castor oil, eating the wrong things. She closed her eyes. "It's all my fault," she thought.

As if he sensed what she was thinking, the doctor tried to reassure Arlene. "These are problems that sometimes happen. It's nothing you did. With the millions of things that can go wrong, we're always amazed so much goes right. Remember no one is perfect. For some of us they are minor things—our teeth are a little crooked, our eyesight not quite what it should be. But even with our imperfections, we manage to lead pretty good lives. Be glad that the problem your baby has is correctible."

Arlene stared down at her hands. Despite his reassuring words, she knew she had not wanted the baby, that she had hated the thought of having part of Joel inside her. Her hate must have had some effect.

After a few days at home, Arlene felt slept out and bored. Barbara had trouble keeping her home for the two weeks the obstetrician had suggested. Arlene couldn't wait to go back to school. Arlene's first day back in class was a disappointment, however. The girls weren't as eager to talk to her as they had been to others who had given birth. Moreover, new students had entered and the teachers seemed busy with them. When the second day of school was equally disappointing, Arlene decided to leave early. She spoke to the nurse about going home.

"Why?" the nurse asked.

Arlene shrugged, "I'm tired, I guess. The doctor said I should be taking it easy."

"If that's the only reason, fine," the nurse said. "However, I think there's more to it than that."

"I dunno," Arlene said, shrugging and looking away.

"I think you better stay at least for the group counseling," the nurse said. "I'll be attending that session," she added.

Normally, the girls suggested the group discussion topics. This day, however, the counselor started out by saying Arlene had wanted to go home early. "She's been persuaded to stay for a special reason," she told the group. "Maybe we can help her and help ourselves." The nurse then discussed premature birth and the meaning of physical disabilities such as the twisted foot Arlene's baby had. The counselor asked the girls how they felt about what had been said and what their fears were for themselves and for Arlene.

The staff of the special school sense that the girls have withdrawn their support from Arlene at a time when she needs it. Anxiety about their own situation coupled with discomfort over anything abnormal has made the girls turn away from Arlene. Such discussions also may be held prior to the return of the young mother, particularly if a baby has died.

Arlene was at first surprised and embarrassed that the counselor had singled her out. But as she listened to the other girls speak, she began to realize that it wasn't that the girls didn't like her anymore. They had been avoiding her because of something much more complicated. Arlene learned that many of the girls were worried about things they too had done while pregnant—intentionally or unintentionally—and possible effects on their babies. Almost all had some private fears, some about dying themselves. Very few had been able to discuss these fears before.

The counselor helped everyone realize how normal it is for every mother to worry about whether her baby will be all right. She also pointed out that most babies are healthy, and undue worrying is not only unnecessary but is harmful to the mother's ability to relax, enjoy her pregnancy, and look forward to the child's birth. "That is," she said, "not to say you won't worry. Everyone does."

The nurse repeated, "With modern medicine, many defects, such as the inverted foot Arlene's baby has, are correctible. Even for the more severely handicapped child, society has means of helping that child toward its potential. But," she also stressed, "the fact is that most babies are born healthy and very, very few mothers suffer any serious ill effects."

The session was going so well that most of the girls were openly disappointed when it ended. Arlene was too. She thought about it all the way home and later told Barbara about the discussion. "It's helped me face up to a lot of things," she said. "I think I will keep the baby. And I'll go home and live with Mom. There could have been a lot worse things wrong with the baby. And maybe life at home will be different because I have a baby."

Barbara wasn't sure she understood Arlene's logic. However, she decided to be supportive. It was the first decision Arlene had made about herself and the baby since she came.

Arlene's baby came home from the hospital two weeks before school was out. Barbara told Arlene she would care for him while Arlene finished out the school year.

"After my baby," Barbara said, "I am sure this one will be a pleasure."

"What do you mean?" Arlene was puzzled, since Jimmy seemed like such a good little boy.

"Jimmy had the colic." Barbara grimaced, remembering the seemingly endless crying.

There is no general agreement about the cause of the colic. Colicky babies cry for prolonged periods of time. Many babies are over the colic by the time they are three months old.

Change of formula, use of a pacifier, and additional burping to relieve air swallowed when crying, and heat or medication may provide some relief. Mothers of colicky babies also need some relief and should plan to let someone else take over occasionally during the baby's colicky time.

It took Barbara more energy to care for Arlene's baby than she anticipated, since a newborn premature baby has to be fed and changed more often. Also, Arlene was reluctant to assume much care. Most often when Arlene was home, she hovered at Barbara's side while Barbara cared for the baby. She did try to help by getting the clean diapers and taking care of the dirty ones. If the soiled diaper had a bowel movement in it, she rinsed it out in the toilet as Barbara had showed her. Then holding on very tightly, she flushed the toilet so that the water would run through and further rinse the diaper. After that, she put it in a pail that had water and a diaper antiseptic in it.

"Careful rinsing and washing of diapers can help prevent diaper rash," Barbara had explained. "If your baby develops a diaper rash, frequent changes including a middle of the night change, no waterproof pants, and powdering with cornstarch after thorough cleansing can help. I sometimes used a protective ointment or exposed the rash to air and sunshine by leaving the diaper off for a period of the day."

The one task Barbara did insist Arlene do when she was home was give the baby his bottle. Arlene complained to Barbara about her arm feeling tired. She shifted positions frequently as she fed the baby.

"Don't expect to do everything just right," Barbara said. "Just because you have a baby doesn't make you a mother overnight. Everything takes a little practice until you get to the point where it's natural and easy."

"But that's why I want you to do it," Arlene said. "You know how."

"The first time you put on high heels, you don't walk quite naturally. But that doesn't mean you can't wear them," Barbara scolded. "After a few times you put on heels and you just don't think anything of it. It's more important where you are going in them. That's the way it is with caring for the baby. How else you gonna learn unless you do it? After you've given a good many bottles, you'll be thinking more about how he's doing rather than how you're doing."

Arlene nodded. She knew what Barbara said must be true. But since she felt nervous and awkward about everything she did, particularly because the baby was so little, it didn't offer much consolation. She was glad to be able to escape to school each day.

Even though new mothers may feel awkward or pressured about feeding the baby, they should never prop the baby's bottle in any way. Babies need to be held when they are fed. The warmth and closeness of the person feeding them communicates to the baby, helping him develop trust and security in the environment. Propping a bottle can lead to swallowing more air, to spitting up, and also to choking.

Arlene hated to see school close. The last day was "baby day" when all the girls came and brought their babies. Most of the girls were back in regular school. The teachers said they looked forward to seeing their former students and hearing how they had been doing.

Arlene desperately wanted to attend with her baby. The doctor had said that newborn babies and, in particular, premature babies were susceptible to infection and therefore should be kept in. "Care should be taken to keep people away from new babies both indoors and outdoors," he had told Arlene. "A four- to six-week-old baby of average weight and development can be taken out in good weather for short periods. But airings for your baby should be handled with restraint until he has had a chance to mature sufficiently. All in all, you will find that he'll be behind other babies the same number of months he was premature. When he is a year old you should think of him as about ten months."

At the last minute, Arlene decided that if she were careful to keep her baby warm and at a distance from the others, she could go. She wrapped the baby in a blanket and got a ride with one of the other students. The girls crowded around Arlene's baby. "I'd forgotten how tiny they can be," one girl whose baby was already crawling exclaimed.

"Is he a premie?" another girl asked.

There was a pause as the school nurse made her way to the center of the group. "Arlene, can you step into my office for a minute?" she said. "I forgot to get some information for the school records." Arlene reluctantly left the circle and followed the nurse into her office. The nurse shut the door.

"Arlene," she said, "the baby is your baby and you are the one who has to care for him. The decisions you make with respect to the baby are yours. However, I must ask you: didn't the pediatrician tell you how dangerous it is to bring a premature baby into a group of people, particularly a group of mothers and babies?"

Arlene nodded. "But it's just for a short while," she said.

"That doesn't matter, Arlene," the nurse said. "Your baby really shouldn't be here."

Arlene was crestfallen. The door had come partly open and she could see that the girls were now sitting on the floor in a circle talking. Some held their babies on their laps. Others let their babies play on the floor in front of them.

Arlene wanted to join them. She looked down at her sleeping baby—so much like a tiny doll in her arms. "I don't have any way to get back home if I leave now," she said.

"I'll drive you," the nurse said. "Just let me tell the head teacher we're leaving."

Arlene stood reluctantly outside the nurse's door. She was

too embarrassed to tell the girls she was going. Finally, she bolstered her courage and walked back toward the group.

"Excuse me," she said. There was so much noise the girls couldn't hear her. "Excuse me," she said in a louder voice. "I just want to tell you I'm leaving. It's been nice getting to see your babies and . . . to the girls I've been in school with—I'll miss you." Several girls looked up and smiled. Arlene quickly turned and started for the door. "Goodbye," she said, not looking back.

"Goodbye," a few voices called after her. The chatter resumed.

Arlene sat miserably silent on the way home. That was her last time at the special school. This weekend she would be going back home. She had nothing to look forward to and it was all the baby's fault. She frowned at him. If she didn't have the baby she could stay at Barbara's. If she didn't . . .

She stopped. She knew none of it was true. If she hadn't had the baby, she wouldn't have gone to the special school. If she hadn't had the baby, she wouldn't have gone to Barbara's. It was just a mix-up. She had gotten the best because of the worst and now she had to leave it. She wondered what would happen to her next.

"I know one thing," Arlene told Barbara later, "I'm going to really take good care of my baby. Some day I'll visit that school again and the nurse will say, 'Look how happy and well cared-for your baby looks. You must be a very good parent. We're proud of you.'"

The next day Arlene moved back in with her mother. Arlene had not expected her mother to be as helpful as she was. A crib had been placed in the room Arlene shared with one of her sisters. By putting a rubber sheet down with a towel on it, Arlene could use the crib as a changing table. Arlene was also surprised how tender her mother was with the baby. Considering how she yelled at all the other kids, it amazed Arlene to see how gently she held and cared for the newest member of the family. Arlene's mother gave the baby a sponge bath. The umbilical cord stump had dried up and fallen off several days after birth, but the doctor had told Arlene to avoid wetting the navel area until it had healed. Arlene's mother cleaned it with a piece of cotton dipped in alcohol.

Pretty soon, I'll be doing all that myself, Arlene thought with determination.

Over the next months, Arlene spent every minute she could with her baby. She threw herself into her "baby work" as she called it. Arlene had been told that holding the baby, talking to him, touching him, patting and stroking him, playing with him were all ways to help the baby learn about himself and the world. She tried consciously to touch him a lot. She put magazine pictures up near the baby's crib so he would have colorful things to look at. She hung a rattle at the side of his crib, showed it to him, shook it for him, and put it in his hand. The baby did not seem to absorb much of what she was doing. However, Arlene knew it was supposed to mean something to him eventually.

All babies need to be touched, played with, loved. However, babies can be very different. Some babies like a stimulating environment—noise and handling. Other babies are easily overstimulated. They need quiet play and gentle handling. A mother has to learn her baby's personality. Arlene is right that, over time, appropriate exposure to sights, sounds, smells, motions and feelings, helps the baby to grow and learn.

Over the summer a number of people came to Arlene's house. The first was a new welfare worker. Arlene's mother had asked for an allotment for the baby, which had been given. Arlene liked the new welfare worker because she was young and enthusiastic. Arlene told her how much the special school had meant to her and how well she had done there. "My teachers said I had good abilities," she said proudly. "They said I should try to finish school."

A visiting nurse came. She told Arlene about the local pediatric clinic and advised her to take the baby regularly for examinations and shots. She also helped Arlene with some of her questions about baby care. The cast had just been taken off the baby's foot and Arlene was particularly pleased when the nurse told her the baby's foot looked fine to her.

Finally, someone from Arlene's old school came. The person from the school seemed satisfied that since Arlene had a baby, she didn't have to go to school any more even though the law stated that young people had to be enrolled in school until age sixteen. The welfare worker had arranged to come at the same time. She was insistent that the school permit Arlene to go back.

"Oh, it's not that she can't come back," the school attendance officer hastened to say. "It's just that she doesn't have to."

"I think she should go back and I want you to be aware that she will be coming back," the welfare worker said firmly.

Arlene's mother was not happy about having Arlene go back to school. "I want to keep an eye on her," she told the welfare worker. "Once she's out of my house, it means she's out of my control." The welfare worker pointed out to Arlene's mother that she had to start trusting Arlene at some point. At last her mother agreed that Arlene could go to school in the fall provided she was home not more than a half-hour after school each day.

When the welfare worker went to the door, Arlene accompanied her and smiled gratefully. "Thanks," she said shyly, "you're not like the others."

Arlene then went back to her room to watch the baby some more. She couldn't quite get over him. He was so like a doll to dress and feed and play with, just as she had done with her own dolls only a year or so before.

One of the good things that happened to Arlene while she

was in the special school was that she learned to trust people and accept what they have to offer. Arlene's ability to share her excitement and concern about her future has stimulated the welfare worker to take extra measures to help her.

CEIL AND RUSS

Ceil felt healthy and energetic during her days in the hospital. After all the upsets of her pregnancy, the change was especially welcome. Russ had offered to pay for a private room, but Ceil's doctor's advice was to at least share a room. "New mothers are not sick," she had said. "You'll enjoy the company." Ceil's main worry was that she'd be put in with someone who would reject her for being young and not married. However, her roommate turned out to be open and enthusiastic. They talked often between visiting hours.

Ceil had never been in a hospital before. "I always think of it as a place for people who are dying," she confided.

"That's the great thing about being here for a baby," her roommate cheerfully replied. "Maternity wards are the happiest places in the hospital. No one is really sick. And most women are pleased to be here—if nothing else, to get a little vacation from their families. Actually," she confided, "I miss my little girl. I'll be glad to get home to her."

"How old is your daughter?" Ceil asked.

"Four," the woman answered. "And, you know, they've been four of the happiest years of my life. I know it's not 'in' these days but I love being a mother. I wouldn't want to be anything else."

Ceil smiled. She looked at the flowers Russ had sent her. It *was* a very nice feeling.

The number of hospital visitors Ceil could have at any one time was limited. Therefore, Russ alternated his visits with Ceil's parents. The first time he came, they went down to the nursery window. A nurse lifted up their baby so they could see him. Russ held Ceil's hand tightly. They both felt very proud. The second time Russ came and they went to look at the baby, the nurse was busy changing diapers.

"I can't tell which one he is," Russ finally said in an embarrassed voice.

"I can't either," Ceil admitted. "It must be because we have to look through the glass and they're so covered up." Nevertheless, inside she was thinking: "They all look alike to me. How awful. I can't even tell which one is my own baby."

During the day, Ceil's baby was brought to her about every four hours for feeding and left with her for almost an hour. Night feedings were handled by the hospital staff in the nursery so that she could rest. At first, when the baby was brought to Ceil no milk was given, since the baby needed a chance to spit up mucus and get his system in order. "What am I supposed to do with him?" Ceil asked nervously.

"Just enjoy him," the nurse replied as she handed the baby to Ceil.

Ceil looked at the scrawny infant in her arms. She wasn't sure how to enjoy him. She was scared to death he was going to cry. If he did, she didn't know what she would do. She tried to feel love. When the nurse came to take him back to the nursery, she was glad.

Ceil is surprised at the appearance of a newborn baby, as are many other parents. The head generally appears much too large for the body. The fontanel, or soft spot, where the bones at the top of the skull have not yet grown together (and won't until about eighteen months of age) may be clearly visible. The face of a newborn has a broad flat nose, receding chin, small lower jaw. The body has a short neck, small sloping shoulders and large rounded abdomen. The legs are more or less bowed. The skin is thin and dry. Fair skin may be rosy red.

"I must be terrible," Ceil confessed to her roommate later. "I know I'm supposed to love my baby and feel motherly. But I don't think I do."

"Well, some people believe in love at first sight," her roommate answered. "But I don't. I think you have to get to know someone to feel genuine love. Once you get to know your baby, you will love him, I'm sure."

"I don't think I know what you mean," Ceil said. "Babies are all so much alike. When I go down to the nursery window, I can't even be sure I'm looking at my own baby."

"Well, you'll soon learn as I did," her roommate said, "that babies are very different from one another. Even in the beginning," she continued, "their personalities start to show through. For example, I noticed when your baby was brought to you, he lay awake very calmly in your arms. You must have heard the fuss mine made, crying and kicking a good part of the time. My last baby was a little sleepyhead. She didn't even wake up some of the times she was brought to me. Very soon you'll begin to notice things about your baby which will make him an individual to you."

Indeed, as the days went on, Ceil looked forward more and more to having her baby brought to her. She was given warmed bottles of milk to feed him. When he took them, she was surprised at the sense of satisfaction it gave her. When the baby cried and she could not comfort him, however, she was relieved when the nurse came to take him away. On the fourth day, Ceil's doctor came to see her for the second time. "I think you can go home tomorrow if you want to," she said.

Ceil nodded. She had had enough of the hospital. She called her parents and asked them to pick her up the next day. It was time to get on with her own life.

In the morning though, Ceil was sorry she had decided to go. "Maybe it's a little soon for me to pick up full-time care of the baby," she thought. Time dragged as she waited for her release. Finally, Ceil's mother came. "I brought the baby's clothes," she said. "After he's dressed, I'll help you carry your things down to the main entrance. Russ and your father are waiting there to help us get out to the car."

When Ceil heard Russ had come with her parents, she winced. She was conscious that her hair needed washing. She felt ugly in the pregnancy outfit she was wearing. "I wish a new mother's shape was the same as before pregnancy," she mumbled.

Then Ceil saw the baby clothes her mother had brought. "Oh Mother," Ceil said. "You brought the wrong outfit for the baby!"

"I'm sorry, dear," her mother said. "I thought this one was the one you wanted him to wear home."

Ceil's voice quavered. "I wanted the yellow one that the girls gave me so I could tell them that the baby wore it home." She stood by feeling helpless as the nurse dressed her baby.

"Have we got everything now?" her mother asked as she picked up Ceil's suitcase.

"Look out," Ceil cried as the suitcase suddenly came open and there was a crash. "Oh no, that was the vase that Russ's flowers came in." She began to cry.

"I'm sorry, dear," her mother said and attempted to pick up the pieces.

"Oh, let's just go," Ceil said sobbing. She picked up the baby and started down the hall toward the elevator.

"What's the matter?" Russ asked anxiously when he saw them.

Ceil didn't want to look at him. She knew she looked awful and crying had only made it worse.

When Ceil didn't answer, Russ turned to her mother. "What's the matter?"

"It's nothing," her mother said. "I think Ceil just needs to get home."

Ceil continued to cry off and on all the way home. She

refused to let her mother hold the baby. She clung to him desperately, hoping that he too would not begin to cry.

Russ sat next to her. He had looked forward to this day. But Ceil seemed so cold and unhappy. He didn't know what to do. He felt very uncomfortable.

When they got home, Ceil went directly upstairs. She put on fresh pajamas and got into bed. The baby was put in a bassinette in her room. Ceil turned into her pillow and began sobbing again. When Ceil refused anything to eat, her mother softly closed the door and went downstairs.

Russ sat in the living room talking with Ceil's parents for a while. Then he left.

Ceil did not fall asleep but lay thinking and sobbing. Everything seemed so awful to her. There she was in her own house, home again, but there was this baby in her room. Her relationship with Russ was so uncertain. He had gone to the prom without her. He would go off to college, probably meet some other girl and marry. She hadn't the foggiest idea of how to care for a baby. How could she ever manage to go to school again? College was certainly out of the question. Everything her thoughts turned to looked the worst she had ever seen them.

Ceil cried off and on through the night. The next day she poured out her feelings to her mother. Even that didn't seem to help. "I don't know why everything seems so awful all of a sudden," Ceil said over and over.

The post-partum depression Ceil is experiencing is sometimes referred to as the "baby blues." It often is experienced by mothers somewhere between the second and the fourth day. Hormonal changes—as the body adjusts to not being pregnant —are a factor. The changes that are taking place in the mother's life style and uncertainty about baby care or the future can also contribute. For most mothers, the depressed feelings pass within a day or two.

As a welcome home present, Ceil's parents had put a rocking chair in her room. Over the next few days as Ceil sat in her rocker, holding the baby, feeding him, talking to him, her life began to look better. She washed her hair, tried on some of her old clothes to see how far she had to go to regain her figure, and began to plan what she would do in the weeks ahead.

Ceil was surprised how strange her world seemed. When she thought back to her pregnancy days, things hadn't been so different after all. She had gone to school, seen her friends, generally done what she wanted when she wanted. Although her shape had changed and she hadn't felt well a good deal of the time, still there had been just herself to think about. Now, however, everything was different.

"This really does take getting used to," she confided to Russ. "I mean having a baby in my room—it's sorta outer space if you know what I mean. And everything more or less revolves around the baby. My family tries to plan meals when they think the baby will be sleeping so I can sit down and enjoy eating. I have to plan when to sterilize the bottles and make the formula. If I go out, I have to plan to do it when one of my parents can watch the baby. I have to plan when I need to be back."

"And the diapers. I had no idea a baby could go through a hundred diapers in a week. A hundred! Can you imagine that? Changing a baby one hundred times! Other than breathing I haven't done anything a hundred times a week in my whole life!"

"What if you had to wash those hundred diapers?" Russ asked.

"Thank you again," Ceil said. "How in the world did you ever decide to get me diaper service as a present?"

"Well," Russ looked a little embarrassed. "It wasn't my idea. My mother thought of it. But I could see it might be the only way I'd get to see you." Russ sat in the rocker giving the baby his bottle. "Am I holding him okay?" he asked nervously.

"The doctor told me," Ceil replied, "that you can either hold him as if he were being breast fed—that is, half-sitting, leaning back in your arms with his head resting on the crook of your arm, or hold him in a more upright position with his head cradled in your hand. So what you're doing is fine." Ceil didn't feel she was very good at holding the baby, but when she saw how awkward Russ was, she realized how far she had come in even a few days.

"Look how he's taking the formula," Russ said with pride. "He's really hungry."

"When he finishes," Ceil told Russ, "he has to be bubbled."

"Bubbled?" Russ grinned at the expression.

"Bubbled means burped," Ceil explained, sharing his amusement. "You can sit him upright and lean him forward a little bit and rub or pat him gently on the back. Or you can hold him with his face against your shoulder and pat his back. You can also lay him on his stomach across your lap and rub his back. Pictures generally show people holding babies on their shoulder," she added, "but I think just sitting him up is much easier. When he's this little though, whatever you do, you have to be careful to see that his head is supported."

Babies are not able to control their own bodies at first. Over the months, starting from the head to the hands to the trunk and legs, they gradually gain control over body motions.

A baby cannot at first hold up its head and thus the head must be carefully supported. Toward the end of the second month, the baby may be able to hold up its head although it will toss and jerk about. The baby can turn its head from side to side. If the baby is on its stomach during the third month, it will use its arms to push up its chest and hold its head high. By the end of the fifth month, its back is straighter and it can sit up with support. The baby starts to roll. The next month finds the baby rolling from back to front. By the end of the seventh month, the infant may sit unsupported for about a minute. During the eighth and ninth months, the baby learns not only to sit by itself but often begins crawling on hands and knees. The infant learns to push itself into a sitting position from lying and go back to lying again. By the end of the tenth month the baby can stand by holding on to something and can lower itself to a sitting position. In the eleventh month, the infant may stand alone and sidestep, holding onto furniture. Some babies start walking during the twelfth month.

It is important for young mothers and fathers to remember that the age when babies roll over, sit up, crawl, stand up, and walk varies greatly from baby to baby. Some babies skip crawling and begin walking first. Most often, parents whose babies develop rapidly tend to take pride in this, while those whose development is slower often worry. It would be more useful if parents understood that no two infants are exactly alike at a given age. Each develops in its own way and at its own pace. Being "ahead" or "behind" is not a helpful yardstick. As long as the baby is within general "norms," parents should relax and enjoy watching the baby progress as an individual.

"Why does he have to be . . ." Russ hesitated, "bubbled?"

"Babies swallow air when they eat," Ceil replied. "The doctor said that if I think he has swallowed a lot of air, I should burp him halfway through the feeding. If not, then just at the end. Sometimes when he bubbles, he spits up like a lot of babies do, so watch out."

All of a sudden the expression on Russ's face changed.

"What's the matter?" Ceil said.

Russ didn't answer. But he continued to look strange.

"Oh Russ," Ceil burst out laughing. Then she added apologetically, "I forgot to give you a waterproof lap square. I'm sorry. I always put one in my lap so if he wets it doesn't get on me. Oh dear, your pants!"

But she couldn't help laughing again. "The expression on your face. It's . . . It's too much."

Ceil's mother poked her head in the door. "What's going on?"

"Oh Mom," Ceil said. "I forgot to give Russ a lap pad."

"And no plastic pants over the baby's diaper?"

"No, one of the baby books said not to use them all the time. It said plastic pants can make the baby hot, and heat and moisture can cause diaper rash."

"Well," her mother said, walking into the room, "the ones the baby has have openings at the side so I don't think you have to worry about that. Here," she finished, "if he's done feeding, Russ, why don't you let me take him so you can sponge off your pants."

Ceil frowned. She didn't like being criticized in front of Russ.

As her mother disappeared out the door, Ceil called urgently after her. "Don't change his diaper now. It's right after feeding and if he's not been burped enough, a lot of milk may come up because of his being on his back."

Ceil sighed. She wanted to share the baby. She could sense how eager her mother was to handle the baby. But she had just had the baby. The baby wasn't awake that much and it seemed she gave him up a lot—to her mother and her dad. Ceil frowned again. She really wished her mother hadn't taken the baby. She and Russ could have managed.

Russ sponged off his pants and then sat back down in the rocking chair. Ceil perched on the bed.

"How funny," Russ mused. "When you and I were going together, there was no earthly way that your parents would have let us sit together alone in your bedroom. Now they don't even give it a thought. They're off downstairs with the baby. Things have really changed."

Ceil and Russ talked on. Ceil especially was full of thoughts about the baby. "You know, the thing that bothers me most," she said anxiously, "is his crying. I know that even healthy babies cry a lot. The woman in the bed next to me at the hospital told me just to relax and expect it. She said if I let it bother me, it would be hard to be a good parent. However, she also said that crying can mean different things and I would learn to tell."

"All his crying sounds alike to me," Russ commented.

"Me too," Ceil confessed. "I've read that they cry most often because they are hungry. At least during the first couple of months, they cry automatically when they are hungry. After that, they may replace crying with fussing when they're hungry. Most of the time if he's crying and I feed him, then he's okay. But sometimes it means he's got a wet diaper or he's having a bowel movement. One book said they can start crying or fussing as much as a half-hour before they have a bowel movement." Russ looked a little uncomfortable at the discussion of bowel movements so Ceil hurried on.

"But the problem is that crying can also mean he's too hot or too cold or he has indigestion, the sheets or his clothes are wet or wrinkled, or something's wrong with his position, that he can't move his arms or legs. Or it can mean there's too much noise or too bright a light or he's overtired. Or," she sighed, "it can mean he's feeling mishandled—like sometimes it takes me too long to change his diaper and he starts to cry." Ceil noticed Russ shifting in his chair. She wanted Russ to be as interested in baby care details as she was. It disappointed her that he wasn't.

"The bad thing," she finished saying, "is that I always think there's something terribly wrong. And sometimes there is something wrong but it's not terribly wrong if you know what I mean." When Russ didn't respond, Ceil added, "I guess what it boils down to is, I'm scared of not doing everything right—of something happening to him. All that's wrong is, say, maybe he's wet, but I react like he's going to die any minute. Sometimes I just pray he won't cry." She paused, then said wistfully, "I suppose it will get better."

"Look," Russ said. "You're going to be a great mother. I

know it. So stop worrying. You already take care of him like a pro," he said, pretending to throw the baby into the bassinette basketball-style.

Ceil laughed. It was so good to be with Russ as herself again—not pregnant. She was sorry when he had to go. Now that she was feeling better, she longed for the companionship of people her own age. The doctor, however, had suggested that Ceil hold off most company for a while and get as much rest as she could. The baby was being fed six times a day, every four hours: roughly two, six, and ten o'clock in the morning, two in the afternoon, and then six and ten o'clock in the evening. Some mornings Ceil's mother took over the 2:00 A.M. feeding so that Ceil could have more rest, but it was still strenuous.

"I don't know how I'll ever be able to go to school," Ceil had already told her mother. "I had no idea babies were so much work. I thought about doing it all but just not day after day after day after day. Like it really never stops once it starts. And just when it seems I adjust to one schedule and can pace myself to do things around it, the baby shifts into a new routine and wants to sleep and eat at new times."

A baby's early months are spent primarily in sleeping—fourteen to eighteen hours a day. The baby's sleep, however, is interrupted by a frequent need for food. At first it eats roughly every three or four hours around the clock (or six times a day). Then the baby begins to stretch out its sleep over the night period so that it moves to five feedings (including a late night feeding and a very early morning feeding). By the end of the third month, the baby is sleeping a long, full night (twelve hours) and requires four feedings, beginning in the early morning and ending in early evening.

Ceil is feeding her baby on what is called a flexible demand schedule. Small babies experience hunger pangs and cry to indicate their hunger. When they are given food, it relieves the uncomfortable feelings hunger caused. Thus, responding to a baby's demand for food, as Ceil is doing, does not spoil the infant, but instead helps it to learn to trust people to meet its needs. As babies grow, they can be helped to eat at certain times and sleep at other times. The growing flexibility on the part of the baby combined with the flexibility of the parent in seeing that its needs are met leads to a mutually satisfying relationship between them.

Ceil's baby began to fill out. His appearance became so familiar to her that she wondered why she had once thought he looked like any other baby. And just as everyone had told her she would, she began to recognize his different cries. She could tell when she needed to rush to his side and when she could relax and get his bottle ready. Ceil loved nuzzling and cuddling her baby. She sat in her rocking chair and made up songs to sing to him or sang what she remembered of nursery songs.

In the third month, the baby started making little cooing noises. Ceil laughed and called him her little coo-coo. "The summer is going so terribly fast," she told him. "What will I ever do when I have to leave you, coo-coo, and go back to school?"

Russ's summer job kept him from stopping by on weekdays. Only rarely did he appear on a weeknight. Mostly he came on weekends.

Ceil sensed that Russ might have come more often except for the atmosphere in her house. Ceil's brother was home from college for the summer. He was openly hostile toward Russ and made it clear that he blamed Russ for having made Ceil pregnant. Ceil tried to reason with her brother but he would not listen. She knew he had always been very fond and proud of her. "It just blows my mind—you being a mother," he said one time and walked out of the room in disgust.

Ceil knew her brother's world was very different from hers now. He was far from settling down. At college he was just beginning to explore himself and his life, just beginning to make sense out of his future. She knew that to him her situation was unimaginable and a disaster. Her brother's attitude was the only really dark side of Ceil's early months of baby care. Her brother's presence was a constant reminder that life could have been and, according to him, should have been, very different.

Toward the end of the summer, Russ brought Ceil a mobile he had made for the baby. Ceil was disappointed when she first looked at it—all flat things dangling at different lengths from strings. She couldn't even see what they were. She tried to be polite. "What are they?" she said.

"It's an aquarium," Russ said proudly.

"Oh," said Ceil. "I see." Secretly she thought it was ugly.

"No, you don't see," Russ said. "The baby does."

Ceil was puzzled.

"Look, I'll show you," he said. "Lie down on the floor."

Wondering, Ceil obeyed.

Russ held the mobile over her.

"Oh," Ceil clapped her hands. "It's wonderful!" Above her, swimming lazily, were pink, blue-green, red, and yellow fish with assorted stripes and dots.

Russ explained as he helped her to her feet. "You see, most of the junk I saw in the stores was rigged so it looked good to a person standing by it. I guess that's so people who see it will buy it. But if it's really for him to look at, things should be hung so he's the one who sees them."

Young parents often make the mistake of equating home-made or improvised with "not as good." It is important to learn that homemade may not only be "as good" but better. Russ has, on his own, learned another important point. Many of the store toys are designed for parent-appeal. That is, since adults are the ones with the buying power, toys often are made to appeal to their interests, tastes, and ideas of usefulness. A graphic illustration of the difference between a child's interest and that of adults occurs when the parent finds that the very young child often prefers the wrapping paper and box to whatever item is in it.

A sensitive adult who tries to understand things from the child's point of view can offer the child interesting and fun things whether purchased or homemade from ordinary, safe household items. For example, pots and pans may have a fascination for a small child that no store-bought toy has. The child sees the parents using them; they can be put one inside another, covered with lids, banged, stacked, arranged, pulled, pushed, filled and emptied. The child's imagination is endless.

"We'll have to hang it out of the baby's reach," Ceil said, getting a chair to stand on. "Mobiles can be dangerous if pulled down."

Russ nodded. Then as they stood admiring the hung object, Russ said, "There's something I've been wanting to ask you. Would it be okay if the baby spends a day at my house before I leave for college? My parents will help take care of him. It would give you a day off and me a chance to be with him full-time."

Ceil didn't know why she was surprised at his request. Although she immediately said yes, as the day approached, she found that the prospect of leaving the baby with Russ aroused unexpected feelings. "If we had gotten married," she thought, "there wouldn't be this situation of a day here, a day there, my house, his house. I really don't want the baby to go even for the day. Could I be jealous of his parents having the baby with them?" she wondered. "Oh I don't know. I just wish he hadn't asked." However, Ceil had bottles, blankets, and a written notation of helpful information ready when Russ came. "It's not as if the baby will be frightened," she told herself. "He knows Russ; it'll be okay."

Even though Ceil went to the beach with her girl friends, the day dragged. She was home two hours early. At last the baby arrived. Ceil had almost never been so glad about anything. Yet she was grateful she hadn't made a fuss about

Russ's taking him. Secretly, she was also glad that Russ was going away to school and would not be asking for the baby again.

It's so funny, she thought to herself, how a person can develop such strong feelings in such a short time. When the baby was brought to me in the hospital, I thought, So this is my baby. Everything was so strange. I was glad to have him go back to the nursery, especially when he cried. Now I know him so well, he's just a part of me. And when he cries, that's the time I want to be with him most.

ERICA AND GARY

Erica decided to breast-feed her baby. "I know babies do as well on bottles," she said to Lizzie, "but I want the whole experience of being a mother." Erica was surprised, however, when the baby was brought to her after the first day for breast-feeding. She knew her breasts did not yet contain milk.

A mother's breasts do not produce milk until two to five days after childbirth. Instead they contain a creamy yellow liquid called colostrum, which is high in protein. Thus the nursing mother feeds her baby on colostrum at first—generally five minutes or so on each breast each time the baby is brought to her. At some feedings, additional liquid in a bottle, such as glucose (sugar) water, may be given. The baby does not need any other food until the mother's milk is available.

Even though one of the hospital nurses showed Erica how to lie down to breast-feed, Erica had trouble making herself comfortable and placing the baby in a good position. "For something supposed to be so natural," she observed, "breast feeding feels terribly unnatural."

"Don't be discouraged," she was told. "It will seem much easier in a week or so."

After a few days, Erica was allowed to sit on the edge of her bed. A pillow was used to prop up her arm as she held the baby. It was much easier to nurse that way. However, she worried about feeding and caring for the baby after she was home. The hospital pediatrician was little help. Even though he came each day to tell Erica about the baby, he always seemed to be in a hurry. "Just fine," he would say. "Your baby is doing just fine." Then he would turn to go.

Erica tried to hold back her questions. "What about the baby's crying?" she finally blurted out. "How will I know if something is really wrong?"

"Oh don't worry about that, you'll know," the doctor replied. "There will be plenty of people around to help you, too."

Erica was crestfallen. He didn't understand. The last thing in the world she wanted to do was to ask her mother anything. She had had enough trouble with that during her pregnancy. Who else was there? Lizzie didn't know and Gary surely didn't. Erica wanted to protest. "But I don't want to ask anyone. Don't you see? I want to know myself." But she didn't say anything. What a horrible man, she thought. I wish I had someone else to talk to.

Most new mothers have some anxiety about their ability to competently care for their new baby. Young mothers, however, may have special concerns. Criticism concerning their pregnancy and the taking on of the responsibilities of parenthood at a young age may have increased their anxiety. They may desperately want to prove to others that they can be good mothers. Patience in answering their questions, and reassurance concerning their deeper fears about their ability to be a good parent is very much needed to get young mothers off to a good start.

It seemed to Erica that up until childbirth everything had been going well. Now it was all falling apart. "My stitches hurt so much. I didn't know it would be like this," she complained to the new mother in the bed next to hers. "Do you ache as much as I do?"

"No, I guess I don't. But tell the nurse," the woman added sympathetically. "She can give you a painkiller."

"No one told me it would be like this. Maybe it's just me," Erica muttered. When they went to the hospital lectures on child care, however, she saw several other new mothers hobbling along as if their bottoms were as sore as hers. Like Erica, they sat on foam pillows with the center cut out and envied the mothers who didn't seem to need them.

"Well, it's not just me then," Erica said to the woman gently lowering herself onto the chair next to Erica's. "How long will it take before we feel better?"

"It took me about two weeks last time," the woman replied.

"I've been reading baby books till I'm blue in the face, but it's so different when you have the real thing in your arms," Erica said, glad to have someone new to share her feelings of concern with.

The other mother nodded. "I've forgotten so many things. Even if you've had a baby, these demonstrations help. Ask whatever questions you have, too. I didn't the first time. I was sorry later."

By the third day, Erica's milk had started. Erica successfully fed her daughter in the morning. The baby slept through the next time she was brought to nurse, however, and nothing Erica could do seemed to awaken her. When the pediatrician came to see Erica later, he noted, "The baby didn't gain after that last feeding."

The tone he said it in convinced Erica that she had failed. Erica wanted to protest, "Of course she didn't gain. How could she? She slept all the time." Instead she sat silently in her bed. The pediatrician gave her a piece of paper that had some instructions about vitamins written on it and left. Erica buried her head in her pillow. How could what was supposed to be such a wonderful experience be so awful? "I won't be able to nurse. My stitches hurt like mad. How will I ever manage the baby?" She began to sob. "I want Gary. I want to go home."

Erica, like Ceil, is experiencing a post-partum depression. Many of the concerns she has are common to new mothers. Others are unique to her. Awareness that such depression is often experienced by mothers in the first week or so after childbirth and that it can quickly pass might be of some help. Assurance of back-up help with mothering at this point may also be important. For example, knowing how to contact a responsive medical person or knowing that acceptable home help is available can ease the concern.

By the end of the next day, Erica began to feel happier. A new pediatrician came in. He seemed relaxed and much more ready to sit and talk. He began by telling Erica his sister had just had a baby too. His whole family was excited, he said. Erica poured out her questions to him. She was disappointed to learn that he would not be back the next day.

Because her stitches were so uncomfortable, Erica decided to stay in the hospital an extra day. Gary approved. But when he went to pay the hospital bill so she could come home, not only was the cost of the extra day more than he had planned but so was the entire hospitalization.

"Didn't you get the hospital's sheet that tells about costs?" the cashier asked.

Gary shook his head. "I don't know. Maybe I did. It doesn't matter now." It was clear he had misunderstood that there would be a room charge for the baby as well as for Erica. Also, he hadn't planned on medication costs. He dreaded the thought of the statement from the anesthetist, which was to be mailed separately.

Gary decided not to tell Erica about their new money problem. In a couple of weeks, he thought, when she's feeling like herself again. Then I'll tell her.

Erica arrived home eager to begin mothering. She was glad to be out of the hospital and on her own. Being on her own, however, meant asserting herself in the face of advice from her mother, her grandmother (who had come for the summer), and even her father. It was not easy.

"Thank goodness, I'm breast-feeding," she told Gary. "It's less expensive than bottles, and certainly easier than all that sterilizing stuff and fixing formula. Most important, Mom and Grandma can't take over. I know I am going to have the baby all to myself at least a few times each day." She added thoughtfully, "The only thing I'm sorry about is that you can't feed her too."

"I'd look pretty silly with breasts like yours," Gary said wryly.

"No, you know what I mean," Erica said. "I mean you could give her a bottle."

Some pediatricians advise giving a breast-fed baby an occasional bottle so that if the mother needs to be away, the baby will accept bottle feeding. The mother can either use her own milk for such a bottle (by squeezing the milk out of her breasts by hand into a sterilized cup) or else use formula milk.

"Well, I tell you," Gary said. "You get the milk down her and I'll get it up."

"What do you mean?"

"I'll do the burping," he said.

"It's a deal," said Erica, watching with pride as Gary supported the tiny infant on his lap and gently rubbed her back until she burped.

Now that Erica was home and her milk supply had increased, she was beginning to look forward to each nursing time. This, despite hints from both her mother and grand-mother, that she might not have enough milk.

"The nurse who helped me get started on breast-feeding at the hospital said to watch out for people who would tell me I couldn't breast-feed," Erica told Gary. "She said other women—sometimes even husbands—don't realize deep down inside that they're a little bit jealous of the close relationship. The nurse said all mother's milk is about the same in quality and there should be no reason why I couldn't breast-feed. The only thing I have to do is make sure I don't get overworried and do get plenty of rest."

Nursing mothers also need to increase their food intake. In general they need to add calories—in the form of meat, fish or eggs, milk, yellow and green vegetables and citrus fruits. The amount of additional calories should increase with the baby's weight. Nursing mothers should also drink extra liquids.

Who can rest with a noisy little thing like this around?" Gary said, holding up the baby and wriggling the baby's nose against his. "Hiccups, wheezes, coughs, sneezes! I couldn't believe the sounds she made last night!"

"I read in one of my baby books that all newborn babies make a lot of strange sounds," Erica said, then laughingly added, "You know, I really wanted to have the baby in our room. But now, I think I'll be glad when Grandma leaves at the end of the summer for more reasons than one. I can see why a baby should have its own room."

The baby burped again. Gary smiled. "Hey, that was another good one." He looked at Erica. "What's next?"

"Well, the baby scratched her face this morning so I think we'd better trim her fingernails."

Gary looked at his daughter's tiny hand and the paper-thin nails. "I'd be scared to do it," he said.

"Well, I'm scared to do it too. But I don't want her

scratching her face. You hold her on your lap there. They say to do it while a baby's asleep but she's so full and contented, I think I'll do it now." As Erica manipulated the blunt-ended baby scissors, Gary watched in fascination. "You know, that takes real courage."

"Uh huh," said Erica as she finished up. " 'Mother Courage,' that's what you can call me."

Gary laughed. "And now?"

"Her first tub bath?" Erica said.

Gary groaned. "There's a lot more to this baby care bit than I thought."

They filled a small basin with about three inches of comfortably warm water. With one hand supporting her head and the other supporting her bottom, Gary gently lowered the baby into the small basin, which he had lined with a towel to keep from being slippery. "Okay," he said. "Now you take over."

Erica supported the baby's head on her wrist and arm while firmly holding the baby up by one shoulder. With her other hand Erica rinsed off the baby's face with clear water. She patted it dry. Then she leaned the baby back slightly so soapy water would not run into its face and soaped the baby's scalp. She rinsed it with clear water squeezed from the washcloth. Then she soaped and rinsed the front of the body. She sat the baby up and supported her under the chin while she soaped and rinsed the back. "Now here, you get her out," she said when she was done.

Gary lifted the baby out of the tub with the safety hold he had used in putting the baby into the bath. "You know it's ridiculous that it takes two of us to do this," he said happily, helping to pat the baby dry.

"Well," Erica said. "As soon as I build up confidence I'm sure I'll be able to do it myself. It's just that right now I feel better having someone to help me." Indeed, Erica found shortly that she had gained enough confidence to study the baby books less and rely more on her own instincts. She also became so used to handling the baby and so attuned to the baby's moods that she wondered why she thought she had needed help to begin with. But she continued to ask Gary to help care for the baby.

Around the fourth week though, Erica experienced her first "real scare" as she called it. A rash appeared on the baby's face and neck. "I wonder what's the matter. Maybe I'm doing something wrong," Erica worried. She reread her three different baby books and studied all the reasons for rashes. Finally, as the rash appeared to worsen she became concerned enough to make a special trip to the pediatric clinic. The doctor there assured her that the rash her baby had occurs in all newborns and would disappear by the time the baby was eight or ten weeks of age. "The best treatment is to leave it alone," he said. Erica was much relieved. She also asked about the baby's eyes and was told not to be concerned about them either. "Although the baby's hearing is fully developed at a very young age," the doctor said, "the eyes of the young infant do not focus and may appear crossed at times."

"I can't believe there's so much to learn," Erica told the doctor. "I keep getting sandbagged by thousands of details about things I never even dreamed I'd want to know."

"Well, ask away," the doctor said. "If we can't knock off a thousand, we can at least go for a hundred."

Erica grinned. "Well, one more anyway. What about using a pacifier?"

"Well, the baby has a built-in pacifier, her thumb, which she can use when she needs. And most babies do need extra sucking. The main objection to a pacifier is that parents may continue to use it after the baby no longer needs it."

"Okay," Erica said. "I'll choose after I've thought about it. And thank you. It's just that there's so much to find out and learn all at once."

As Erica put on the baby's sweater in the clinic waiting room, she noticed the wide difference in the appearances and actions of the babies there. She also noticed the differences in the appearances and actions of the parents.

Erica's baby kicked and fussed as her bonnet was put on. "My little live wire," Erica said as she bent over her. "I'm glad I've got you." A broad smile spread across the baby's face. "Ohhh, a smile!" Erica laughed. "A smile for me. I love you!"

Erica picked up her daughter. She began to sing a little song as she carried her out to the car. She also danced a little step. "You may think your mommy's a little cracked. But I'm just happy. Happy you're fine. Happy I'm fine. Happy, Happy, Happy."

Babies are as different as adults. Over the course of the first year, parents and babies learn about one another's personalities and work out ways of living together. If a baby is loud, easily upset, very active, or irregular, it takes a parent with a great deal of energy and patience to meet the challenge. At times, such babies can leave parents feeling less successful as parents than they may actually be. On the other hand, babies that adapt easily, are quiet and regular, also affect the parents' reactions, feelings, and behavior. Such parents may have an easier time. Erica's baby is not an "easy" baby, but Erica is eagerly accepting the challenge.

Erica's natural instincts have her talking to the baby, singing to the baby, and providing pleasant motions for the baby. Young mothers and fathers often make the mistake of thinking that it is silly to talk to a baby who "can't understand." Such stimulation and communication are important to the baby's development. Parents can talk to their babies while changing diapers, dressing them, giving them a bath, feeding them, playing with them. What is said is not as important as the tone of the voice and the fact that the parent often looks at the baby to reinforce the communication between them.

As the weeks went by, Erica was surprised at the amount of

energy she had. She had been told that just as it was important for mothers to see the doctor during pregnancy to be sure that the baby was growing well, so it was important to see a doctor after the birth of the baby to be sure that the mother is returning to her prepregnancy state. "One of the things I want to do," she announced immediately after her sixth-week postpartum check-up, "is to get my figure back. The doctor says I'm fine and if I do some basic exercises, I'll be back to my old self in no time.

"The other thing I want," she hesitated, "is to have an evening out. Do something with Gary—just the two of us."

"Well, we can help with that," Erica's mother said. "We're not here to be built-in baby sitters, but we can certainly see that you get an evening out once in a while."

As she got ready to go, Erica felt like a schoolgirl on her first date. "Now I know how long my pregnancy really was," she said smilingly to Gary, ". . . forever." As a treat, they went to a movie downtown rather than one at the local movie house. Afterwards they stopped at a snack place that was popular with many of Erica's old school crowd. Several people they knew waved at them or said "Hi." However, no one came and sat with them. They both felt an unexpected loneliness.

"I can't believe it," Erica said. "I've only been out of school a couple of months but I feel old and out of touch."

Gary nodded. "I wish we knew other married couples our age."

"Well," Erica said. "Of the two girls in my class who got married, one moved away and you know I can't stand the other one." They sat for a while longer, talking occasionally, and then went home feeling let down.

Perhaps it was the disappointment of the previous evening carrying over, or the fact that Gary was grouchy when he got up, but Erica found everything going wrong the next day.

"Mother," she finally said exasperatedly, "let me mix the cereal the way I want to. It'll be okay."

"I was just trying to be helpful," her mother said in a hurt tone.

"I know," Erica answered. "But I can do it and it's okay this way."

Erica's grandmother wandered into the kitchen. "The baby was fussing so I turned her over."

"Oh Grandma, you didn't!" Erica said. "She was fussing because she wants her dinner. She didn't need to be turned over."

"Erica, your grandmother was just trying to be helpful," her mother reminded her sharply.

Erica nodded. "I'm sorry, Grandma," she said.

She put a small amount of rice cereal into a little dish and picked up the demitasse spoon she had for feeding the baby.

At one time babies were not put on solids until around one year of age. However, most doctors now have them start somewhere between two and four months. Generally, the baby is given a single grain cereal as a first feeding, although bananas or applesauce may also be used. Feedings should be kept small. The parents should watch to see if there is any sign of allergy or indication that it is hard for the baby to digest the new food. They should also wait about a week before trying another solid so that if the baby cannot tolerate a food, it is easy to determine which food it is.

"It certainly is early to start feeding a baby solid food," Erica's grandmother commented to Erica's mother. Erica went out the door and up to the bedroom where the baby was fussing. "There, there," she said. "I know you didn't want to be turned over. Here, I'm going to give you some nice cereal." Erica supported the baby in her arms and reached over and got a little cereal on her spoon. She slipped it into the baby's mouth. The baby gagged and began crying.

"Tastes funny, doesn't it?" said Erica soothingly. "But you'll get used to it. You'll even really get to like it." She put some more on the spoon and gave it to the baby. More crying.

Erica's grandmother poked her head in the door. "Just not ready for it yet."

"Grandma, please!" Erica said. Her grandmother's head disappeared and Erica heard her muttering as she went down the hall.

Erica turned back to the baby but her own enthusiasm for beginning solids had waned. "I'll try again tomorrow," she murmured, leaning back in the chair and beginning to nurse her baby.

The doctor had said that she should start the baby on solid food. And she had talked to another girl at the clinic whose baby had started on solids at this age. However, maybe her grandmother was right. Maybe her baby was a little too small yet. She sighed. She wanted so much to be a good mother and to take care of her baby the way she should. It was all so confusing. Sometimes her mother said one thing and her grandmother said another. Other times they both agreed, but what they said was different from what the books said. Sometimes the books were even different from one another.

When Erica got her information from a doctor, she felt best about what she did. She had faith in the pediatricians at the clinic. But she didn't always know what they would say. Occasionally, she lied and told her mother and grandmother that a pediatrician had said something he hadn't. She didn't like lying but sometimes she was at her wits' end.

Erica sighed. "I don't know whether I can make it or not. And poor Gary gets pushed out with three mothers for this baby. Maybe it will be different when my grandmother leaves. I hope so. I'm really getting crushed and so is my baby. Sometimes I think why not just give up. Let them take over. It would save a battle and I could just go back to living my life. It sure would be easier."

One of the main concerns about "multiple mothering" is inconsistency. An infant needs to learn to trust its environment. For example, if one person gives a pacifier to a baby when he cries, and another either does not give it or takes it away, this can be confusing to the infant.

6. PARENTHOOD:
The Next Six Months (4-9 months)

ARLENE AND JOEL

When fall came, Arlene found she couldn't wait to get back to school. The newness of caring for the baby had worn off and she looked forward to getting out each day and being with kids her own age again. Now that the baby was slightly older, her mother didn't seem as tolerant of Arlene's handling of the baby. She often told Arlene what to do. She also expected more of Arlene around the house. The nagging had started again too. "Arlene, you already made one mistake," her mother had told her as she got ready to leave for school the first day, "now don't make another."

"What do you expect me to do?" Arlene had finally snapped back. "Say to the baby as it grows up, 'you're a mistake'? Besides, I'm only going to school. You'd think I was going camping with the football team." Arlene walked out the door without saying goodbye to either the baby or her mother.

Arlene was determined to make good in school. She tackled her schoolwork with the same enthusiasm she had initially given the care of her baby. The successes in the special school were still fresh in her mind. But after a few weeks, going to school and coming home to care for the baby began to wear on Arlene.

The teachers in her school were not nearly as complimentary or understanding as they had been in the special school. Furthermore, now that her mother had taken over care of the baby, it seemed to Arlene that all she did was run and get bottles or wash dirty diapers. Her mother seemed to be having all the good times with the baby while she was stuck with the "yuk" work. And her mother was now acting as if it were *her* baby! Arlene began to long for a way out.

Finally, Arlene discovered she could get away from the house if she volunteered to do errands for her mother—go to the store, pick up things at the cleaners—and take the baby along. After a full day of child care her mother was glad to have the baby out of the house for a while. Also, she thought the fresh air was good for the baby.

At first Arlene just dawdled along the way, looking in store windows. Unless her mother needed something for dinner, as long as Arlene was back by dinner time it didn't seem to matter how long she was out. Arlene loved the attention she and her baby received from people who stopped to look in the buggy. When they admired the baby, Arlene glowed with pride.

One Saturday afternoon, Arlene found herself taking the buggy to the Bot. Joel had skipped town—at least that was the word when his payments stopped—so there was no fear of running into him. The girls at the Bot crowded around. Arlene woke up the baby to show it to them. Several girls wanted to hold him and Arlene let the baby be passed around. When he began crying very hard, though, she took him back. She held the baby for a while trying to soothe him. Finally, she sat on the park bench with the girls and rocked the baby to sleep in the buggy. The girls asked her what it was like to have a baby. Arlene was the center of attention.

After a while, a couple of fellows came by. They stopped to talk and then went into the pizza place. The girls decided to follow. Arlene was torn. She wanted to go with them but she didn't know what to do with the baby. She decided that if she parked the buggy right in front of the store and went in for a short while, it would be all right.

Arlene came out a half-hour later. The buggy was nowhere in sight. Arlene panicked. She knew she should never have left the baby by himself. He must have been stolen. She ran into the middle of the street and looked up and down. She couldn't see the baby anywhere. She ran back into the pizza place wild-eyed.

"What's the matter?" someone asked.

"My baby's gone!" Arlene cried. Everyone ran outside.

Suddenly someone shouted. "Here he is!" The buggy was neatly parked around the corner of the store. Arlene could barely hold back the tears. One of the girls who had left the group earlier came down the street. "What happened?" she asked. When she was told, she went over to Arlene. "Oh Arlene, I'm sorry," she said. "When I left the store the baby was crying because the sun was shining on his face. So I put the buggy around the corner in the shade." Arlene realized that the girl had tried to be helpful but she couldn't thank her. She felt too upset.

For several weeks after that incident Arlene was very attentive to the baby and stayed away from the Bot entirely. Soon, boredom and frustration at home along with problems in schoolwork led Arlene into going to the Bot again. When she went indoors, however, she always took the baby in with her. To keep the baby from annoying her so she could stay longer, she sometimes gave him teaspoonfuls of Coke and bits of potato chips to suck on.

Having had a baby made Arlene more acceptable to the Bot crowd. If she didn't come to the Bot, the group told her they had missed her or they hadn't had as much fun without her. When the group or a part of it went off to do something, they always urged Arlene to come. With the baby it was impossible, but no one held it against her.

Arlene desperately wanted to find some way to do things with the Bot crowd. Because she was finally a part of the group, the baby began to be a drag on her. One evening, Arlene particularly wanted to go bowling because a new fellow at the Bot was going. He seemed to like her. Arlene debated. If she asked her mother, she knew her mother would say no. Her mother didn't trust her. "The one way you're going to learn responsibility, young lady, is to have it," her mother often said. "Now you got yourself a baby and you're going to take care of it." Her mother just wouldn't understand.

When her mother, by coincidence, turned out to be going out that evening too, Arlene's heart jumped. Once the baby was asleep these days, he slept a long, full night. She would have time to put him in bed and still go. Arlene swore the other kids to secrecy. "You tell," she said, "and I'll see you regret it for a long long time."

Despite Arlene's nervousness, it all went like clockwork. She got the baby to sleep on time; her mother left on time. Arlene went with a chill of anticipation running up and down her spine. The new fellow, Bud, picked her up around the corner. Arlene had only bowled twice before in her life, so she didn't do well on the lanes. In spite of that, she had a wonderful time. The kids laughed and clowned around. Bud spent much of his time with Arlene showing her how to bowl better. He wasn't all that good himself, but he knew a lot more than Arlene.

Arlene was very disappointed when the bowling alley closed. "I could have done that another two hours," she said.

"With your bowling, Arlene," someone said, "it probably would have taken that long to get a score."

Arlene laughed, as did everyone else.

"Where do we want to go now?" one of the girls said.

Arlene sighed. She wished she could be going on with them but her mother would be home in another hour. Her arrangement with Bud had been that he would take her home right after bowling regardless of what the other kids did. She was grateful when he kept to his word and didn't press her about going elsewhere with the group. As Arlene got out of the car, one of the girls in the back seat called, "Arlene, try. Maybe next time you can fix it so you can come somewhere else too."

Arlene nodded. "I'll try," she said. She hurried down the block and into the apartment. She felt wonderful. It was the biggest lift she'd had in a long time.

That night as Arlene lay in bed, she replayed the whole evening, particularly her relationship with Bud. It was very unlike how it had been with Joel. She had been awed and impressed with Joel. She had felt like a little girl on the sidelines watching her superhero. With Bud it was different; they were more like equals and he seemed just as attracted to her as she was to him.

The next day Arlene floated on the memory of the night before. Within a few days, however, everything had settled into a routine again. The weeks went by and there were no other opportunities. Arlene continued to go to the Bot in late afternoon. But whenever she heard that the group had done something nice in the evening or on the weekend, it made her miserable.

Arlene was very frustrated with school. No one paid much attention to her and she wasn't learning. That day she had been told she might not pass English. On the way home she kicked angrily at the snow that had fallen all day. She wouldn't be able to go to the Bot. The buggy wouldn't go in snow and it was too far for her to carry the baby. Arlene took off her wet clothes and hung them up.

"Don't leave your boots dripping in the front room, Arlene," her mother yelled. "Put them in the back hall."

Arlene grimaced. She hated to be told what to do but she particularly hated to be told to do things she had intended to do anyway. "All right," she yelled back. "You'd think I didn't know anything."

Arlene played with the baby for a while, but she was preoccupied with the snow and the Bot and the upcoming holidays. Finally she got the baby's dinner ready and put him in his highchair. Before she could pick up the spoon, he dropped it over the side. She picked it up and put it back on the tray. He immediately dropped it again.

"Now stop that." Arlene picked up the spoon and filled it with food. But the baby grabbed it before she got it to his mouth. When Arlene jerked it away, he began to cry.

"Now eat this," Arlene ordered loudly, filling the spoon again. The baby turned his head away and pushed with both hands. His dinner dish went over the side of the highchair and down on the floor. Beets splattered over the kitchen walls, the floor, and Arlene.

"Oh, now look what you've done!" Arlene angrily snatched the baby out of the chair and began to spank him. The baby's screams and Arlene's yelling brought her mother rushing to the kitchen.

One of the ways babies learn is by dropping things and watching them fall. At this particular age, spanking the baby does not help because the baby does not understand why it is being spanked. Arlene at first saw the baby as doll-like. Now she is assuming that he is purposely misbehaving. She has yet to see him as a developing human being with his own pattern of growth and his own set of needs.

"Arlene, for heaven's sake," her mother said, taking the baby. "What's the matter with you!"

Arlene looked at her mother and ran crying to her room. She was sorry she had hit the baby. She was sorry she had lost her temper. But most of all she was sorry for herself. Sorry she wasn't doing well in school. Sorry she was tied down with the baby. Sorry she couldn't go out and date like other girls. Sorry she was alive.

After Arlene stopped crying, she could hear her mother talking to the other kids and the noise of dishes. The baby had stopped crying and she guessed they were getting ready to have dinner. Arlene wanted to join them but that meant getting the baby back, or helping with dinner, or doing something. She couldn't face it. Instead she curled up on her bed and stared at the empty crib next to it. Finally, she felt guilty and got up. The family was sitting down to eat. Her mother was holding the baby on her lap as she ate.

"I'll take the baby now," Arlene said. Her mother handed the baby to Arlene without saying a word.

Arlene got a bottle for the baby from the refrigerator and walked back to her bedroom. She changed the baby and got him into a clean sleeper. Then she sat on the edge of her bed to give him his bottle. He held it too. Arlene leaned over and put a kiss on his forehead.

"Tiny, helpless little man. I'm so sorry I spanked you. I'm sorry. I just . . ." The tears started to fall again. She felt terrible for having hit such a defenseless little person. "I want so much to be a good mother, but I really am an awful one," she whispered to him, her voice quavering.

Over the next few days Arlene tried to be extra nice to the baby. She played with him constantly whenever she was home. Then one evening her play was interrupted by a phone call. "Hello," she said hesitantly. She felt her face flush. It was Bud. He said he hadn't seen her at the Bot to tell her, but Saturday the group was going to some friend's uncle's house for the afternoon. He said something about an ice-skating pond out back and they'd cook hotdogs over a fireplace and be back before dark. "If you can go," he finished, "meet us at the Bot around noon."

Arlene hung up the phone. She wanted to walk into the living room and ask her mother if she could go. But what if her mother said no? She knew how her mother felt about things. If her mother said no, then her mother would be watching her. She decided not to say anything.

"Who was that?" her mother called.

"Oh, one of the kids from school," Arlene lied. "Lost his English book and thought maybe I had picked it up with mine."

"Why'd he think you?" her mother asked.

" 'Cause we piled our books on top of one another's at the lunch table," Arlene added, grateful she could think of something so quickly.

"Incidentally," her mother said, "with the holidays coming, they need some extra help where I used to work. So I'm going to be starting Saturdays now and maybe do some weeknights closer to Christmas. As soon as you get out of school for vacation and can take care of the baby, if they need me, I may even do days."

Arlene's heart leaped into her mouth. "Okay, Mom," she said. That meant her mother would be gone on Saturday.

Arlene waited until her mother left that Saturday, then took her sister aside. "Now don't forget, when he wakes up from his nap, change his diaper and play with him for about an hour. Then give him that dinner I showed you." Arlene knew it was a lot for her sister to remember. However, the baby was napping now. There really weren't too many hours he would be awake and have to be watched. "When you put him to bed, change his diaper once more, you understand? And don't you dare ever tell Mom I wasn't here," Arlene finished. For a moment Arlene thought she better not go. "Just get out of the house," Arlene told herself. "Once you do, you'll feel okay."

It turned out to be a far better afternoon than Arlene had even dreamed. Whoever owned the house wasn't home, so the kids had the whole place to themselves. It was a perfect setting: an ice-skating pond out back, paths through a small woods, and a big fireplace in the living room. Arlene had never been anywhere as nice. Most of all she liked being with Bud. When the hifi music in the living room got so loud that neither one of them could hear what the other was saying, they went upstairs to one of the bedrooms to talk. They talked for a while, then somehow one thing led to another and they had intercourse.

It wasn't at all like the way it had been with Joel, Arlene thought on the way home. She sat in the back seat of the car. Bud's arm was around her. It was friendly and warm and they were equals.

"And I'm home in good time," Arlene thought happily when the group dropped her off around the corner from her building. "Long before Mom." Before she even opened the apartment door though, Arlene knew something was wrong. She could hear the baby crying and the kids all talking. She didn't stop to use her key; she banged on the door. When Arlene got inside she found her sister walking up and down with the baby. The baby had a red swollen bump on his head.

"What happened?" Arlene asked angrily, snatching the baby.

Her sister looked very frightened. "I put him on your bed to change his diaper and the telephone rang. When I went to get it, he fell off on the floor."

Babies can never be left unattended. If the telephone or doorbell rings, the baby should not be left alone. Babies have no way of knowing what can happen if they roll over or explore. A parent should either put the infant in its crib or playpen, or pick it up and take it along when leaving the room. Even when in the room, a parent must be careful. For example, a mother or father should not turn away while diapering the baby. It can too easily roll off a surface even when the parent thinks it cannot.

Arlene was able to quiet the baby but she was terribly worried. The bump looked so big. She couldn't wait until her mother got home. "What should we do?" Arlene asked urgently the minute her mother stepped in the door. Arlene was so upset she didn't care if her mother found out she had been gone. However, her mother didn't ask who was caring for the baby when it happened.

"First thing in the morning, we'll take him to the baby clinic," her mother said.

"But this is Saturday," Arlene reminded her. "It's not open on Sunday."

"Well, he looks okay to me," her mother said.

But Arlene was so persistent that her mother finally told her to take him to the emergency room of the hospital. The doctor who examined him assured her that the baby was in good condition. Nevertheless, Arlene lay in her bed that night feeling terribly guilty. But then it seemed she felt guilty about everything these days. She remembered back to the afternoon. Her baby's fall had changed her feelings. Oh no, what if I get pregnant again? she thought for the first time. Now she had her period to worry about too.

After a serious fall, if a baby vomits, gets drowsy, or has pain or headache, it is wise to get in touch with a doctor. If the baby seems drowsy because it is his normal bedtime, a parent can let the child go to sleep but should rouse him every thirty minutes. If the baby can't be awakened, a doctor should be called. If a baby loses consciousness after a serious fall, a doctor should see the baby immediately since this can indicate concussion.

Parents should be prepared for emergencies. The telephone number of the baby's doctor and a poison control center should be posted by the telephone. Parents should know what to do in case of burns, choking, or poisoning. In their medicine chest they should have a syrup of ipecac to induce vomiting in the case of certain types of poisoning, and any other medicines their doctor recommends they keep on hand. They should also have a rectal thermometer.

CEIL AND RUSS

Ceil always had a sense of nervous anticipation when school began. This year her feelings were compounded. At times she felt she wasn't ready to go back to school. "I'm going to miss so much of my baby's development being away each day," she told one of her girl friends. "I know my mother will take good care of him. Still I wish I could be there to do it. I guess I also feel very guilty about my mother. She's going to have to give up so many things in her life to be home with the baby each day. On the other hand," she was quick to add, "I can't tell you how much I look forward to the freedom—simple things like walking faster than a buggy pace, being someplace where I don't have to have one ear cocked all the time in case the baby cries."

In many ways Ceil felt very much older and more mature. Yet she also felt scared and shy inside. She missed her bouncy confidence of old and the feeling that she knew where she fit in the world. She wondered how the teachers would treat her.

The first day of school was a confusing whirl for Ceil, as it appeared to be for the other students. Ceil became very conscious of her figure. She still wasn't back to prepregnancy size, but then she hadn't exercised very hard either. "If I'm not so slim, I won't be so attractive to boys," she had reasoned. "And if I'm not so attractive, I won't have to face how I might feel about them or how they might feel about me." When she compared her figure to that of the other girls, however, her competitive instinct was aroused. "I've just got to do something about my shape," she said to herself. When she got home, she took out an exercise book.

Ceil was surprised how rapidly she adjusted to the school routine. As a matter of fact, school seemed very much like it had been before her pregnancy except for three things. One, Russ wasn't around. Two, she didn't engage in outside activities and dating. And three, she used every minute of her study hall and part of her lunch hour to work on her homework.

Ceil's home life, however, was very much different. Ceil was up early with the baby and busy until bedtime. It wasn't just the care of the baby but all the extra work that went with it—extra washing, extra food preparation, helping her mother with the things her mother couldn't do during the day because she was caring for the baby. On top of it all, Ceil found she tired more easily than she used to. "I always thought you had a baby and that was that," she told her mother. "I had no idea it could take as long as six months before you really felt up to your old self."

In the midst of all the adjustment, Ceil found herself asked to a football game. He was a new boy in school—a change in school boundaries had meant there were several new kids in school. Ceil knew he was aware she had a baby because his family went to the same church as hers did. And there wasn't a soul in church who didn't know—some local gossips had seen to that.

Ceil hesitated. "I don't know," she said. "I've got a lot to do these days."

"C'mon," he said, "everyone needs to get out once in a while."

"Well," said Ceil, "I'll let you know tomorrow." On the way home she debated the subject over and over in her mind. Her understanding with Russ was that he would date. That was all part of college—going places and doing things with new people. She just hadn't imagined she would need to think about it so soon.

Ceil didn't know how to feel. Part of her said, "Go. He's a neat guy. It will show everyone that just because you've had a baby, they shouldn't count you out." On the other hand, she thought, I shouldn't be going out. I should be at home with my baby.

When Ceil finally raised the subject with her parents, she was greeted with shocked looks and an embarrassed silence. In their faces, Ceil immediately read something she hadn't thought of. Why, she said to herself, they don't trust me. They think I'm going to go out and do something dreadful— maybe even get pregnant again! Her back arched. She had mentioned it as a trial balloon to clarify her own feelings. The fact that their resistance wasn't because of her responsibility at home or her image at school, however, made her angry. Ceil went on the offensive. "After all you do know this boy's parents. I wouldn't want them to think we're snobs. A football game certainly can't be that harmful. Besides, other than the day Russ took the baby this summer, I haven't gone anywhere or done anything. It's the first thing I've asked to do."

In the end her parents said yes. Nevertheless, Ceil didn't feel triumphant. She was still unsure herself.

Some young unmarried mothers and fathers have a close relationship that continues through the pregnancy and afterward. They do not feel that they want to or need to look beyond it for male-female relationships. Other young single parents will want to reach out for new companions, both as friends and as potential mates. Parents of such young parents may have a difficult time accepting that a teenaged mother, for example, may want to begin social relationships reasonably soon after the birth of her baby. Young parents cannot live in isolation forever. The more experience they have in meeting and knowing people, the more they will be able to make competent judgments about their choices of friends and mates. At times, outside assistance—a professional counselor from school or the community, or a relative or close family friend— may be needed to help the young person's parents understand the importance of social relationships.

Many times, young parents need new interests. Learning a new skill or developing a new hobby that can be shared with others may be one acceptable way to begin social relationships. Participation in group activities may seem initially more appropriate to the young parent's parents than dating.

As the week passed, Ceil was surprised how much she looked forward to going out. She wished she could have spent more time getting ready. Because of the baby care, she always had to do hair, makeup, and dressing in one-quarter of the time needed.

Ceil thoroughly enjoyed being out at the game except for the warm hugs her date gave her. She continually pulled away; she didn't like to be that friendly on a first date. Later, on the way home, she discovered to her horror that the affection he showed at the game was just a preliminary to sexual advances. Finally she understood what his invitation and actions had been all about.

"Get your hands off me and take me home," she said in angry disgust.

"You bitch," he sneered. "You did it with other guys, why not with me!"

Ceil felt sick all over. Once inside her house she ran upstairs without stopping to say hello to her parents. She went into the bathroom, turned on the water loudly, and cried. When she heard footsteps in the hall, she quickly washed off her makeup.

"We heard you come in," her mother said. "Did you have a good time?"

"Oh yes." Ceil opened the bathroom door so her mother could see her but kept her face partially hidden in a towel to hide any sign of crying. "But I missed the baby so much, I just rushed upstairs to peek in on him."

"Who won the game?" her mother said.

"Oh, they did," Ceil answered quickly, patting her face with the towel. "But it was a good game, we almost beat them." Inside, however, she was crying, "Nobody won. I hate men. I don't care if I never ever go out again as long as I live."

As the weeks went by Ceil tried to forget what had

happened. Russ would be home for Christmas and Ceil couldn't wait to see him. His letters had been infrequent but full of warmth when they did come. The baby was saying "dada." Since Russ had not been around, Ceil realized how much certain sounds must be just a normal part of the baby's development. However, she also knew Russ would be elated if the baby said "dada" when he was around.

As early as the second month, a baby begins to make sounds that will eventually lead to language. Vowel sounds such as *oo* and *eh* are repeated. By the end of the third month, the baby is putting another sound with the vowel to say sounds such as *ma, la,* and *goo.* Over the next few months he adds other sounds and begins to give them expression. The infant can make sounds indicating pleasure and displeasure. By the eighth month, the baby is making two-syllable sounds, such as "dada." It is also learning the meaning of the sounds the adult makes. Although the baby cannot yet say them, it can respond to familiar words, such as its own name, "bye-bye," "no-no," "mommy," "daddy," and "bottle." By the tenth month, the child is using at least one word appropriately. At one year of age the baby is using at least three words appropriately but knows many more. It can respond to such simple sentences as "Give me the teddy bear."

Christmas vacation brought some surprises for Ceil. She had expected to have free time because she was not going to school. However, her mother turned over complete care of the baby to her. After having had the baby only on weekends and briefly after school, this was a shock to Ceil. She had forgotten how demanding the day-after-day care of the baby was.

If Ceil wanted to go anyplace, she had to take the baby with her. Ceil had a backpack. Since she hadn't used it regularly, however, she could carry the baby only about a half-hour before she tired. She had to judge her time carefully, too, to get him out and then back home by nap time. If she were gone any length of time, she had to take not only the baby but various supplies, such as bottles of milk or fruit juice and extra diapers.

Ceil tried to understand that her mother needed the time off to do the shopping and visiting she usually did at Christmas. However, Ceil resented having no time to herself. When she and Russ saw each other, it was at her house and mostly over the baby's head. Although she liked being with Russ and the baby, she would also have liked some time to relax with Russ alone. There was nothing to do but make the best of it.

"Want to feed him?" Ceil asked Russ.

"Doesn't he feed himself now?" Russ asked.

"No," Ceil laughed. "Babies don't feed themselves completely, that is with a spoon, until they are at least eighteen months. But he's been anxious to start doing it himself, so along with what I feed him, I give him finger food to handle by himself—round cereal and bits of cheese."

"He certainly seems like he wants to feed himself," Russ commented.

The baby grabbed at the spoon whenever Ceil got it near his mouth or else turned his head away.

"There was a major revolution around the sixth month when he could sit propped up by a blanket," Ceil said. "For the first time his hands were truly free so he could really use them. To keep his hands occupied during feeding at first I gave him a cup and spoon. That wore off, however, so now I give him something to fit into something—like large buttons to put in a jar."

"He sure is different," Russ commented. "Last time I was here, he was just a bottle baby."

During the first month of a baby's life, its hands are held in a fist. By the third month a baby's hands are mostly open; it can briefly hold a toy, such as a rattle, when it is placed in its hand. Around the fourth month, an infant starts to reach for objects. By the fifth month, the baby is able to grasp objects by holding its hand as though it had on a mitten. At the end of the sixth month, it has become better at reaching for an object and transferring it from hand to hand. The baby's eyes and hands are working together now. In the seventh month, the two-handed play signals the beginning of pushing, pulling, banging, and pounding. By the eighth month, the infant can feed itself a cookie and hold its bottle. In the ninth month it may be able to use the index finger and thumb like pincers, putting objects together. The baby enjoys activities such as dropping things into a cup and then removing them. By one year of age, an infant can manipulate the thumb and forefinger to pick up small objects.

Ceil's big evening out was to be the New Year's Eve party Russ's family always gave for their friends and relatives. The day before, however, the baby became listless. His feet, which were normally cool to the touch, felt hot and dry. Ceil was home alone. She got out her baby books and hurriedly looked up how to take the baby's temperature.

The best method for taking the temperature of a baby or small child is with a rectal thermometer. After shaking down the thermometer, put vaseline or cold cream on the bulb. Take off the baby's diaper. Place the baby on its stomach on a bed or in his crib or on your lap. Slide the bulb about an inch into the baby's rectum. Do it slowly and carefully. Let it follow the natural curve of the infant's rectum. Don't push it or the baby could be hurt. Hold the legs and buttocks firmly so the baby won't injure himself. Hold the thermometer lightly so that the baby won't push it out. It takes at least one minute to get a rectal temperature. Rectal temperatures read about one degree higher than oral temperatures.

The baby did have a high temperature. It was the first time he had gotten sick. Ceil tried to remain calm. Walking back and forth holding the baby, she read about fever. "Fever itself is not an illness," the book said. "It is the illness that must be cured. Attempts may be made to lower the fever, however, to make the child more comfortable."

Ceil had no idea what the baby's illness might be. She called the baby's pediatrician. He wasn't in his office and the half-hour it took him to call her back seemed like forever. The doctor asked Ceil if the baby had rapid or labored breathing, was pulling on his ears as a sign of earache, had been vomiting or coughing, or had severe diarrhea.

Ceil said no, feeling that the baby's condition probably wasn't so serious if he didn't have any symptom that the doctor asked about.

"Use baby aspirin," the doctor instructed after asking a few more questions, "but only in the amount I tell you. Extra fluids are also good. If the fever does not go down and the baby seems really uncomfortable, you can put him in a lukewarm bath. That will help bring the temperature down. Call me in the morning," he finished, "if the baby is not significantly better."

Ceil gave the baby his aspirin. As much as she wanted to "mother," there were times when she felt she needed others around to help her and worry with her, if necessary. She was tremendously grateful when her parents came home.

In the morning Ceil discovered that the baby had come down with a cold. She called the doctor and said the baby's fever was down but he apparently had a bad cold and diarrhea.

For the diarrhea, the doctor suggested taking the baby off milk temporarily and giving him fewer solids. "Give him jello or applesauce at first if he gets hungry," he said. For the cold, the doctor suggested using a vaporizer. He said that the safest kind is cold mist. "Moist air is especially important for an infant," he told Ceil. "It is hard for him to breath through his mouth and he doesn't know yet how to blow his nose.

Keep up the extra liquids too," he stressed. "Also keep him rested and evenly warm.

"And," he said, "you'll find that not only when babies are sick, but as they get better, they are often cranky and difficult. They need extra affection, extra attention, and lots of patience."

Ceil nodded on the phone. She was determined to be a good mother. But inside she groaned, "Oh why did this have to happen on New Year's Eve?" Nevertheless she dialed the number of the baby sitter and cancelled.

"I'm sorry we have to go out this evening, dear," her mother said when she learned of Ceil's plight. "But we made this commitment quite a while ago. Otherwise we'd be glad to baby-sit."

"Oh, I know, Mom," Ceil said. "I could go but I just don't want to leave him with a baby sitter when he's sick."

"I understand," Ceil's mother said, "And I think you're wise."

Around midnight Russ called Ceil from the party and said "Happy New Year!" It seemed to Ceil that the whole disappointing holiday was summed up by that call.

Vacation was over the following week. Ceil hated to have Russ go back to college. It seemed she had hardly seen him. Yet she herself was anxious to get back to school. "How can I have so many different sets of feelings?" she thought. "I do love the baby. I love taking care of him, playing with him, being with him. But going back to school that first day will be such freedom; I can hardly wait."

However, getting back to school wasn't exactly what Ceil expected either. There was talk of skiing and skating. "I don't know," Ceil said to one of her girl friends as they put on their coats after school. "Maybe it was because the holiday was such a bummer, but I feel so left out of everything."

Her friend nodded sympathetically. "Listen, do you have time to stop by the auditorium before we walk home?"

"Why?" Ceil asked.

"I just want to hear the tryouts for the junior class play."

Last year, that was Ceil's chief ambition—to have the lead in the junior class play. This year she had been so preoccupied that apparently she had even missed the notices of tryouts.

They walked into the back of the darkened auditorium. "Look," her friend said, "Betty is trying out. God, I hope she doesn't get it. She's so stuck up now. If she gets the lead, I'll throw up."

"She's not really that good either," Ceil said. "Listen to that phony expression she puts into everything." They listened some more. "I could do a lot better than that," Ceil whispered.

"And look how he's smiling," her friend noted, pointing to the English teacher who was in charge of producing the play.

"Well, I can't see why he thinks she's that great."

"Ceil, why don't you try out?"

"Oh, I can't," Ceil said.

"Why not?" her friend said. "It won't do any harm just to try out."

"I couldn't—I mean it takes time for rehearsals and all that."

"Look, just read the part," her friend urged. "I can't stand the thought of Betty not having any competition at all. Go on . . ."

"Well," Ceil hesitated.

"Go on," her friend urged.

Ceil got up and walked down the darkened aisle and spoke to the English teacher. "I'd like to read for the part too," she said. Betty finished and the teacher nodded to Ceil to go up on stage.

Ceil's hands were shaking. She picked up the book Betty had put down on the chair and began to read. As she read, Ceil's nervousness disappeared. Her voice poured out in rich tones. She felt she was the character. When she finished, she stood holding onto the book as if transfixed.

The sound of clapping came from the auditorium. Ceil looked up startled. A number of students, including some of the fellows on their way to basketball practice, were standing in the back. Ceil was embarrassed. She put the book down on the chair.

The English teacher came up on stage and turned to the group of students who had been trying out. "All right," he said. "Thank you all for coming. I'll post the selections for parts tomorrow. Now remember, if you are picked, it means rehearsals three nights a week and on Saturdays. The last week we will rehearse every night and on both Saturday and Sunday."

Ceil gulped. She had no idea the play would take that kind of time commitment. She walked toward the back of the auditorium. Her friend met her coming up the aisle.

"Ceil," she said breathlessly. "You were spectacular. I mean really spectacular. You should have seen the guys that came in. They were stunned. I mean they just stood there and none of them said anything. You've got it. I mean you've got the part cold."

Ceil barely heard what her friend was saying. She had a rush of emotions. Reading the part had revived all her feelings and desires to be in the play. But the amount of time involved overwhelmed her. She had no idea it would mean that much rehearsing. To do the play and carry her homework meant that there would be no time for chores or baby care for the next two months. She couldn't ask her parents to care for the baby all day and all night too. If only some way . . .

Ceil was very nervous when she got home. "How's the

baby been, Mom?" she said, but found she didn't listen to the answer.

"Now we're going out for a while this evening," her mother told Ceil after dinner. "Just running over to the neighbors. We'll be back somewhere about nine or ten." Ceil nodded.

Ceil turned on the television. The baby bounced on her lap. Ceil loved it when he bounced. He was so lively and so much fun. She moved away from the television and sat on the floor in front of the hall mirror. The baby seemed to enjoy it even more when he could see himself bouncing. Sometimes he bounced for fifteen minutes. Where oh where does this tiny tyke get his energy? Ceil wondered.

"Bouncy, bouncy baby, boop, booooop, boop." Ceil sang a made-up little rhyme in rhythm with his bouncing. The grin on his face broadened.

Finally it was seven o'clock, the baby's bedtime. The baby now slept in Ceil's brother's room since her brother was back at school. The minute Ceil put the baby down, he began crying. "Oh those teeth," she said. "Will they never get here?" She got the baby up and rubbed his gums with her finger.

Teething may begin at four months and last until the child is almost three years old. Most babies begin getting their teeth at six or seven months. For many babies it is a painful process. Loss of appetite, irritableness, increased crying and loss of sleep may all occur at such times. Rubbing the baby's gums with a clean finger, or giving him safe things to chew on can help. Teething rings filled with water that can be kept in the refrigerator until cold are helpful. Upon a doctor's advice, aspirin may also be given. Since the baby is working his mouth more, drooling may increase. However, drooling in general starts at about six weeks in most babies and is not directly related to teething.

Ceil walked the baby back and forth until he quieted. She

tried putting him down again. She had a math exam to study for. When the baby had cried hard for ten minutes more, she tried rubbing his gums again and walking him. He quieted once more but did not fall asleep. Putting the baby in the buggy and rocking him didn't seem to help either. An hour passed and every time she put the baby down he cried. As she walked she thought about the play. She wanted to do it so badly. Finally, around nine o'clock the baby fell asleep on her shoulder. She walked him about five minutes more just to make sure he was truly asleep. Then she put him down in his crib and tiptoed out of the room.

Ceil went downstairs and opened a Coke. She plopped down on the couch and put her feet up. She didn't see how she could ever concentrate on studying tonight. She kept thinking about how much she really wanted to do the play. She wasn't dating, she wasn't doing anything. But there was no way she could ask her parents to take care of the baby for that many hours. Particularly when he was so fussy. But she wanted to be in that play. And if she didn't take the part, it would mean that Betty probably . . . Ceil's thoughts were interrupted by the cries from upstairs. She got up off the couch, her fists clenched. She pounded up the stairs. "God damn it!" she said.

She opened the door to the baby's room and turned on the light. His cries grew louder. She stormed over to the side of the crib. She looked down at his waving arms and feet, his flushed face. His cries filled her ears almost to bursting.

"Whaahhhhh," Ceil began to scream back at him as loud as she could. "Whaaahhh, Whaaahh."

Suddenly, Ceil's mother and father appeared in the doorway. After a moment of indecision, Ceil's mother walked in and took Ceil in her arms. "Ceil, come on into my room," she said. As she passed through the doorway, she told Ceil's father, "Take care of the baby."

"What's going . . . ," he started to question.

Ceil's mother shook her head. "Just take care of the baby," she said firmly.

Ceil was holding her head and crying. She sank down on her mother's bed. Her mother sat on the bed beside her patting her back. Ceil pushed her hand away. "No," she said. "No, leave me alone." Then she sobbed harder. Ceil's mother sat patiently.

Finally Ceil stopped shaking. "I'm so sorry," she said. "I'm so sorry. I don't know. I get up at 5:00 A.M., feed the baby, take care of him, go to school, come home, take care of the baby, do homework, do cleanup, go to bed, get up at 5:00 A.M., feed the baby, take care of him, go to school, come home, feed the baby, do homework. I'm so tired of it all I can't stand it anymore." She began to sob again.

"I know dear; it's a lot. We're trying to help as much as we can."

"Oh Mom," she said. "I know you are. I mean you care for him all day. It's just that . . . Oh, I don't know." Then Ceil told her mother about the play.

"Well, maybe we can arrange that," her mother said. "You need time to be a person too. You can't just be a schoolgirl and a mother. There are some things that you must take the time to do just for yourself."

Ceil shook her head slowly. "Oh thank you, Mom. I want to. But I can't. I mean I really wouldn't be happy doing the play either, because it would take so much time and I can't stick you with that much baby care. Plus, I do love my baby and I would miss so much if I didn't spend evenings seeing him and playing with him. He's changing so fast. As it is, I'll probably not be around when he starts to crawl or takes his first step. I'm going to miss all those important events in my life and his. So I want to be home as much as I can. It's just that . . ."

"Just that there are times you wish you weren't a mother and could live the life you might have been living if you didn't have him."

"Oh, Mom," Ceil said, "Is that so awful? I'm so confused. I do love him."

"No, Ceil," her mother said. "That's not so awful. I think that's why a lot of women wait to have their children—so that they get a lot of the things they want to do done before they get tied down with babies. And it is being tied down. There's no way around it. You aren't as free.

"If you're ready for it, if you've finished school, if you have had a chance to test yourself out in the world—sort of like seeing if you can get the lead in the play and do it, but maybe having a job or traveling or meeting and knowing numbers of people—whatever, then I think there's not such a restless feeling. But believe me, all mothers at times feel they've got too much child care and not enough of other things that they want. I know I did."

Ceil had never thought about her mother having to care for her and her brother when she wanted to do other things. "But you've always been so active. I mean, from the time I was little I can remember you joining clubs and doing other things."

"You're right, I've done a lot. Because I wanted to. But there were times I would have done more things, or different things. And there were times when doing the things I did wasn't easy—when I worried about taking time away from you two."

Ceil was silent.

"Anyway," her mother said, "I think the upshot of this will be that we have to get you some more time for yourself. Maybe I'd forgotten until now how much I felt at times that I needed time off for myself. Your father was able to give some of it to me. And your aunt helped me out. Even if you don't want to do the play, I think you should regularly have one afternoon a week when you don't have to come home but can go places after school or do whatever you want. Even if it's just coming home and going up to your room and reading a book.

"Yes, you should have it. I think we've all been expecting too much. A good thing to remember is that you need to take care of yourself before you can take care of other people."

"Oh, Mom, I can't," Ceil said hesitantly. "I can't ask you to do that."

"Don't worry," her mother replied. "Maybe we'll get a sitter if I don't feel I can do it. Maybe your cousin would like to baby-sit one afternoon a week. We'll work something out. That will be my concern. Yours will just be to use that time to be the teenager you are."

"Oh Mom," Ceil gave her a hug. "I love you. I won't do the play. But one afternoon would really mean a lot to me."

"Now," her mother returned the hug. "Let's see what's happened to the men of the family."

Ceil stood up. She smiled. "Dad probably is frantic."

As they walked down the hall, however, they became aware of the quiet. Cautiously, they peeped into the baby's room. There in the rocking chair was Ceil's father and the baby. The chair was tipped back and they were both sound asleep.

This whole thing has got to be a dream from beginning to end, Ceil thought. "My father asleep in a chair with my baby. *My* baby. I've got a baby! It can't be me. It can't be my life. . . ."

ERICA AND GARY

"Erica," her mother said firmly. "If you pick that baby up all the time, you'll spoil her."

"Mother, I won't," Erica said, getting up.

"Now that your grandmother's gone for a while," her

mother added, "and the baby has the guest room, I think we can have some order around here. We don't need to have toys and bibs all over the living room."

Erica picked up the bib from the end table and the teddy bear off the floor and went upstairs. It was so hard to keep everything straightened up. Whenever she brought the baby down for feeding or just to be sociable, blankets, rattles, everything came down with her. And when she took the baby upstairs, there was no way it could all go back up at the same time.

There were other problems too. She knew the baby's crying at night annoyed her father, but the baby was going to cry sometimes. And when her mother's afternoon bridge group came, or if her parents entertained, the noise sometimes woke the baby. She couldn't tell her parents to stop living. After all, it was their home. And then there were the fights—dumb fights with her mother about things like how warmly the baby should be dressed or if she should be covered.

"What's the matter, sweetie?" Erica said as she entered the baby's room. "Mommy's here. I'm not going to spoil you. You're just trying to tell me something. Are you hungry?"

Young parents, in particular, are often concerned about having a "spoiled" child. A child cannot be spoiled by answering its legitimate needs. Indeed, more problems will result if the child's cries are misunderstood or ignored. Looking first for hunger, then for discomfort or pain, and finally for fussiness in the younger baby may help a parent determine what is wrong. Sometimes, picking a baby up and cuddling it for a minute is all that is needed to calm the child down again. Unless the baby is immediately picked up each time it cries, there is no need to worry about spoiling it. Some babies cry as they settle down. If a baby continues crying hard for ten minutes, the parents should examine the child and its physical situation carefully even though they may have done so once already.

The older child may express needs in other ways than by crying. The baby may cling desperately to the parents or otherwise act very dependent when the parents would expect that the child should have progressed beyond this stage. Specialists feel that such behavior often occurs just before the child takes a new developmental step—such as crawling, walking, or talking. Reassurance in the form of extra cuddling or other responsive measures can help the child through this difficult period and increase its ability to move out. Such reassurance will not spoil the child at all. Knowledge of the reasons for a child's behavior can help the parent get through such stages with more patience and understanding.

Erica picked up her daughter and sat down to nurse. "I try to help around the house," she thought to herself. "But regardless of how much I do, I feel more and more like a charity case. And as much as I try to get along with my mother, angry quarrels break out more and more often. I just don't know what to do."

"Erica, don't forget to give the baby her vitamins!" Her mother's voice came from downstairs. That did it.

"Gary," Erica said later, "we have got to get out of here. I mean it. I just can't stand living here anymore. Mom is driving me wild. And I'm tired of trying to live my life upstairs. I want a downstairs. I want to be able to shout if I want to, and cry if I want to, and I want to be able to laugh. And I want to choose my own food and eat my own meals when I want to eat them. I have got to get out of here."

"Erica, we haven't got the money," he said. "We'd have to get furniture. Most apartments require a deposit of an additional month's rent. We still have some bills to pay off."

"I don't care," Erica said. "I want out—*out!*"

"But where are we going to get the money?"

"Well, if we got an apartment closer to where you work, we could sell the car." She rushed on. "We don't really use it that much. With the baby we're in every night; we don't go anywhere. Most of the time it just sits there."

Gary was stunned. "Sell the car?"

"Yes, sell the car. What's so terrible about that? A car is a car. But I'm me and this baby is your baby and we live like two—oh, I don't know—mice in somebody's attic."

"I need the car," Gary said. "How will I get to work?"

"As I said, we could look for someplace where you could either walk to work or be on a bus line. Look," Erica said forcefully, "we don't need the car. We do need to get out of here on our own!"

Gary sat down. Erica was obviously terribly upset. But his *car*. It was his car. There were so many feelings tied up with that car. "Erica, the car . . . ," he said. "The car, I don't know . . ." His voice trailed off. Maybe it still represented a wisp of California to him. Maybe it was still what identified him as a man when he changed diapers, made the bed, or did other things to help out Erica.

One of the problems young fathers appear to have is the taking on of what they identify as non-masculine tasks before they have become completely secure in their own masculinity. Fathering a child, while superficially demonstrating masculinity, does not apparently answer many of the deeper needs young men have in their quest to establish masculine identity.

The very next day, Erica asked her mother to watch the baby for the morning. She didn't like to do it because sooner or later her mother would remind her of "all the baby-sitting" she'd done. But Erica needed complete freedom for a few hours. To Erica's amazement, the second apartment she looked at was exactly what she wanted. It had two bedrooms, although the second bedroom was so tiny that it was hardly fair to call it a bedroom. Yet it was perfect for a baby. Gary's place of work was only a thirty-minute walk or short bus ride away. Erica called Gary and he agreed to look at the apartment after work. She waited breathlessly for him to get home.

"Well," she whispered when she met him in the front hallway. "Did you see it? What did you think of it?"

"Yes," he said. "It's nice, but it's expensive."

"I know," Erica said. "It's more than we had thought about paying, but when you get your raise things will be better. And it's available now. Not too many people move out of that building, the man told me. So if we want it, we better take it now. He couldn't promise there would be any others available this year."

Gary lay awake late into the night. He had hoped to get completely out of debt and have some money saved before they moved. Yet Erica was right, it was a nice apartment. And certainly he was tired of living with her parents too. Of course, he wasn't home as much as she was, so he didn't have to put up with as much as she did. Finally, he got up and wandered down the hall.

The only light in the bathroom was the night light, yet Gary immediately saw that he had walked in on Erica's father. "Oh, I'm sorry," he said, terribly embarrassed. "I guess my mind was somewhere else."

"It's all right," Erica's father said. "I'm almost through. I'll be out in a minute."

Gary stepped back outside the door. That did it. He'd tell Erica. They'd take the apartment.

Erica's parents, especially her mother, acted hurt when they learned of the move. "Why so soon? How are you going to manage? You said you'd be here till after the first of the year at least. What about the money you owe?"

Now that they were getting out, Erica felt she didn't have to be so defensive. She tried to smooth things over as best she could. "The kind of apartment we wanted just happened to be available," she said. "And don't worry about the money. We'll manage. Gary's going to sell the car. The apartment is right on the bus line."

Gary had a guilty look on his face. He hadn't yet decided to sell the car. Erica was right. They did need the money. However, maybe they could make it and still keep the car. But once Gary and Erica moved into the apartment, they found that so many things they had taken for granted had to be bought. Just for the kitchen alone, they spent an amazing amount of money. Can openers, measuring spoons, and other items added up to bigger sums than they had planned. They tried to keep everything at a minimum but even so there was so much they needed to set up housekeeping. Moreover, Erica insisted they leave the twin beds at her house.

"If I am going to have my own place, I refuse to sleep in single beds any more," she said. They bought a mattress and put it on the floor in the bedroom until they could afford a bed.

It seemed to Gary that Erica was always asking him for money. Most of the time it was for a very good reason. One time, though, he found that a salesman had sold Erica thirty-five dollars worth of baby pictures.

"Look," Erica said, parroting back what the salesman had told her. "The baby will only be this age once. And just one print alone would be fifteen dollars. This way we get three large and two wallet-sized ones."

"Erica," Gary sighed, "I don't care how much you save, we haven't got that kind of money."

Later on it was Gary's turn to explain. "A big screen *color* television?" Erica had noticed the kind of television before Gary had even gotten it out of the box.

"Well," Gary replied. "We said we'd get a TV. I mean, we're home every night and don't do anything. And this one . . . the man said it was a special deal. If you bought the color television, you got this portable radio too."

"But we didn't need a portable radio," Erica said. "We have your stereo."

"But we have nothing in the kitchen so I can listen to the morning news at breakfast," Gary said defensively.

"I know," Erica said. "But if you'd gotten a small black-and-white TV like we planned, with the difference in cost, we could have gotten a portable radio for every room in the apartment."

"Yeah," Gary finally said, "I guess you're right. But I bought it and it's a beautiful television. So let's not talk about it any more."

When all the bills came in at the end of that month though, Gary threw down his pencil in disgust. "We just can't make it. Bills from the pediatrician, the television, paying off the hospital bill. Oh well," his mouth turned down, "that's it."

The next day when Erica took the baby for a walk, she saw their car parked on the street with a "For Sale" sign in the window.

Young people are particularly vulnerable to all kinds of high-pressure sales tactics. Consumer education is very much needed to help them manage on what, most often, are limited resources. Many times adults neglect to give young people needed advice because they assume, particularly if the young people are married and living on their own, that they are competent in areas where they have had little experience.

But at least to Erica, every sacrifice to be in their own apartment was worth it. One of the first things she did was to "baby-proof" the apartment. Only after she found the baby sucking on a large button-eye that had come off a teddy bear, did she think to baby-proof the toys.

Baby-proofing toys is a constant process for parents. The tasting, biting, and gumming of babies starts around the third month and lasts until the second year. When children are small, almost everything goes into their mouths. Also, babies tend to fall often, frequently on top of their toys. Therefore, babies should not be given toys with sharp or rough edges, nor toys with parts small enough to be swallowed. Toys should be smooth-edged and, regardless of material (wood, plastic, metal, or cloth), should be sturdy. Broken or cracked toys should be removed from play until repaired. Also, toys should be appropriate to the age or development of the child. Both outgrown toys and toys that are too advanced can frustrate a baby. Too many toys at one time can also annoy a child.

Baby-proofing an apartment, house, or room—putting small breakable objects away, arranging furniture so that a baby cannot pull it over on top of itself, putting caps on electrical outlets so that a baby cannot poke into them, putting medicines and cleaning supplies out of reach (and sight), and so forth— also means peace of mind for parents and greater freedom for the baby. Although small children still have to be watched, baby-proofing living space helps to eliminate the number of times a parent must say *No!* to a baby.

Being in her own apartment made many things easier for Erica. She was able to organize and plan her own day. She felt she had more time with the baby. She fondled and kissed her often.

Erica found she could watch the baby endlessly. When she saw the baby patting a spot of sunshine on the floor, her eyes filled with tears. Being a mother meant experiencing such joy-filled precious moments.

"I wish you could have been here today," she'd say to Gary. "The baby pulled herself up for the first time on the couch. But then she didn't know how to get down and finally started to cry till I helped her sit back down. But then she got right back up again. I spent half the afternoon helping her down."

"You mean, I'm going to have to teach her that too?" Gary asked.

"What do you mean, *too?*" Erica asked.

"Well, I taught her how to crawl, didn't I?"

Erica laughed, remembering the one Saturday afternoon

Gary had spent on his hands and knees. The baby had been rocking back and forth on her hands and knees all week trying to go forward. Erica never knew whether Gary's demonstration really had made the difference or whether the baby was just ready. Anyway, at the end of the afternoon, the baby had at least gotten her hands going with a little bit of leg motion and the next day she actually crawled.

Erica took the baby for a stroller ride every day. It was Erica's chance to get out as well as the baby's. Particularly on days when the baby was fussy, she found that the best way to change the baby's mood was to get outdoors. Often it changed her own mood favorably too. Erica particularly needed to get out whenever the baby was in a clinging stage. The constant demand for attention or to be picked up left her wanting to scream.

Erica's one regret was that she had no friends in circumstances similar to her own to talk to and do things with. The check-out clerks in the grocery stores became substitute friends and shopping became an entertainment. She went to the store almost every day to buy some item. Finally, Erica met another young mother in the grocery store. Her little boy was about the same age as Erica's daughter. The two mothers decided to see each other. Having someone to talk to and a person to call if she was worried about something made a wonderful difference to Erica. They talked about everything from the games they played with their babies (peek-a-boo, pat-a-cake) to what to do about constipation ("Give your baby an ounce or so of prune juice," the other mother said.)

The one negative aspect of their friendship was that Erica's baby was crawling and the other mother's baby had not yet started. Erica was disappointed when the other mother seemed to resent this and made remarks that took much of the fun out of the relationship.

All mothers, particularly new mothers, enjoy having a chance to exchange information about their children's progress. Unfortunately, sometimes the sharing can turn into a competitive comparing. Mothers need to remind themselves that babies develop differently, each at its own pace. For example, having a child who walks early is a source of false pride for parents. As one wise pediatrician told a mother, "She's probably got eighty years to walk, so why rush a couple of months. Let her walk when she's ready."

Because of her limited number of friends, Erica depended mainly on Gary for her social needs. Sometimes when he got home she talked nonstop, starting with when he walked in the door, through dinner, until he finally would say in an exasperated tone, "Let's just watch this program, okay?" Erica would then realize what she had been doing and try to be quiet. Often she found she couldn't wait for the commercial so she could begin talking again.

Despite Erica and Gary's joy in the baby and the pleasure of being on their own, financial pressures were ever present. It wasn't so much the big things that got them down now but the five dollars here and the three dollars there that added up. They agreed not to give each other birthday or holiday presents, but felt too insecure not to give such gifts to their parents. Money always seemed to be the problem and the solution. "If only we had money," Erica said for the hundredth time. "It would make such a difference."

"Look, I'm sorry. I'm sorry, I'm sorry! I'm doing the best I can," Gary said. "I just don't make more."

"Oh honey," Erica said, and she was immediately sorry she had raised the subject. "I didn't mean it that way and you know it. I just meant . . ."

"I know," Gary said.

Finally, however, they both felt so overwhelmed that Gary found a part-time job at a gas station weeknights and a half-day on Saturdays. He made less than at his regular job, but it helped out.

"We're right back where we started when I was working and going to school and you were working," Erica said. "We didn't see each other very much then and we promised each other it was just for a little while."

"Well, if I get a good raise in the spring, maybe this will have been just for a while too," Gary replied. "In the meantime, what else can we do? It would cost you more to pay somebody to care for the baby than you could earn if you went to work."

"Yes, I know," Erica said. "I guess we haven't got any choice. I keep thinking I am going to spend less but regardless of where I think I've cut, the money just gets spent."

Erica had just weaned her daughter from the breast to a cup. She found she felt better—not that she had been feeling bad, but she had an upsurge in energy. Because of the two jobs, however, Gary had less energy. Erica began to be restless and bored. She wanted to get out and away from the baby occasionally. Gary was more and more eager just to stay home on weekends and sit and watch television. He also wanted to go to bed early. At times on weekends Erica nagged him to go out. When they did go somewhere, however, since they had no money for a baby sitter, they had to take the baby. When she got fussy, it annoyed Gary.

Erica hated to ask Gary to care for the baby by himself, but sometimes she so ached to get out that she did. She waited until the baby napped and Gary was settled in front of the TV, however, before she left. Often she came back much later than she had promised. Regardless of what she did—whether she went downtown to look in store windows or went to a museum—she had difficulty coming back on time. The freedom was a narcotic.

It was at those times that she remembered her decision to move away from her parents' house. "If we had stayed," she mused, "I could get out without having to ask Gary to baby-sit when he's so tired. Or if I needed to come back late, there would be other people to take over." She sighed. Life was always such a mixed bag.

7. PARENTHOOD:
Through the First Year (10-12 months)

ARLENE AND JOEL

Everything happening to Arlene seemed to be going wrong. She felt helpless in her situation. She had so little bargaining power—with her mother, with school, with anyone. "As soon as I turn sixteen, I'm going to drop out of school and get a job," Arlene thought. "Then at least I'll have some money." In the meantime though, she felt she was sinking. Finally out of desperation, Arlene called the head teacher of the special school she had been in. "If I get pregnant again, can I come back?" Arlene asked.

"Well, we'd like to think you would not become pregnant again, Arlene. Are things not going the way you want them to?"

"Well," Arlene hesitated. "I guess not."

"Tell me about it," the teacher said.

Arlene plunged into a mass of details and not in any proper order. "Please, I want to come back," Arlene said at the end. She bit her lip waiting for the answer.

"Well, Arlene, I do think you need help," the head teacher told her. "Would you let me think about what you've said? I promise to be back in touch with you in a couple of days."

Arlene felt disappointed as she hung up the phone. But at least the teacher had said she would think about it.

Just as she had promised, the teacher called back. "Arlene, I've had a chance to talk to the welfare worker who works with your family."

Arlene said, "Oh, *her*."

"I think there are some things that can be done to help you. The welfare worker promised me she's going to come to talk with you tomorrow. I'll call you again sometime next week to see how things are going."

Arlene sighed. "Welfare worker, yuk!" Granted she was the nicest one they had ever had, but Arlene didn't trust them any more than her mother did.

When the welfare worker came, the first thing she said was, "Arlene, I wish you had called me." Arlene looked at the ceiling.

"Or maybe you think I should have called you." The worker sighed. "It's just that they give us so many people to try to help. But, regardless, I'm here to try to help you now. The head teacher can't really do much because she's in another school district. However, she talked to me about how much progress you had made at the special school and how much she thought you had to offer. She urged me to try to help you and I want to do just that.

"Now first off, the teacher told me some of your problems but I'd like to hear about them from you."

For the second time in a week Arlene went over the troubles in her life. When she mentioned that she was worried about being pregnant, the worker looked surprised. "I thought you told the visiting nurse you were taking birth control pills!"

"Well, I was, but they ran out."

"Why didn't you get some more?"

"I don't know," Arlene said. "I got them from the clinic I

went to when I was living with my sister. I didn't know anyone to go to here."

"You could have asked someone," the worker said gently.

"I know," Arlene said. "But I didn't plan on ever needing them. And . . ."

Many young people find it difficult to prepare for events they either don't want to have happen or don't believe will happen. Thus many young mothers refuse birth control on the grounds that "I'm not going to be having intercourse" or "I'm sure I won't get pregnant." They are probably also reacting to societal norms that frown upon sexual activity among teenagers. As one girl put it, "Let's face it, if I use birth control, I'm a bad girl. If I don't, and get pregnant, I'm a good girl who got caught." However, as we have seen from the lives of the young people in this book, that is far too simple an approach for the complex set of circumstances that surround an early pregnancy. There are many people, including a new life, to consider.

"Never mind," the worker said. "The important thing to do is to get you a pregnancy test to find out if you're pregnant and to get it done early enough so you have some options."

"Options?" Arlene said.

"Abortion," the worker said.

"Oh."

When they finished talking, the worker told her, "Arlene, I've already started to set up an interagency case conference about you."

Arlene looked worried. That sounded bad to her. "You wouldn't take my baby, would you?" she said.

"No," the caseworker explained. "Actually the problems you have need solving from a lot of different groups. The idea will be to get them together so we can work things out."

"What will they say about me?" Arlene asked suspiciously.

"Well, for one thing, if your mother does go back to work, as you say she wants to do, you'll need someone to care for your baby so you can continue to go to school. Another consideration is that if you're having trouble in school, you may need some tutoring help. If you're not using birth control and want to, the health people should know about it. The focus of the conference will be on how everyone can best help you."

Arlene hesitated. "Okay," she finally said. She was nervous but pleased that so many people were going to be talking about her. "When will they do it?"

"I hope next week," the worker said. "I have been having a little trouble getting everyone together but it looks like next Tuesday will be good."

"Will you tell me what everyone says?"

"Of course."

Some communities have held inter-agency conferences to tackle the problems likely to be faced by numbers of young parents or young parents-to-be—help with child care while they are in school, for example. Solving such problems in this manner avoids the expense of individual case conferences and hopefully arrives at solutions for many young parents. Arlene is lucky that the welfare worker has taken such time and interest in her. Most young parents get fragmented help at best, and very few have a comprehensive approach taken to their problems.

When the welfare worker reported back, she talked to both Arlene and her mother. "Here's what we would like to suggest," she said.

Arlene looked at her mother nervously. She knew her mother blamed her for all this attention. "It's getting me a bad reputation for not being able to handle things in my own family," she had told Arlene.

"First of all, to free your mother from having to care for your baby and also to give you a greater responsibility in the care of your child, we would like to suggest you have your baby cared for in family day care. The welfare department will pay for it."

"What's that?" Arlene's mother asked suspiciously.

"Well, there are several kinds of day care. There's home day care where someone cares for the baby in its own home—such as you have been doing," the worker said to Arlene's mother. "Home day care can be care by a relative in the home, or it can be care by a paid person who comes into the home.

"Another kind of day care is group day care where large numbers of children are cared for in a group. Group infant day care centers are hard to find and the cost of caring for infants in such groups is very expensive. I have heard that in some cities where they have special programs for pregnant school-aged girls and young parents, group infant day care centers are operated in connection with either special or regular school programs so that girls can continue in school. But we don't have that here."

"I wish we did," Arlene said.

"Now the kind of care I am suggesting is family day care. That is where a mother takes care of one or more children in her own home. She has a license to do that and is paid for it."

"I once thought of doing that," Arlene's mother said. "But I was told I had too many kids of my own."

"Part of the purpose of licensing," the welfare worker said, "is to assure that the mother can give the time needed to care for the children. If she has small children of her own at home, they must be counted as part of the number of children she is caring for."

"Where does this mother live?" Arlene asked.

"Well, we haven't selected one yet," the worker said. "That's something I want you to help us do. The advantage of family day care is that we can try to find someone in the neighborhood near your home or closer to school, whichever you think is best for you.

"I will want you to talk to the mother. She should be someone you feel is going to care for your baby the way you want him cared for. Not only should you feel you can respect her but you must have the feeling that she is a person who is going to respect you too."

Arlene felt very good that she was to be consulted.

"Also, if you want," the worker continued, "I can let you talk to other mothers who are having, or have had, their child cared for in the day-care mother's home. You can find out how they feel about that particular mother."

Although licensing requirements are supposed to ensure an appropriate home surrounding, the young parent should also see that the home and conditions are adequate. For example, is the home large enough to accommodate the extra children being cared for? Is there enough fresh air and light? Will there be a quiet place for the baby to sleep and can the baby have its own crib? Are the number or kinds of children (too many young infants, for example) too much for the day-care mother? Is the day-care mother someone able to take instructions from a person much younger than herself? Does she like children? Does she like what she is doing?

Whether using paid baby sitters in their own homes or day-care mothers, young parents would do well to get recommendations from those who have used the person before. In addition, the young mother should look for someone who is dependable and who has experience in caring for young children. Plans must be made for care if either the infant or the person giving care gets sick.

"Now another thing we will get worked out, with your approval of course, is to rearrange your school schedule so that you can finish with your classes earlier. Through a volunteer program there will be someone at the school to help you with your homework before you go home. That way, although you won't be through a great deal earlier, you will come home having your assignments done and ready to care for your baby.

"Next fall, if you find you can handle your school program and the family day care has worked out, you might want to work part-time in the afternoons, both to give yourself some work training and experience and to make some extra money for your baby's needs."

Arlene listened with growing amazement. She could hardly believe all the things the worker was telling her.

"Now, one more thing," the worker said. "There is an adolescent clinic at the university hospital. This is not the city clinic you would normally go to. It will be farther for you to go. However, they have group meetings for young people like yourself. Most of the kids who go there are using some kind of birth control. You can get support there, I believe, for some of the problems you are facing."

"Arlene doesn't need birth control," her mother said. "She's not messing around with anybody anymore."

Arlene looked at the worker. She hadn't told her mother about her recent brush with another pregnancy. Her period had come before she went to get the pregnancy test. It had seemed best to go on as if nothing had happened. If the worker told, she knew her mother would be terribly upset.

"If Arlene goes there," the worker said, "it doesn't mean she has to choose birth control or necessarily needs it. However, it is a good idea for Arlene to have others to talk to about how she wants to plan for her future."

"Oh," her mother said.

Arlene breathed a secret sigh of relief.

"But that does bring up one more point," the worker said. "I do think Arlene needs some time for social things."

"Arlene's got a baby," her mother said. "She doesn't have time for just hanging around corners anymore."

"However, Arlene does need a chance to be with people her own age," the worker said. "Unless she gets to know and be friends with a variety of people, when the time comes for her to form lasting friendships or to marry, it will be very hard for her to choose the right people."

"Hum," Arlene's mother said. Arlene was pleased with the worker.

The worker continued. "Arlene should be able to date if she wants. If you don't want her to go out, then perhaps she could have some of her friends come over here."

Arlene winced. She knew the worker had overdone it then. If she just hadn't said that.

"I run my own house," Arlene's mother said. "I'll decide who can come here and who can't." The tone of her voice signalled to everyone that the conference was over.

Later, Arlene thought, that except for that last part, it had really been a good discussion. She felt very involved in what was going on.

The next few months were quite different for Arlene. The day-care mother's home was not as convenient to either her own home or school as Arlene would have liked, but she really liked the day-care mother. The day-care mother asked her opinions about everything and genuinely seemed to want to care for the baby in the way Arlene desired. Arlene felt more responsible for the baby than she had when he was being shifted between her and her mother. She gained respect for her own opinions. Whenever she watched the day-care mother with the children, Arlene found that she learned things too.

Two afternoons a week, Arlene picked the baby up near dinner time rather than right after school. One was on the afternoon she went crosstown to the clinic and the other was on her free afternoon. The worker had arranged that Arlene have one afternoon free to do whatever she liked.

Arlene tried hard to make the family day-care arrangement work, but it didn't always go smoothly. Having to get up, get the baby dressed, get over to the day-care home, and get to school on time put a strain on Arlene. Sometimes in her rush to get out the door, Arlene would find that she had forgotten to bring some of the things the baby needed. The day-care mother had to gently remind her not to forget the next day. Sometimes too, Arlene had trouble getting back across town from the clinic sessions on time. If she particularly enjoyed her free afternoon, she was often late. The day-care mother had children of her own to care for and was anxious at the end of the day to have her own home back again. As nice as she was, she became irritated when Arlene did not pick up her baby on time.

With the tutoring, Arlene did a little better in school. Still she did not feel learning was as meaningful as it had been at the special school. Sometimes at home in the evening she wished there was someone to talk to about her school work, but her mother seemed uninterested.

Arlene looked forward to the group sessions at the clinic. They gave her an opportunity to get to know kids outside her neighborhood. She often spoke out. Because of her experiences with group discussions at the special school, she knew how to participate. Whenever she saw someone shyly sitting, hardly saying anything, she thought: That used to be me. How different I am now.

Arlene decided to use an intrauterine device for birth control (I.U.D., everyone called it). "I'd rather use the pill," she told the group, "but I'm always forgetting to take something to the day-care mother's house or to school. I suppose I'd forget to take my pills too." When she said it, she laughed. She didn't feel critical of herself. That was another change. She was more comfortable with who she was.

When one of the girls in the clinic group asked Arlene if there were anything that could have been done to prevent her pregnancy, Arlene said emphatically, "If I knew then what I know now, I never would have gotten pregnant." Then she grew thoughtful and almost sad. "I guess for me it would have been best to have had an abortion or else to have put the baby up for adoption. But so many funny things kept going on in my life, it never worked out."

"Why do you say it would have been best?" the girl asked.

"Like now, good lord, it seems I've got so long to go to graduate," Arlene replied. "And when I think that my baby will be about ready to start school when I finish, I can't believe it. And well, when I think of carrying on the way I am for four more years, I don't know. It's just that day after day it's get up, take care of the baby, go to school, come home, take care of the baby, go to bed, get up, get the baby ready, go to school, pick up the baby, go home, take care of the baby, and on and on and on. I think a lot about dropping out of school."

"Maybe you should put the baby in temporary foster care or something," one of the girls suggested. "I heard about someone who did that."

"Or maybe you should just have him adopted now," another girl said, "if you feel that way."

"I just don't know," Arlene said. "I've thought about all that. One thing, I don't think my mother would ever let me give him up now. She's got a thing about that. And I must admit it would be pretty hard for me to do it too. But a couple of times, I've done things that I know are very bad for the baby and I suppose bad for me too. I'll just have to see how things go." Arlene grew thoughtful. "When I was thinking about having him adopted when I was pregnant, a woman at the adoption agency said to me: 'Sometimes you have to love your baby more to be able to give him up' or something like that. Anyway I do love him now."

Everyone was very quiet.

"But maybe some day, I'll be at that point."

"What point?" one of the boys asked.

Arlene hesitated. "Of loving him so much I'll be able to

see what's really best for both of us—keeping him or giving him up."

When Joel was finally located and asked about Arlene and the baby, he shrugged his shoulders. "What do you want from me?" he said. "That's her problem, not mine."

Then he went on. "It cost me plenty too. The hospital costs. And then that kid of hers—he had something wrong with him—a foot or something and that cost money too. That's why I finally split—I could see that it was the kind of thing that could go on for the rest of your life."

Finally he added. "Look, I get along the best I can. The girl I am living with now is okay. But nothing for me is long-term. I've seen too much of life to get caught in that bag. It's a day-to-day existence, man. You better believe it."

CEIL AND RUSS

Ceil sat in the doctor's office with her baby. During the first six months, she had taken him for a check-up every month. Now she was taking him every six weeks.

She remembered the first visit. She had timed it carefully so that the baby would not be hungry or tired. But the doctor was late in getting to his office. Then the nurse had her undress the baby while the doctor saw another child. Being undressed made the baby feel uncomfortable and he began to fuss. By the time the doctor came, he was crying loudly. Ceil tried to ask the doctor her questions, but in her concern for what the baby was feeling and what the doctor must be thinking she forgot most of what she wanted to know. Ceil was angry at the doctor for being late. She was angry at what had happened. It shattered her newly-formed confidence about mothering.

Since that time, though, Ceil and the doctor had become good friends. She had probably telephoned him too often but he seemed to understand. "As long as you know," he said, "that I can't raise your baby. I cannot be a substitute mother. You're the one who's going to do the things that will keep the baby well and happy. And you're the one who has to make the decision each time about whether or not a doctor is needed."

Still the doctor was the one counterbalance Ceil felt she had against her own mother's knowledge about how to care for the baby. When Ceil didn't want to turn to her mother, she turned to the doctor. She couldn't help her feelings. Taking advice from the doctor allowed her to feel independent and responsible. Taking advice from her mother often made her feel dependent and childish.

This time, however, Ceil didn't know who could solve her problem. Around his tenth month, the baby had started to show a marked preference for Ceil's mother. For example, the baby was afraid of the vacuum cleaner and other loud sounds. Also, whenever strangers appeared he acted terribly frightened. When he cried and needed to be held, he turned to Ceil's mother. Ceil felt rejected and hurt. As a result she had become increasingly rude to her mother.

"My mother is taking my baby away from me." Ceil's lip trembled as she said it.

"What do you mean?" the pediatrician asked.

"You don't know what I go through," Ceil told him. "If I am going to be a student with a baby and come home every day and take care of him and spend my weekends with him rather than going off with the other kids, at least I want him to be mine."

"I think at this point," the doctor said gently, "you are perhaps thinking more of yourself than of the baby."

The last thing Ceil needed was to be told she was in the wrong. She looked away. She was sorry she had ever brought it up.

"I am not saying your own feelings are not valid," the

doctor continued. "However, at times of stress, if the baby feels more comfortable turning to your mother, it doesn't mean your mother or the baby is trying to do something to you. Ceil, babies grow in security and love. Without that they cannot venture out into the world and learn. Developing trust in its environment may be the single most important thing that happens to a baby in the first year of life. There may be times," he finished, "when you have to put aside your own feelings to meet the baby's needs."

"But I do that all the time," Ceil snapped. Nevertheless, Ceil finally had to admit that her mother was not doing it purposely. Her mother was about as noninterfering as a mother could be under the circumstances. She asked Ceil if there was anything special she wanted done with the baby each day, consulted her about what foods to give him, and generally made an effort to let Ceil know that she realized Ceil was the baby's mother and the one responsible for the decision-making.

"I guess I really do understand," Ceil said. "It's just that sometimes I resent not being able to stay home and be with the baby. The baby goes to bed before seven o'clock. My mother gets him so much more than I do. She'll probably see him take his first step and I won't. Maybe you don't understand but that's hard on me. I feel I'm missing a lot with my baby.

"At the same time," she continued, "I know that if I quit school and stayed home with him, I'd start resenting that I wasn't going to school. Also I'd probably feel then like I ought to be out working. It's very hard not having any money of my own right now."

Ceil sighed. "I just wish I'd waited to have him when I could be with him all the time. Do you know what I mean?"

The pediatrician nodded understandingly. "Mothering can be a wonderful experience. However, life circumstances seldom make it the exact experience women want it to be.

Mothers with more than one child complain to me how they feel guilty because they aren't spending as much time with their second child as they did with their first.

"Women with small children who have to work have many of the same feelings you do. They often wish they could be at home with their children. And many of them have to worry about how well the baby is being cared for in their absence. That's something you are lucky enough not to have to do.

"Women who are free to stay at home with their children sometimes talk to me about feeling trapped, about feeling less of a person because they relate to young people all day."

"I guess because I know my situation so well," Ceil said, "I think I'm the only one who has problems."

"That happens to all of us," the doctor said understandingly. He turned to the baby. "Now, let's take a look at this young fellow. Is he crawling and into everything these days?"

"Into everything?" Ceil said. "That's an understatement. He's into things I didn't even know existed."

"How do you handle his curiosity?" the doctor asked.

"Well, the best thing I've found is that if he really shouldn't get into something, I divert him. I show him, or suggest something else I know he'd like to do. That way I don't have to say No so much. I've learned something else too," she added. "Lots of times, I find I'm about to say No, and I catch myself. Sometimes there is no *real* reason why he can't look at, or get into, whatever it is.

"One time I stopped and mentally pretended to run my hand over everything in the room—floors, walls, objects; and then everything I could see out the window—trees, grass, streets. I realized all of a sudden that I knew what everything felt like. Then I tried to see if I could imagine what everything would taste like. And that was even more spectacular. I knew the taste of metal, wood, glass, plastic, brick—even things like tree bark. I could also tell what the sound would be like if any of the objects I saw fell. So I

figured that at one time in my life, besides using my eyes to
see things, I had listened to, felt, and tasted my whole
environment too. To him everything is new. I can see why
he's so curious."

"Of course, in all his exploring, you have to protect him,"
the doctor said. "Because it is all new to him, he doesn't
know. He doesn't have any idea of what could happen."

"Oh I do watch him," Ceil said. "It's just that often I find
that if I do let him do something, like say, feel a plant—I
help him so he doesn't hurt it—then he doesn't very often
bother the plants. He knows what they're like.

"And one more thing I've found," Ceil said, "is that
because I don't say No all the time, when I do say it he's
starting to pay attention. The other day he even stopped
what he was doing when I said No."

At around ten months, babies do have some self-control in
response to an adult's *No*. By twelve months, they can follow
simple requests, such as "Give me the cup." However, young
parents tend to overestimate the baby's ability to understand.
The young parent may give a command that the baby does not
understand and assume that the baby is being naughty or
stubborn because it does not obey. Babies need to be pro-
tected. As they grow older, they need to have limits set. That is
part of the security of their world. But adults also need to
understand that the world is very new to the younger baby,
who as yet understands little of the world and none of its
reasoning.

On the other hand, Ceil's own interest and curiosity about
the world have helped her to understand this on her own. In
particular, she understands that when a baby reaches for, gets
into, and does things of concern to adults, the baby is not being
bad. Indeed, this is a very healthy sign—a sign that the child is
curious and interested in its environment, and has the self-
confidence to want to reach out and explore.

"He's a very healthy young fellow," the doctor said. "I
want to give him a shot before you go, though."

"I hate that," Ceil said. "I feel so sorry for him."

"The hurt or crying from an injection will last only a moment or two; the protection may last his lifetime. Some of the diseases he has already been immunized against are very serious. Some, like polio, can be crippling. Others can cause him to die."

"I know," Ceil replied. "I didn't mean 'don't do it.'"

During its first year, a baby will receive immunizations against diphtheria, tetanus, whooping cough (pertussis), polio, and measles. The first three injections are usually combined in one injection, called DPT. Some of these immunizations require booster, or follow-up, shots for effectiveness. At one year the child is generally given a test for tuberculosis, also.

The doctor gave Ceil's baby his shot. The baby cried for a minute and then was distracted by Ceil's hopping around with him.

"Stop and make another appointment with the nurse on the way out," said the doctor. "And don't worry, that baby knows you're his mother."

Ceil smiled. "Okay," she said. "See you next time."

The last three months of the school year went smoothly for Ceil. "Only a little bit more and I'll have made it through my first year as a schoolgirl mother," Ceil told one of her girl friends. "Last summer, I never thought I could do it."

"I hear you've started going out again," her friend said.

"Well, not really going out," Ceil said quickly. "It's just that Frank and I decided to do a special project for social studies class. He came over to my house several times and we found we like talking together."

"What will Russ think?" the girl asked.

"It's not anything like it was with Russ," Ceil said. "As a matter of fact, I've grown to respect Russ in a lot of ways I didn't appreciate before. But Russ is away at school and I don't really know what our future's going to be like. It's just good to have boys for friends as well as girls."

"What do your parents say?"

"Well, they haven't said much. I think they don't want me to miss out entirely on 'being young'—whatever that means. At the same time they realize and I realize that life isn't the same for me as it is for other girls. Having Frank to drop by and talk to is really great for me. He doesn't mind the baby. Sometimes if he comes by before the baby's gone to sleep, we just play with the baby. I guess in some ways he's acting as a father for the baby or another brother for me. I don't know which. Anyway for as long as it lasts, it's nice."

"That's good," her friend said. "For a while this spring I was worried about you. You acted . . . sorta funny."

"Well," Ceil said. "For a long time this spring, I really didn't like having anyone, even my girlfriends, come over. When the baby was up it was hard to be me. A baby is so demanding and has so many ways of getting attention. I couldn't fully participate in what was being said."

"But we used to talk about your baby and play with him too," her girl friend protested.

"I guess it's hard to explain," Ceil said. "But as much as I liked to share the baby, I needed more for you all to talk about other things. Anyway, for some reason, with Frank it is different. It just goes the way it goes. That's the best I can say."

"Do you think you might marry Frank?" her girl friend asked.

"No," Ceil said. "We don't have that kind of relationship. Not that I haven't thought of it. Sometimes I would give anything to be married and have this thing settled. You know, a father for the baby and all that. I can see where it would be easy to rush into it. I do believe all babies should have fathers."

"I guess marriage when you have a baby is a little different."

"Well, when you already have a baby a person isn't just marrying you, he's marrying your child too. If he doesn't like your child, the marriage won't work. If you marry him just to get a father for the baby, that won't work either. Let's face it, for one thing I'm not physically attracted to Frank. I think a marriage without that would, in the long run, have a pretty difficult time surviving. Not that that is the most important part, but it's a part.

"Anyway," Ceil hastened to add, "the baby does have a father—Russ. And he will grow up knowing Russ is his father. I just have to work things out around that."

"Maybe you'll marry Russ someday," her girl friend said.

"Oh, sometimes I think I will. But I have a mixture of feelings toward him that are hard to understand. Like, I'm the one that refused marriage when I was pregnant. But at times I resent him for getting off scot-free if you know what I mean. Sometimes I wish that if I had to have gotten pregnant, it would have been by someone I didn't even know so I wouldn't ever have to think about Russ." Ceil paused. "Other times, I think that if I'd done that, I'd feel guilty toward the baby. At least I can tell him I was in love with his father when I conceived him."

"If you had it to do over, would you get pregnant again?" her girl friend asked.

"I love my baby very much. Some of my most beautiful experiences have come from being a mother," Ceil said thoughtfully. "The only thing I can tell you is that my whole life has been changed. A lot of the things I want to do are just going to have to be done differently. Like if I go to college, it will have to be a local college where I can commute daily, rather than go away to school. Meeting people is so different. It's hard to keep exposing your self-esteem to other people's opinions. I know who I am, what I did, and why I did it, but. . . ." She hesitated. "I never know what other people will think."

"What do you care what they think?" her girl friend protested.

"It's not as easy as that," Ceil countered. "Take my father. I love and respect him. But I know he still thinks I should act like my pregnancy was a terrible mistake. And if I meet a fellow I think I might really like, I can't help but worry about what his reaction is going to be when he finds out I have a baby."

"I see," Ceil's friend said slowly, but Ceil wasn't sure she did. Maybe it was something you had to experience to know.

Ceil had ambivalent feelings about Russ's coming home for the summer. She had achieved a balance in her life and was afraid of his upsetting it. It turned out that he was equally uneasy about seeing her.

On his first visit of the summer, Russ brought a present—a child-size sweatshirt with the name of his college and 19?? on it.

"Is that for me or the baby?" Ceil asked.

Russ paused. "I hadn't thought of that. I guess," he added, "like Cinderella, if you can fit into it, it's yours." Ceil and Russ both laughed, but underneath they knew their conversation was on two levels.

Their uncomfortableness with each other disappeared, though, as soon as Ceil brought down the baby.

"He's got so much personality," Russ said continually. When the baby threw a ball at him, Russ beamed. "Did you see that? He's only a year old and did you see the way he threw that ball!" The pride showed in his voice.

Russ momentarily envied Ceil for having his son with her. He wished she had been doing something terribly wrong so that he could take the child away. Then he thought, "What if they really were mistreating him and I couldn't do anything about it? And what would I really do with him? It's best this way."

As the weeks went on, Russ realized he felt differently about Ceil than he once had. She seemed so serious now. She had always seemed to know where she was going. Now she was preoccupied with hanging on and getting there. He admired her but missed the girlish naiveté and flirting that had been in her personality before. Even when she laughed and was having a very good time, he sensed a new maturity.

Russ also felt more mature. But it was not in the same ways. Ceil seemed more settled. He felt more ready to go out and take on the world. His life was different now—new friends at college, new experiences. Russ could tell he was a long way from getting serious about any other girl. Not so much because he had strong feelings for Ceil, but because the close brush with settled responsibility made him want to avoid it for a very long time.

"I don't feel totally like a parent because I don't see my son often enough," he said. "The next time I become a parent, *if* I do, I want to have the time for it, the money for it, and I guess the desire for it."

Russ sat on the porch talking with Ceil. After the tension of their first few meetings of the summer, they had fallen into a comfortable pattern. Russ thought they had a good relationship. "A funny thing happened to me yesterday," he said. "I met that counselor I worked with last year—you know, the one who sat down and talked with me when we were having so many problems. Anyway, apparently he's trying to counsel kids about sex. He asked me if there was anything that anyone could have done to prevent the pregnancy.

"I told him I supposed I could have been more careful. I certainly knew about condoms and other birth control methods. I was anxious to prove myself as a man. I told him I really cared about you. But it was very important for me to experience that part of life. I wasn't old enough to take responsibility for you. I had a hard enough time taking responsibility for myself then. So I just let things happen."

Russ paused, then went on. "If anyone had asked me then, I would have said I was very responsible. But I have a very different idea of what that means now. Funny, you know, you have your whole life ahead of you when you're young. You don't realize how what seems simple at the time can change your whole life. Maybe only living through all the changes, or seeing how things are never going to be the same—like for you, Ceil—makes you wiser. Although I would tell other kids not to become parents while they're young, I'm not really sure it's anything you can tell kids and have it make sense—sense enough to change their actions, I mean."

Russ hesitated. "If he'd asked you if there was anything anyone could have done to prevent your pregnancy, what would you have said?"

Ceil was very thoughtful. "Someone else asked me something similar recently," she said. "No, I guess there isn't anything anyone could have done. But I would advise other kids not to do it."

"Same here," Russ said. "Isn't it funny?"

"Yes," she said and reached for his hand. "It's funny."

They both sat in silence, lost in thought. Then Ceil roused and spoke. "Enough of that. Back to reality. I hear our son waking up inside. Now, if you're here for the day, you can help. Would you rather change his diaper or put a load of his laundry into the washer?"

ERICA AND GARY

Erica got off the bus in front of her mother's house. She wished she had stopped somewhere for a Coke. It would have given her some time to think before she picked up the baby.

She didn't know what she would say to her mother. But before she even said hello, she blurted it out. "I'm pregnant again."

"Pregnant!"

She's as surprised as she was the first time, Erica thought. Only this time I'm surprised too.

"I thought you were using something," her mother said.

"We were," Erica replied. "Gary always used a rubber."

"You know condoms aren't the most reliable method, Erica," her mother said. "I thought you were going to use the pill or an I.U.D."

"Well," Erica looked embarrassed. "There was a sort of misunderstanding." Erica flushed with the memory of her earlier deceit. "Gary doesn't trust them. Anyway, it really doesn't matter now. I'm pregnant."

"How are you going to manage? You're barely making it now, if you're making it at all, I imagine."

"Oh Mother, just don't start up now, okay?" said Erica. "I've got enough of my own without your adding to it. How's the baby been?" she said, reaching for her daughter's jacket. As usual, the sooner she got out of her parents' house the better she'd feel. Poor, in debt, whatever, it always felt so good to be out of that house.

"Oh, she's been a dear," her mother said, grateful to have something else to talk about. "But really, Erica," she added. "I think you ought to use cloth diapers like I did. The disposable ones are so expensive."

"I just use disposable ones when I'm going to take her some place, Mother," Erica said in an annoyed tone. "Besides, with the money I pay out each time to use the laundromat, I'm not sure it is so much more expensive."

That's the way it always was. Whenever she was with her mother, there was always some criticism.

"Well, I've got to get home and fix Gary's dinner. Thanks for watching the baby for me." Erica stood up.

Suddenly her mother leaned over and hugged her. "I know you are trying to make a go of it on your own, but your father and I are here if you need help."

"Thanks, Mom," Erica said. She wished she could have said it more warmly. Her mother did mean well. It was just that any help always meant so much criticism and interference.

On the bus trip across town Erica tried to weigh her feelings. She looked down at the small person seated on her lap. Her daughter was growing up. She had started to walk already. Erica felt a strange mixture of happiness at her daughter's progress and resentment of the new demands the baby's independence brought. Also, Erica missed the dependence of a small baby.

"Will I be able to have enough time and love for two children?" Erica sighed. It did seem soon to be having another baby. And she would have two in diapers since most babies, she knew, weren't ready for toilet training until they were eighteen months of age or older. "At least having two so close together means they can play with one another," she rationalized. By the time Erica got home, the first shock had worn off.

After dinner, when Erica told Gary about it, Gary hit the ceiling. "Oh my God," he said. "How are we going to pay for another one?"

"Well, I'm covered by your health insurance at work now," Erica said.

"But you know that won't pay for all the hospital and doctor costs. And we found out how much it really costs to care for a baby these last couple of months." The tone of Gary's voice scared Erica a little.

"But we already have a lot of the things—crib, playpen, highchair," Erica argued.

"Sure, but if the new baby uses the crib, we have to get another bed. And it means vitamin drops, pediatric visits, food." Gary sank down in the chair. "If only we had some of the money back we shouldn't have spent."

"Like what?" Erica asked.

"Like we bought too many clothes for the baby at first. She outgrew some of them after wearing them only once or twice."

"But this baby can wear them."

"Yeah, once or twice. And what about those baby pictures?" Gary added.

"What about the color television?" Erica countered.

"Oh, shut up!" Gary stalked out of the living room.

Erica heard him go into the bathroom. The shower water seemed to run forever. After it stopped, Erica waited for him to come back into the living room. Eventually, she realized that he must have gone to bed. She got a blanket and lay down on the couch. She was cold and uncomfortable and lonely. Finally she went into the bedroom and crawled under the covers. She put her arm around Gary but he shrugged her away. She turned on her other side. She thought of her daughter, of herself, and the new life inside her. She felt terribly alone.

During the next couple of weeks things didn't seem to get any better. Sometimes Gary did not come home for dinner between his two jobs. Other times he came home later than usual after the night job. Whenever Erica asked him where he had been, he turned her question aside, or else was silent.

Erica's first pregnancy had been so pleasant that she was surprised to find herself with morning sickness. She felt very tired as well. It was difficult to rest because her daughter was lively and energetic.

"She's into everything," Erica told Gary. "I don't mean it badly. I know she's just curious, but I can't turn my back for a minute. And we don't have that much to get into. If I take her to the park, she picks up dirt, sticks, everything, and puts them into her mouth. She runs after every dog she sees. She hates to sit in the grocery store cart now but if I put her down, she's disappeared in a minute. I just can't keep track of her. It's exhausting."

Gary looked at her unsympathetically.

"I guess only if you cared for a little baby day after day would you realize," Erica said defensively. "You never relax, I mean even for a minute. You have to be on the alert all the time and it's very tiring. I mean even when she's napping, I try to nap but I'm always half-listening in case she wakes up. And I don't really sleep well until you get home and. . . ." Erica's voice trailed off. She could tell his attention was elsewhere. It wasn't any use saying anything more.

"Have a good day?" she asked, trying to at least have some conversation.

"Good enough."

"I hope you finish early tonight," Erica tried again. "There's a great late movie on. I'll make some popcorn."

"I don't know when I'll be home," Gary mumbled.

"Well, try to make it home for the movie, huh?" Erica said. "It'll be more fun to see it if you're watching too."

"Look, I said I don't know when I'll be home," Gary said more firmly. "So don't wait up."

Erica drew a breath. But the feelings she was trying to hold down just wouldn't stay down. Something gave. "You didn't hear a word I said, did you?" she yelled. "When I told you I was tired, I never get any real deep sleep, I don't feel so well with this pregnancy, I never can relax with the baby. You never heard any of that, did you? You don't listen and you don't care!"

"And what the hell, you think with holding down two jobs—I work all day, come home to your complaints, and go back and work all evening just to pay your lousy bills. And you think I'm not tired?"

"*My* lousy bills? Who bought the color television we're still paying for?"

"If it weren't for the television, what else would we have? Somebody who bitches all the time about how rough they have it!"

"Well, if you don't like it here, why don't you just get out?" Erica yelled.

"That's a damn good idea!"

Gary stormed into the bedroom. Erica followed and watched while he picked out some underclothing and a couple of shirts and shoved them into an old suitcase.

"Don't forget your sport shirts," she said. "With all your playing around, I wouldn't want you to look like you had any responsibility."

Gary glared at her, slammed down the lid on the suitcase, and walked out.

Erica stood motionless in the doorway. After a while, she did the dinner dishes without being aware she was doing them. Then she sat quietly in the living room, her face expressionless, too numb for tears.

The next few days without Gary were frightening to Erica. When she told Gary to get out, she knew what she really meant was "stay and take better care of me." She felt very helpless being on her own, especially while she was pregnant. How much it had meant to know that there was someone who cared about her, who was interested in their daughter. Even if he hadn't been home much, she had felt his support. Now there was nothing and she was lost.

When Erica heard from someone who worked with Gary that he was planning to go to California, the bottom fell out. She no longer had any energy for her daughter. Everything she did was mechanical. She mechanically changed the baby's diaper. Erica wanted to respond to the baby but she felt hollow inside. Even her smiles were forced. If Gary really did go, what would happen to her? The thought of moving back in with her parents made her sick to her stomach. To be made dependent on them, possibly for years and years, with her mother saying "I told you so" and trying to tell her how to care for her children. She didn't think she could stand it.

Erica called the welfare department. They told her to come in and see them. However, from what they told her on the phone about eligibility, she knew she would have to move out of their apartment. Even if she found the cheapest place she could, it would be difficult making it on welfare. And she had heard that once you got on welfare, it was almost impossible to get off. Like it was the bottom and you just stayed there. No one in her family had ever been on welfare. What would they think if she ended up there?

But the end of the month was coming, and she had no money for the rent or for food.

In desperation Erica went to the minister who had married them. He suggested that she have Gary come in and talk with him. When Erica finally reached Gary at work, he refused. "Don't give me that Jesus song and dance," he said.

The minister then arranged for them both to see a marriage counselor. "Perhaps," he suggested, "if Gary feels it's someone who doesn't know either of you—someone with an open viewpoint, he might come."

Gary reluctantly agreed. He missed the first appointment but came to the second one.

As they sat and talked with the counselor, Erica and Gary began to understand each other's point of view a little better. Erica was surprised to learn that Gary was jealous of the time she was able to spend at home and be with the baby. He thought she was having all the fun while he did nothing but work. Also, she learned that he felt that she was so involved with the baby that he was pushed out of the relationships with either of them. Having another baby just meant a further barrier to their being together again.

Gary, on the other hand, was surprised to learn that Erica was jealous of his working. "You never said you wanted to go to work," Gary said in a surprised tone.

"It's not exactly that I want to *work*," Erica said. She talked about her experiences at the dry cleaning store. "I met people who got to know me," she said. "I felt liked and needed." She discribed how lonely and isolated she was at home with the baby. "Gary," she said, "you're constantly meeting people, having new experiences, growing, learning. I'm being left further and further behind."

After two such sessions, Gary decided to move back in and give things another chance.

But living together for Erica and Gary now meant an uneasy truce. Both desperately wished they had taken advantage of the counseling offered to them before they were married. They agreed that it probably would not have changed their decision to marry but it might have helped them avoid some of the situations in which they found themselves.

The cost of the new baby was constantly on their minds. Money always seemed the answer to their problems. If only they had enough money, things would be so different. Their continuing sessions with the marriage counselor had made them aware that more than money was involved. But if they only had enough money, they felt, at least they could focus on their other problems. Without the money they needed, it took much of their energy just to survive.

The counselor recommended that Erica change prenatal clinics. "There's a clinic that has a special program for problem pregnancies."

"Mine is not a problem pregnancy," Erica said stiffly. "Gary and I are married and we're having our second baby, that's all." The counselor's recommendation brought back a rush of feelings that Erica had had with her first pregnancy.

"Erica," the counselor said gently, "I thought that one of

the things we've been discussing in our sessions is that everyone encounters some kinds of problems in living. Nobody's life goes like clockwork. It's how you handle the problems, your ability to see options and alternatives; it's your ability to make decisions and stick to them or change them if needed that's important. Don't let yourself become the problem.

"Now," he continued. "You are taking on a new baby soon after the birth of your other baby and you do have to manage with little money. Is it so terrible to think that you could use help?"

Erica nodded slowly. "I guess I want to be so independent. It's hard for me not to think of getting help as a loss of self-respect, a loss of pride."

Erica went to the clinic. To her surprise she understood for the first time that pregnancy seemed to cause some readjustment in every family—even families of older people and people with enough money. She began to feel a little less inadequate when she saw that problems were a part of life and everyone had them.

The discussions with other mothers were helpful as was the information provided by the program staff. The program doctor said he wanted Erica to watch her diet very carefully during this pregnancy.

Doctors are concerned about rapid repeated pregnancy in adolescence. The young mother's body has its own growing needs to meet. The first pregnancy creates additional demands. A young mother's body is likely to be overtaxed if it has to meet the requirements of a second pregnancy too soon.

A nutritionist showed Erica how wise buying and careful preparation of food could stretch her food dollar and actually improve the nutrient value of the food. Erica had never paid much attention to the nutrition of their meals.

She fixed what Gary and she liked. She realized, however, as her daughter moved off baby food and onto the same things they were eating, that it was best for the whole family to change their eating habits. "Not just for cost but for the way you feel," the nutritionist regularly reminded her.

The group discussions with the other mothers were sometimes painful. They caused Erica to think about many things she didn't want to think about. As she told Lizzie, "If I could have listened to all of those mothers at the clinic before I became pregnant the first time, I might not have become pregnant. Pregnancy seemed like the answer to a lot of problems then. But I think it created more problems than it solved. And yet I love my daughter so dearly, I just can't imagine my life now without her."

Lizzie was home for summer vacation and had come for dinner. They stood talking in the kitchen while Erica made a salad. "It's just that I didn't see what opportunities there were," Erica continued. "I felt my life was going to be: get married, have a home, have children, and that was that. It never occurred to me that it might not work out. It never occurred to me that I really could or would actually *want* to do something else."

"And now?" Lizzie said.

"Well, things between Gary and me are okay these days but they're not guaranteed, if you know what I mean," Erica replied. "This pregnancy is putting a strain on both of us. What if marriage doesn't work for us? What if I am going to be alone? For the first time, I've had to think seriously about what I would want to do to earn a living or to make money to help support my family if I had to. And for the first time, I realize I never prepared myself to do anything. Not even mentally, let alone with training of some sort."

"Well, I haven't either," Lizzie protested.

"But you're going to school. Besides, the thing is, if I do end up having to work most of my life, I wouldn't want to do just anything," Erica said. "I'd like to do something that I would enjoy, that would be something I could feel proud of doing. But I just haven't even thought of what that would be or how I get either the training or experience to be able to do it."

"I guess you've gone through a lot this year, Erica," Lizzie said.

"I was really a very different person when I got pregnant," Erica responded. "Having a baby and being married does change you. Particularly, I think, when some of it doesn't go well." She hesitated. "I'm mixed-up about what I want to say."

"Have you changed your mind about—well, Gary?" Lizzie asked.

"No, I do love Gary and I really do want to be married, have a home, have children," Erica said quickly. "But maybe if I had been who I am now back in that last year of high school, I might not have started out the way I did. But I did and I do like it. I mean I love being with my daughter and caring for her, playing with her, teaching her things." Her face beamed with pride as she spoke.

"Well then, I'm not sure I understand," Lizzie said.

"At the same time . . . ," Erica fumbled for words. "I realize I have got to be a person in my own right too. I have got to keep growing myself. And I'm not sure how to do that."

"But you've always been in control of things," Lizzie said.

"I sometimes think that during this last year I've been afraid to be as strong as I am," Erica said, "because I felt that if I were weaker or more helpless it would tie Gary to me more. I see now all the dependence I've been dumping on him—care of me, care of our daughter, and now the care of our new baby—plus being my only real friend. Do you see what I'm saying? He's had to carry everything. I now feel I've got to reach out, get to know people, do things so I can bring some new interests home. And I don't know how I'm going to find the time to do that with two small children and no money even to take a bus anyplace."

Lizzie sat silently.

"So all I am saying is," Erica finished, "that I've got to grow even if it works the wrong way and splits me from Gary. I can't not grow. And I've got to be sure I take responsibility for my own growing so I'm prepared for whatever happens in life. I will have two children you know." Erica's chin trembled. "But Lizzie," she added suddenly, "I've just *got* to make things work here. I've just *got* to."

Lizzie put her arm around her. "If you're that determined, Erica, you will. I know you will."

After dinner, while Erica put the baby to bed, Gary talked with Lizzie in the living room.

"You heard things have been rocky?"

"Yes," Lizzie said. She started to say something else but Gary interrupted.

"I know I wasn't really ready for marriage," he said. "I always expected to marry Erica anyway, so when she became pregnant it never occurred to me not to do it. But at the same time, I had some things that were important for me to do, for a person to do. Like that trip I was going to take to California with my buddy. When I gave those up, it seemed as if I gave up not only my dreams but a certain part of myself. I always thought of marriage as something I would do. But it wasn't the same as my dreams, if you know what I mean."

Lizzie nodded.

"It's funny how things have gone," Gary said to her. "I guess I found it hard living with Erica's parents and I built up a lot of resentment. Erica and her mother seemed to really shut me out after the baby came. It was better for a while after we moved into this place. But then, I don't know, everything just got to be too much. Nothing was fun anymore. And I couldn't see the future as anything but more of the same. I don't know right now what exactly is going to happen to Erica and me."

"Listen, I'm sure things are going to be okay." Lizzie tried to be encouraging.

"You know I moved out for a while? I was even going to go to California. But there's no going backwards. I am a different person than I was before I got married. Going to California now and trying to play the carefree guy just wouldn't work. I'd always have Erica and the two kids at the back of my mind. There's no going back. But right now it's a little hard to think of where forward is.

"I never dated many other girls besides Erica. I've got to admit now, sometimes when she's dragging around the house complaining, and the baby's fussy, I wonder about it. I go to work and see other girls, dressed up, having a good time, laughing. I wonder what it would be like to know them."

Lizzie was silent. Gary looked at her.

"If I could have it to do over again, I guess I just would be more careful. I should have used a rubber that night Erica got pregnant. Later Erica told me she had lied to me about the pills. I never did quite figure out why. She knew we were going to get married some day. I don't know why she felt she had to do that. Anyway, maybe I would have been smarter even not to have had sex. That may seem odd but there are things a guy can do without having to run the risk of a girl's becoming pregnant."

He sighed. "But it's no use having regrets. And there's no going back. I guess this is just a low period for me. The boss at my regular job told me today that there's going to be an opening in the sales department at the end of the summer and he's going to consider me. That would mean I could probably make enough money after a short time to give up the night job—maybe even before our second baby comes."

"Perhaps if you can get that job and have some more free

time for Erica, the baby, and yourself, things will get better," Lizzie said. "Right now you're just so tired that you don't feel like you have anything to give anybody."

Gary nodded. "But you know," he added, "even as I sit here griping, I know it isn't all the way I say it is. Sometimes, I see those single guys at work. They're standing around trying to figure out what to do in the evening. I know they're bored as hell. And I walk out the door and come home. My little girl runs to greet me. And then I see Erica and she's gotten fixed up. Even though she's pregnant again, she can look pretty good when she wants to. And maybe she's made something I really like for dinner. And I think I love her so much and I love our daughter so much . . ." His voice drifted off.

"No," he finally said. "Once something's started, you just can't go back. And it would be too hard to start over. No, I've just got to try to make this thing work somehow."

Erica came into the room carrying a white box.

"Lizzie, remember when you gave me your bouquet that night you graduated? I want you to know I saved it. See?" Erica held out the open box.

Lizzie looked in. "That was a long time ago, wasn't it?" she said softly.

Whether or not the marriage of Erica and Gary will survive is an open question. They married before they got to really know themselves or had a chance to test out their potential. They took on responsibility for children before they had a chance to work out mutually satisfying ways of living and growing together. Erica has learned that her assumption that children bring people together can be as false as it is true.

However, Erica and Gary are both determined young people. They have already shown a great deal of strength in overcoming some of the problems in their marriage. Experts often point out that more than half of those who marry while still of school age divorce within five years. We would do well to remember that in spite of the obstacles society puts in their way, the marriages of almost as many do survive.

Young parents have a spontaneity, flexibility, naturalness, and enthusiasm that can stand them in good stead in their tasks as parents. They have a capacity to grow and learn. Families and institutions that touch on the lives of such young people need to support their many strengths. The young parents will benefit, and ultimately so will their children and society.

Index